SAINT PETER

A Biography

✝

MICHAEL GRANT

SCRIBNER
New York   London   Toronto   Sydney   Tokyo   Singapore

SCRIBNER
Rockefeller Center
1230 Avenue of the Americas
New York, NY 10020

First Scribner Edition 1995
Published by arrangement with George Weidenfeld & Nicolson Limited

SCRIBNER and design are trademarks of Simon & Schuster Inc.

Manufactured in the United States of America

1 3 5 7 9 10 8 6 4 2

Library of Congress Cataloging-in-Publication Data
Grant, Michael, date.
Saint Peter: a biography/by Michael Grant.—1st Scribner ed.
p. cm.
Includes bibliographical references and index.
1. Peter, the Apostle, Saint. 2. Christian saints—Palestine—Biography.
3. Apostles—Biography. I. Title
BS2515.G65   1995   94-39660   CIP
225.9'2—dc20
[B]

ISBN 0-684-19354-X

Contents

List of Illustrations   vii
Preface   ix
Map 1   Palestine and the surrounding territories   xi
Map 2   The Roman Empire   xii

PART I   HOW DO WE OBTAIN INFORMATION?   1

Chapter 1   The problems of research   3
Chapter 2   The sources   26

PART II   WHILE JESUS WAS ALIVE   51

Chapter 3   The calling of Peter   53
Chapter 4   Peter's weaknesses and strengths   65
Chapter 5   Peter and Jesus   73

PART III   AFTER JESUS'S DEATH   87

Chapter 6   Peter and the Resurrection   89
Chapter 7   The leadership of Peter   103
Chapter 8   The speeches attributed to Peter   111
Chapter 9   Cornelius: Peter and the Gentiles   116
Chapter 10   The clash with Paul   122
Chapter 11   Paul and James   132

PART IV   ROME   145

Chapter 12   Peter in Rome   147

Chapter 13   The death and burial-place of Peter   152

Epilogue   159

References   168
Table of dates   183
Bibliography   186
Index   205

Illustrations

1 From the Missal of Abbot Berthold of Weingarten, 13th century. J. Pierpont Morgan Library

2 *Jesus and the Twelve Apostles*. Pala d'Oro, San Marco, Venice

3 From a 13th-century German psalter. Fratelli Fabbri, Milan

4 *Jesus giving the Keys to Peter*. Painting by Perugino, Sistine Chapel, Vatican

5 *Peter holding the Keys of the Kingdom*. Sculpture at Moissac, France

6 *One of Peter's Denials of Jesus*. Catacombs of St. Domitilla

7 *Peter and Malchus*. 15th-century French ivory of the betrayal of Jesus. Weidenfeld Archive

8 *Martyrdoms of St. Peter*, alabaster relief of Nottingham School. Victoria and Albert Museum, London

9 Alabaster panels of St. Peter and St. Paul. English, c.1400. Weidenfeld Archive

10 *Martyrdom of St. Peter and St. Paul*. 15th-century manuscript in Biblioteca Laurenziana, Florence

11 From the Bronze Doors of St. Peter's Basilica, Rome

12 Marble statue of St. Peter. Vatican

13 *Peter enthroned*, central panel of altarpiece; school of Guido da Siena, 13th century

14 *Healing of Lame Man by Peter and John at the Beautiful Gate of the Temple* (Raphael *Cartoon*). Victoria and Albert Museum

15 Peter's (adopted?) daughter Petronilla admitting Veneranda to heaven. Catacombs of Domitilla, Rome

16 Old St. Peter's: interior, painting in left aisle of church of S. Martino ai Monti, Rome

17 Old St. Peter's from a drawing by Maarten van Heemskerk, 1533

Preface

I owe grateful acknowledgments to the late Sir John Barnes, to Mrs
Maria Ellis and to Lord Gilmour. I also want to thank Miss Jennifer
Ellis for looking up references, Mrs Charmian Hearne for seeing
the first stages of the book through the press, Mrs Hilary Laurie for
adding helpful proposals, Mr Malcolm Gerratt for offering many
valuable suggestions of which I have taken the fullest advantage,
Mrs Erika Goldman of Scribner's for offering constructive ideas,
Mrs Arabella Quin for her editorship, and my wife for giving assistance of numerous kinds. I owe the proposal that I should write the
book to Lord Longford (on the top of a London bus).

I hope that what I have written is not altogether unoriginal, and
that it has contributed certain unfamiliar points of view, and brought
together material – notably in relation to Peter's associations and
background – that is not customarily found under one cover. Nevertheless it would be both ungenerous and inaccurate to deny that I
have made use of earlier books, and gained great benefit from them.
A list of the literature from which I have profited in this way is
given in the Bibliography. However, I should like to mention here
four works which I have found particularly useful; I have not always
noted these debts in detail, since I judged that to do so would hold
up the flow of information that I have sought to provide. The books
in question are *Peter in the New Testament* edited by R.E. Brown,
K.P. Donfried and L. Reumann; *Peter: Disciple, Apostle, Martyr* by
O. Cullmann; *Simon-Petrus* by R. Pesch; and *Simon Peter: From
Galilee to Rome* by C.P. Thiede. (I have also ventured to echo some
of my own earlier books, especially *Jesus* and *Saint Paul.*)

I have added supplementary notes, mainly bibliographical in
character, at the end of each chapter, while detailed references appear

at the end of the book. Translations of the Old and New Testaments are taken from the *Revised English Bible: with Apocrypha*, Oxford and Cambridge University Presses (1989) (New Testament, 1990), to which I owe gratitude.

Michael Grant
1994

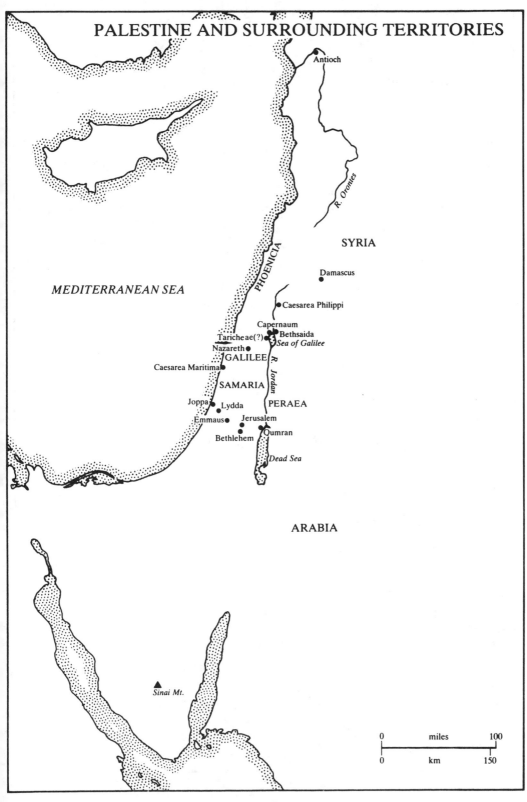

PALESTINE AND SURROUNDING TERRITORIES

MAP 1

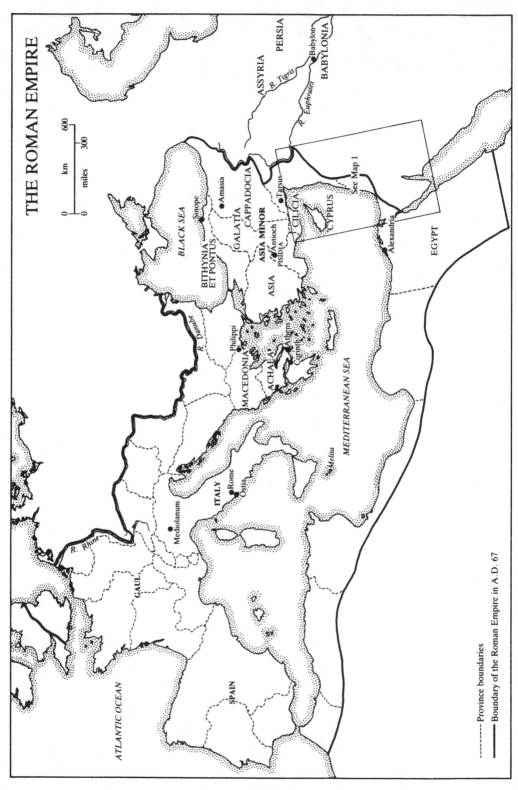

THE ROMAN EMPIRE

PERSIA

ASSYRIA

R. Tigris

R. Euphrates

BABYLONIA
•Babylon

km
600
300
miles
0
0

BLACK SEA

•Sinope

•Amasia

BITHYNIA
ET PONTUS

GALATIA

CAPPADOCIA

ASIA MINOR

•Tarsus

•Antioch

PISIDIA

CILICIA

CYPRUS

See Map 1

ASIA

Alexandria

EGYPT

R. Danube

Philippi•

MACEDONIA

ACHAEA

Athens•

Corinth•

MEDITERRANEAN SEA

•Melita

ITALY

•Rome

•Ostia

Mediolanum•

R. Rhine

GAUL

SPAIN

ATLANTIC OCEAN

------ Province boundaries

——— Boundary of the Roman Empire in A.D. 67

MAP 2

Part I

HOW DO WE OBTAIN

INFORMATION?

Chapter 1

THE PROBLEMS OF RESEARCH

Peter is one of the central figures of the Christian religion and also, inevitably, a key figure of the entire world of today, with which, whether people are aware of the fact or not, that religion is inextricably fused. And yet he remains a shadowy, legendary personage. Some declare, indeed, that it is impossible to recover any true picture of him and see what he was really like. But up to a point, by carefully investigating what we are told and not told, it appears to me that this can be done, or at least attempted. Cardinal Henry Newman had something to say about this. 'He who made us,' he said (though not everyone will agree when in this way he blames our historical problem on God), 'has so willed that in mathematics indeed we should arrive at certitude by rigid demonstration, but in religious enquiry we should arrive at certitude by accumulated probabilities.' And in the case of Saint Peter the probabilities – even if that is often as far as we can go – exist in abundance.

This is so much the case that Peter has come down to us as an astonishingly complex and many-sided man. 'In early Christian thought, as attested by the New Testament, there is a plurality of images associated with Peter: missionary, fisherman, pastoral

3

shepherd, martyr, recipient of special revelation, confessor of the true faith, magisterial protector, and repentant sinner.'[1]

His role, in fact, was unique. He was an apostle of the living Jesus, indeed the foremost of his apostles – *the* apostle. And then after Jesus's death he was the leader of the Christians who survived. He was therefore mentioned in the New Testament nearly two hundred times, a good deal more frequently than all the other apostles put together. Nine of the twenty-seven New Testament books have something to say about him. 'He certainly possesses a much greater significance in the foundation of Christianity than we are accustomed to assume.'[2] It is quite wrong for us to allow him to stay in the shadow of Paul, in which he so often remains hidden.

Or rather, wrong though it is, we find it hard to do otherwise because, unlike Paul, Peter did not leave a great body of letters written not long after the life of Jesus had come to an end (the only two letters ascribed to Peter are of disputed authorship, cf. Chapter 2). Another reason why the true Peter is so hard to recover is that the New Testament writers who so abundantly refer to him are discordant about the part or parts that he played and about what sort of man he really was. No wonder Pope John Paul II, in 1978, referred to 'the mystery of Peter's role in God's design for the universal church'. Peter and his role were, and remain, uncertain and disputable. That is another of the reasons why, although there are modern *Lives* of Peter, they are infinitely fewer than those of Paul.

But all this uncertainty presents a vigorous invitation to accept the challenge and try to discover all that we can about Peter himself and his historical existence.

His *historical* existence, I say, because his life, as it has come down to us, is abundantly set about by miracles.

Even if some of the miracles attributed to the lives of Jesus and Peter are exorcisms and healings which could, by some stretch of the imagination, be regarded as historical, based on the two men's exceptional curative powers (which were also attributable to other Jews, notably Pharisees and Essenes), most still remain acts of supernatural agency, 'against nature' in so far as we comprehend its

4

manifestations, so that they are outside the historical picture. Peter's 'escape' from imprisonment is a conspicuous example. Students of history, therefore, are not able to take these miraculous happenings into consideration. They can believe in such stories, if they wish, but they do so as a matter of faith and not as historians. Or they can disbelieve them, if they prefer. In either case, it is their duty to attempt to *find out what happened*, within the realms of historical fact and possibility.

The miracles ascribed to Peter go back directly to, and are inspired by, those stated to have been performed earlier by Jesus. The latter, therefore, deserve fuller analysis, if we are to understand the ancient picture not only of Jesus, but of Peter as well. In the case of Jesus, what stands out is that the *reason* for his special fame during his lifetime and after his death was his supposed miraculous power.

He was famous as a healer, but he was also famous as a worker of miracles in other senses of the word. That, we are assured, was clear enough to the writers of *Mark* and *Matthew*, who describe him as 'Lord' because of the miracles he was supposed to have performed. The same belief was explicitly expressed, so it was said, by Peter, immediately after Jesus's death. 'Men of Israel,' he is quoted as saying, 'listen to me: I speak of Jesus of Nazareth, a man singled out by God and made known to you through miracles, portents and signs, which God worked among you through him, as you well know.'[3]

Biographers of Jesus have sometimes excised this miraculous material from their narrative, in order to make it sound more credible to modern ears. But any such attempts conflict strongly with the ancient accounts that have come down to us. In the four Gospels, no fewer than 232 miracles are reported. Take *Mark*, for example. Out of that Gospel's 661 verses, as many as 209 deal with miraculous doings. And *Matthew* and *Luke* carry the same tendency still further, *Matthew*, in particular, emphasizing the theme to an extraordinary extent. 'It is hard to find a non-miraculous kernel of the Gospel.'[4] And that is why Peter, too, was credited with miracles after Jesus's death. He was believed to have been following his great predecessor's tradition.

The ancient evangelists did, however, appreciate that this meant straining their readership's credence. *Matthew* and *Luke*, for example, make some effort to omit stories which seem to them unpersuasive, unedifying or impossible to understand. And *John* omits the vast majority of Jesus's reported miracles, retaining only seven, of a particularly stupendous character. However, the last chapter of that Gospel offers the comment that Jesus, with his followers as witnesses, performed many other actions as well, 'which are not recorded in this book';[5] and many of those actions, indeed, were once again miraculous, described by the word 'sign' (*semeion*) which appears no fewer than seventeen times in *John*'s Gospel.

The miracles attributed to Jesus in the four Gospels amount to as many as thirty-five – and a good many more can be added from non-canonical writings. Stories of this kind must have been passed around, in the first place, in the Aramaic language, and they were long kept alive in Galilee and elsewhere. Even Jews who maintained a profound hostility to Jesus believed that he possessed gifts as a sorcerer and worker of wonders.

The Jews had for many centuries accepted the idea that many sorts of miracles, in addition to healings, took place. They were presented as credentials of religious leadership.[6] Elijah and Elisha were seen to have been powerful enough to arrest and change the course of nature itself, and there were specific Old Testament precedents as well as rabbinical analogies for some of the miraculous acts attributed to Jesus, such as the Stilling of the Storm.

The Hebrew word *oth* needs to be continually borne in mind. It means the sign, the *semeion* as *John* translated it, which not only was an announcement and description of a miraculous happening, but also actually helped to bring that happening about. As we have seen, *John* refers with particular emphasis to these signs, and it seems that the writer of that Gospel, and others, believed that Jesus regarded his apparently miraculous actions as possessing a symbolic character. That is to say, he is represented as considering them to be symbols of his unique status, and this is also how the evangelists wished to present these supposed deeds.

This brings us to the question which modern readers mostly want to answer: did the miracles of Jesus, and of Peter for that matter, really take place? We are naturally very ready to conclude that they did not, and we are encouraged in that readiness by Jesus's own conviction of their symbolic nature. Did Jesus himself, or the evangelists, *not* believe that these miracles actually happened, but believe instead that the reports of them were only *symbols* of Jesus's exceptional powers, which were described in the sort of wondrous, superhuman terms which people of the time understood and were impressed by – even, sometimes, with the employment of magical deception by those who narrated such stories?

The answer, 'Yes, they were only symbolical' seems obvious enough to us, but it would not have been easy to make the same answer acceptable to ancient Jews. They would have seen no sharp distinction between what was miraculous and what was not, since they omitted, generally, to distinguish between the natural and supernatural spheres: between what could be seen, in the course of ordinary human lives, and what could not. The point, to them, was that the natural and supernatural were equally real, and both expressions, in their different ways, of God's will.

However, as they were all too well aware, the supernatural and invisible sphere was difficult to describe and delineate. It was no good trying to do so in intellectual, rational terms, for this was a realm which stood outside rationality and logic. In other words, its existence and activity could be conveyed only in figurative language, by all the metaphor and imagery that could be summoned up to express what was virtually indescribable. What had to be expressed was not plain historical fact but a higher and harder sort of 'truth' altogether. These things were inexpressible in any literal phraseology. But the attempt had to be made in order to arouse and inflame people's imaginations. There were numerous Hellenistic parallels, but this point is particularly applicable to the land of Palestine, where words, it has been said, have never been regarded as necessarily a reflection of fact, but rather possess a vigorous existence of their own. This was a region, and an epoch, in which the difference between practical possibility and impossibility, dry historical truth and untruth, does not always seem relevant or deter-minable. What seemed more important was the assurance that the world of natural causation was often invaded by divinity.

The factors involved do not seem so strange to those who study the Talmud and Midrashim – though this is a thing that relatively few people do. The rabbis who composed those writings liked to couch what they had to say not in the shape of hard fact, but in a manner planned to appeal to the imagination of their readers: that is to say, in a form designed for ordinary people rather than phil-osophers or historians.

This meant that the rabbis' teachings were very much inclined to assume the shapes of parable or allegory, or some other sort of striking literary effect, rather than to take the form of bare historical narrative. They did not ask, and their listeners and readers did not ask, whether the things that were talked about *had really happened.* Sometimes, no doubt, they had happened, because Jesus was evi-dently a most successful healer; healing and faith are intimately connected. But on other occasions the point was, instead, to put a message across: to edify rather than offer a historically accurate record. This has caused a good deal of misunderstanding in modern times, when more importance is attached to historical accuracy. However, that was not at all the preoccupation which ancient Jewish writers preferred to maintain.

This is all another way of saying that the miracles of which the ancient Jews so freely spoke, and which were attributed with equal freedom to Jesus and Peter, did *not,* in a historical sense, take place. And indeed, as we have seen, no one would have thought of putting the question in those terms – since historical truth was not, people felt, what really mattered.

When a well-known rabbi was about to die, it was declared that the stars became visible in broad daylight. Of course that did not actually happen, and we are not even supposed to believe that it did. The statement is only another way of saying what a marvellous man the rabbi was. And exactly the same applies to the miracles attributed to Jesus and Peter. Let us consider one of the miraculous actions ascribed to Jesus, in which Peter participated. Peter was asked

whether his master paid the Jewish tax levied to finance the proceedings of the Temple, and the apostle replied that he did. But
when this was reported to Jesus, he offered, we are told, a miraculous
course of action in order to make the next payment both for Peter
and for himself. His proposal took the form of a command to Peter
himself:

> Go and cast a line in the lake. Take the first fish that comes to the hook,
> open its mouth, and you will find a silver coin. Take that, and pay it in;
> it will meet the tax for us both.[7]

Some modern critics have not liked the look of this passage, which
they have considered too banal and crude to be consistent with the
greatness of Jesus. For surely this is a (pious) fable,[8] and the miracle
which Jesus supposedly ordained never occurred; and, he never, in
reality, supposed that it would; nor would anyone else want to
enquire if it really happened, and if Peter was, indeed, able to extract
the silver coin from the fish. What Jesus was said to have been
advising, in a very practical way, was that people must just be
prepared to meet their obligations, to pay their taxes, and to pay
them from the proceeds of the day's work. However, being an
experienced and popular teacher and preacher, who knew that his
listeners liked flights of fancy, he offered this advice not in direct,
down-to-earth terms, but in the metaphorical, imaginative speech
current at the time.

Later too, when Peter, we are told, failed to walk on the water as
Jesus had, there is no need to explain that he 'began' to do so[9],
because this was another pious story – not a miracle this time, but
a miracle that failed to come off – designed, in this case, to show
that Peter's faith needed Jesus's support.

Two conclusions can therefore be reached. First, the miracles did
not happen; neither Jesus nor Peter performed them. But, second,
they cannot just be eliminated from the story to make it reasonable,
because they were part of the thought-processes of the time, and
therefore, even though non-existent as historical facts, they were
parts of history all the same: vital and essential parts of the total

historical picture. Jesus and Peter were upon the earth at a time when, as we have seen, the actual *reality* of the event, in the sense that we should consider valid, was not a primary or even particularly apposite consideration at all, and we should interpret the New Testament accordingly.

Nowhere, it must be said again, was this point of view more strongly in evidence than throughout Palestine – in Galilee and in Judaea. This was a region where there was always profound religious excitement and emotion, and these were at their highest in the period we are considering. Naturally enough, too, this excitement was intensified by the preaching of Jesus. Like the rest of the ancient world, only even more so, Palestine expected miracles – or, rather, expected the more exalted manifestations of life to be expressed in miraculous terms – and so that is what happened: miracles were invented, as embroideries of what seemed to be taking place all around, and as such were put into words and reported.

Nor were the New Testament writers wholly unaware that, as strict historical facts, these miracles did not take place. It looks, for example, as though the author of *John* was conscious that this was so. For example, when he is describing the most unlikely and fanciful of all such miraculous deeds, the raising of Lazarus from the dead, he clothes this description in words which make the whole story sound symbolical.[10]

Once again, however, the question of whether the event actually occurred as a recordable happening would not have seemed of major concern to the ancient Jews, or to the writers of the Gospels. For what the latter, the evangelists, were concentrating their interest upon was something altogether bigger and more significant: namely, the enormous position of Jesus which the miracle stories were imaginatively designed to illustrate. For that reason, it should be repeated, the miracles, although not events in a rational sense, were exceedingly meaningful all the same, because they illuminated the picture of Jesus which contemporaries envisaged – and in consequence they guided the sequence of events that followed, and indeed they helped to produce these events.

Jesus's alleged miraculous doings, to which his special fame was above all else due, were selected by himself and his followers to serve the same purpose as every other element in his life: that is, to symbolize and promote the dawning of the Kingdom of God, which he himself was bringing about. When, as we saw, Jesus was alleged to have told Peter to pay their taxes with a silver coin found in the mouth of a fish, he was saying, in effect, 'Pay the earthly state's taxes. Although the whole matter is not really very important, since the Kingdom of God is upon us, pay it all the same to avoid irrelevant worldly problems.' In depicting the source from which the payment was to come he is deliberately vague, ironical and humorous, because the whole business is of such secondary significance.

Almost all the miracles act out, and symbolize, the present coming of the Kingdom of God, and its complete realization that lies ahead. These supposedly miraculous happenings are signs: signs that the Deliverer is present, and signs of the greatness of his power. It is from Satan that Jesus is to deliver the world in this New Creation he is bringing. Thus when, for example, like God in the *Book of Job* and the *Psalms of Solomon*, Jesus walks on the water,[11] he is demonstrating a triumph over Satanic evil forces: forces which he is hereby reducing to subjection, while at the same time displaying how potent faith can be. The waters appear again when Jesus is alleged to have calmed the storm which made them turbulent.[12] This turbulence, in a Jewish world in which winds and sea were anthropomorphized, stood for the worldly troubles that the Kingdom of God is bringing to an end. In keeping with the concept of *oth*, Jesus is accomplishing two things at one and the same time: he is symbolizing this divine transformation, but simultaneously he is seeming to bring about its arrival.

The Transfiguration should also be included in this category of miracles. It appears in other Synoptic Gospels and elsewhere in early Christian writings,[13] but here is *Mark*'s version:[14]

Jesus took Peter, James [the Great] and John [the sons of Zebedee] with him and led them up a high mountain where they were alone; and in their presence he was transfigured; his clothes became dazzling white, with a whiteness no bleacher on earth could equal.

They saw Elijah appear, and Moses with him, and there they were, conversing with Jesus. Then Peter spoke: 'Rabbi,' he said, 'how good it is that we are here! Shall we make three shelters, one for you, one for Moses, and one for Elijah?' (For he did not know what to say; they were so terrified.) Then a cloud appeared, casting its shadow over them, and out of the cloud came a voice: 'This is my Son, my Beloved: listen to him.' And now suddenly, when they looked around, there was nobody to be seen but Jesus alone with themselves.

This can be considered an incident staged to convince the disciples, a scene produced by a magician, involving a psychological illusion. But it can also be interpreted as a mystical allegory created by the evangelists or their sources, either for typological motives (that is, to relate Jesus to the Old Testament; see below), or to display the eschatological revelation that was being vouchsafed to Peter, in spite of, and in contrast with, his alleged inadequacy and incomprehension. At all events, the description, with its divine commendation of Jesus, cannot fail to confirm rationalist beliefs that these miracles did not really happen.

In the charged atmosphere of the times, and amid the current belief in miracles, the question of whether Jesus was, in truth, performing such a miraculous act did not acquire any prominence, and was, perhaps, beside the point. However, the scene, or the account of it, was engraved firmly on the minds of storytellers, and of those who listened to them and passed on what they had heard, until the tale reached the evangelists, who later recorded Jesus's career.

Nevertheless, a certain air of mystery not surprisingly remained. As the Gospels show, there could be curious diversities of opinion about what had actually taken place when 'miracles' were reported (thus *Matthew* omitted the healing of the blind man of Bethsaida[15] because he did not believe that Jesus's use of saliva was credible).

All these considerations apply equally to the accounts of miraculous doings by Peter himself, with which his career was likewise abundantly studded. True, some of his supposed cures (for example, those attributed to his shadow and others related to clothing that had been in contact with Paul's skin)[16] could be ascribed to the psychosomatic impact of a mesmeric will on hysterical subjects. Yet there remain other miracles allegedly performed by Peter that are plain miracles, like those believed to have been performed by Jesus himself. His 'escape from prison', for example (Chapter 7, note 18), is plainly miraculous and bears an uncomfortable similarity to pagan prototypes (those who choose to believe in it are sometimes driven to suppose that the guards who let him go were drugged). Peter's 'miracles', in general, 'reflect ... attempts to make historical sense of the highly coloured stories which Christians at Antioch, Caesarea or Jerusalem had told about the community's early years'.[17]

The historian or would-be historian can hardly be content to agree with the pagan Quadratus (c.AD 125) that the Christian miracles *did* take place, but were magically produced;[18] nor will he be inclined to accept the assertion of the fifth-century Christian theologian Vincent of Lérins that 'we must keep to what has been believed everywhere, always, and by everybody',[19] or that certain occurrences, not capable of verification by history, could and did take place. Call the so-called miracles, if you wish, 'trans-history' or 'meta-history' or 'beyond history'.[20] But the fact remains that such 'happenings' lie outside nature and rationality, and could only be accepted by *faith*. The would-be historian has to ignore them as events because they need faith to inspire belief in them, and are, consequently, out of the range of the historian's knowledge. However, the fact that people told of them, and often credited them, still deserves his or her careful attention because the credulous attitude of those persons became a portion of history, and influenced its evolution.

One suggestion about the sort of thing that might have taken place goes like this.[21] Let us imagine a group of followers of Jesus collected together and talking. They are keen to listen to any visitor who has stories to tell about the Master, especially stories that they have not heard before. And one such visitor, we may suppose, tells one of the tales he has been told about Peter, of how Jesus made it possible for him to walk on the water (Chapter 4, note 17), at least during the time when he fixed his gaze upon Jesus and continued to move, step by step, nearer to where Jesus was. It was only when Peter let his concentration be distracted from Jesus to the menacing winds and waters that encompassed him that he started to sink, until Jesus raised him up and brought him to safety.

Very possibly there were people present who listened to this story with incredulity, feeling scepticism about whether anything of the kind could, in fact, have actually happened. But it is also not unlikely that some other member of the group declared that he, for his part, believed in the tale because he had had what might be called a comparable experience. That is to say, perhaps, he had been assailed by frightful difficulties which threatened to get him down and submerge him, but found that he could overcome them all, provided only that he kept his gaze fastened upon Christ, and continually endeavoured to move closer and closer to him. It was only when the listener permitted himself to become completely immersed in his own problems and fears that he found himself in danger of being overwhelmed by them: when he looked at Jesus, like Peter, he was all right.

This is, of course, wholly hypothetical. But it may well have been the kind of thing that happened. Factual events, of course, did not enter into the matter at all; we are not being told anything new about the historical Jesus. What we are being told about is the Christian experience. It is perfectly likely that much of it came into being in this type of vivid imagistic form – and was only later transposed into something that was meant to look like a narrative history, but which really was not.

One such occasion was that of the Pentecost 'miracle' after Jesus's death, when everyone 'talked in other tongues',[22] or rather emitted strange, ecstatic utterances (not foreign languages).[23] Ecstatic speech of this kind – not unknown to the Jews – was allegedly practised later by the apocalyptic, prophetic Christian sect of the Montanists (second and third centuries AD) and is still uttered by the Pentecostalists today.

A 'new' tongue meant a redeemed community. Hostile observers thought the speakers were drunk, but Peter protested that 'it is only nine in the morning'.[24] It has been suggested that the facts had been 'amplified by tradition into a rhapsody'.[25] And another sceptical view maintained that a strong wind, the sirocco, provided the psychological background for the wondrous event;[26] those who have felt the effects of the German Föhn will view the latter interpretation with sympathy. The sirocco allegedly affected the disturbed emotions of the disciples – and indeed, it brought them a sort of relief. They had gone through a traumatic period of horrifying depression when the humiliation of Jesus's disastrous death seemingly put an end to all their hopes. But then their spirits had been revived to a fantastic degree by the belief that God had raised him from the dead and translated him to heaven, to be invested with the Kingship which he would soon return to exercise on earth.

To demonstrate these wonders God had sent to the world his *ruah*, his sacred wind.[27] It was a sign, portending what was to come. It elevated the disciples into a high state of excitement; they started weeping and singing and shouting, as if they were drunk. And indeed that is how they seemed, filled with the marvel and glory of what they believed had occurred.

Scholars have tried to define, by one phrase or another, what the miracles really were and signified. They were like myths. The real meaning of a myth, we are told, is not to provide an objective image, but to express man's understanding of himself in his world. The Gospel writers made use of legendary motifs and features to make more visible the significance of Jesus as the divine bringer of salvation. The miracle stories are to be seen as theological statements in dramatized form. A pre-scientific age would not approach traditions of miraculous happenings with the caution, indeed suspicion, which is common in our day, since it would not be looking for the same things.

Often, too, the evangelists had specific messages in mind. The Feeding of the Five Thousand was probably designed to symbolize the Eucharist.[28] The miraculous catching of fish was not only a Jewish sign of God's favour, but a forecast of the disciples' later catching of men.[29] Moreover, Jesus's ten miracles echoed the ten miracles of Moses in Egypt, and Elisha's miracles were another recognized prototype.

By the same token, this was an age of visions. It was not considered at all strange that people should claim to have seen them. They were abundant in the Old Testament, and Jews frequently believed that they themselves had been accorded hallucinatory, often prophetic, visions, although these were not always regarded as reliable. Jesus was said to have had similar experiences. The Jews regarded him as 'possessed', although he would not accept this definition.[30]

After Jesus's death the surviving community of his followers continued to have visionary experiences. The women, it was stated, had a 'vision of angels' at Jesus's tomb.[31] Stephen was also said to have believed he saw visions.[32] And so did the subject of the present inquiry, Peter. The 'angel' who supposedly rescued him from prison[33] after his arrest in AD41/42 has been interpreted as the product of a dream. The empresses Aelia and Licinia Eudoxia dedicated his 'chains' in the Churches of the Holy Apostles at Constantinople and S. Pietro in Vincoli at Rome (AD 439, 449).

Peter himself, it is true, was said to question the meaning of such phenomena,[34] and according to 2 Peter he warned against the possibly misleading character of 'tales artfully spun'.[35] Nevertheless, he saw visions and they fortified his position. Moreover, the belief in them persisted, and the experience of Paul, before the gates of Damascus, was the most spectacular of all[36] – although there was a certain scepticism about whether it really happened.[37]

Yet the scepticism paled before general credulity, and this is the sort of thing, as has already been stated, which presents the historian with an obstacle. It must be admitted that these supposed visions, like 'miracles', affected the course of history (as did those of Joan of Arc). Yet the historian must also maintain the rationalistic attitude that the visions have to be left out of his or her cognizance. Within the realm of rational history, they did not happen – although the belief that they had happened influenced the course of events.

A further factor that has to be borne in mind, and when necessary discounted, is the extremely powerful prevalence, among Jesus and Peter and their Jewish and Christian contemporaries, of typology: the interpretation of texts in the Old Testament (that is to say, the Jewish Bible, since some would prefer not to use the term 'Old Testament', in order to avoid causing offence to Jews) as predicting the prefiguring subsequent and current developments. Thus almost everything that happened to Jesus or Peter, or was done by them, was seen as an echo of the earlier scriptures – often by what seems to us by a far-fetched kind of interpretation. This creates a great gulf between our ways of thinking and those of the authors of the Old and New Testaments alike.

The Jews and early Christians venerated their Bible with a thoroughgoing, literal veneration that caused them to see every event, or possible event, in the light of it. They were able to find what they regarded as substantial and valid links between the contents of this holy book, the Old Testament, and every later happening throughout the entire course of history, right up to their own times and onwards into the indefinite future of the world. These echoes seemed to come from each successive part of the Bible. After the legendary origins of humanity, and the mixture of legend and proto-history that characterized the subsequent books, came the 'tables', which they believed that God, more than a millennium previously, had passed to Moses on Mount Sinai, the two tablets of the Testimony, 'the handiwork of God'.[38] This was the Covenant, the supreme substance of the Jewish interpretation of history, comprising, it would seem, the first five books of the Hebrew Bible, the Torah, called the Pentateuch by the Greeks. Torah is often translated as 'Law', but originally it meant teaching conveyed by divine revelation.

The Torah was all-important, but second to it came those books in the Old Testament relating to the prophets. These revered personages – notably Elijah, Elisha, Amos, Hosea, Isaiah, Jeremiah and Ezekiel, and others too – were ascribed words and deeds which reverberated through the subsequent history of the Jews and early Christians, who continued to interpret everything that happened in accordance with what one or another of these prophets had foretold, or had actually prefigured in their own careers and lives. Another source of supposed predictions and rehearsals of the future was provided by the *Psalms*, known as the Psalms of David because, according to (mistaken) tradition, they were attributed to the authorship of that revered king.

This total reliance on the supposed authority of the Old Testament as a source of foretellings and prefigurations is the phenomenon usually described as 'typology', from the Greek word *typos*, meaning model or pattern. Its significance to the ancient Jews cannot be overestimated, since it came to signify that the Torah, reinforced by the prophets and the *Psalms*, appeared to embody the unique and totally effective expression of the will of God, and the complete revelation of his purpose and intentions, and of everything that he wants people to be and do.

The continuous attention paid to the Bible over ancient century after century was founded upon the conviction that every event and prospective or possible event must inevitably and necessarily be seen as a reflection of what was contained in the scriptural writings. In other words, the whole of human history, so the Jews believed – though Friedrich Nietzsche, like others, has described the idea as wholly ridiculous – was specifically designed and organized by God with a view to the correspondence between what happened now and what had happened in earlier times.

Indeed, what had happened in earlier times, it was believed, had actually been *planned* by God to prefigure all later events, right up to the age in which one was living. The Jews went further still because, although well aware of false prophets and false interpretations of prophecy, they totally excluded from practicability or possibility any current or future happenings which, in their view, had *not* been announced or prefigured in the books of their Bible. This meant that the books in question needed to be interpreted with extreme ingenuity and a fantastic array of subtleties, many involving manipulations of a strained and improbable character, so as to enable their antiquated contents to be satisfactorily 'updated' to provide contemporary meanings and fulfilments.

What is essential, however, for our present purpose is to appreciate also that this attitude was faithfully preserved and maintained by the early Christians – who may even, in some cases, have possessed manuals of Old Testament quotations upon which they could draw. And that was how the New Testament, which these Christians created, went out of its way to present the lives of Jesus and Peter and their companions as an entire compendious series of detailed fulfilments of what the Torah, the prophets and the *Psalms* had laid down and foretold.

To take a few of very many examples, Jesus's rescue of the world echoed Moses's rescue from Egypt, his 'meekness' recalled that of Moses,[39] his ten 'miracles' were not oblivious of Moses's miracles in Egypt or of Elisha's cycle of miracles, and the Messianic associations of the House of David were recognized. Moreover, the Transfiguration, as we have seen, gives a prominent role to Elijah.[40] There are more than twenty echoes of the Old Testament in the accounts of Jesus's death alone. And even the references to the Marys echo biblical prototypes.[41]

Furthermore, there is reason to believe that this was the attitude not only of people towards Jesus,[42] but also of Jesus himself. *Luke* tells us so, when reporting Jesus's sermon at Nazareth,[43] which cited, we are told, a passage in *Isaiah*;[44] and Jesus designed his entry into Jerusalem as a deliberate carrying-out of what *Jeremiah* and *Isaiah* had foretold.[45]

Indeed, there can be no doubt that Jesus had this typological aspect in mind at every juncture of his career. Nor is this in any way surprising, since he was a Jew and felt the same reverence for the Scriptures, the Old Testament, as anyone of the same faith must have felt. Jesus saw himself as a prophet and was taunted by his captors because that was his view.[46] *Mark*, in particular, is profoundly conscious of Jesus's Old Testament links.

All this has to be borne in mind when any examination of Jesus or Peter, or of those who accompanied them, is attempted. And it is of the utmost importance because the belief of the Christians, inherited from the Jews, that the Scriptures were being fulfilled, and must be fulfilled, frequently directed the course of events. At the same time, however, one cannot avoid the conclusion that this makes life very difficult for the would-be historian. In particular, as has already been pointed out, many of the Old Testament passages cited by the New Testament as prefigurations or events or utterances receiving later fulfilment cannot conceivably, by any objective kind of reasoning, be interpreted in any such sense.

Nevertheless, this was the point of view which guided ancient Jewish history – and which guided, also, the thinking of early Christianity, so that any study of Jesus or Peter or Paul has to remember it at every stage. That is to say, to these early Christians the Jewish Bible, the Old Testament, appeared full of prophecies, examples, warnings, patterns of behaviour and other pieces of information which possessed a direct relation to Jesus, although he lived so many hundreds of years after those passages had been written down. And that material equally possessed a direct relation to the early Christians themselves, who belonged to the generations coincident with or immediately following the lifetime of Jesus. Moreover, this seems to have been a conviction that Jesus himself shared.

The inevitable historical problem which is raised by these facts has already been touched upon, but must now be given further attention. When Jesus or Peter or his other followers believed that some turn of events coincided accurately with an Old Testament prophecy or prefiguration, does that signify that Jesus or the others had deliberately, intentionally, arranged what happened in order to ensure that the text in question should receive fulfilment? In the case of Jesus's entry into Jerusalem, it may be supposed that this was the case. And his Nazareth sermon does seem to have been designed (or invented?) in order to fulfil a passage in *Isaiah*; if the sermon took place, and was not a fictitious creation, it and its supposed fulfilment of the Old Testament passage served a convenient purpose, because Jesus reportedly employed the occasion to dwell on the Kingdom of God, the proclamation of which was his principal purpose. But those are not the only two relevant incidents. At every juncture, we have to consider whether what Jesus did and said was motivated by a desire to fulfil the Old Testament; and the same applies to Peter.

Jesus is actually stated, when he appeared on earth again after his Resurrection – at the time when Peter led his followers – to have explained to those who saw and heard him, the passages in the whole of the Old Testament that referred to himself.[47] In his earlier, earthly career, too, Jesus had allegedly emphasized on more than one occasion this same connection with the Old Testament and what it recorded. And, when he was arrested, *Mark* records that what he said was this: *let the Scriptures be fulfilled*.[48] Elsewhere, too, *Mark* leaves us in no doubt that this was Jesus's attitude and intention, for he ascribes to him no fewer than thirty-seven explicit quotations from the Old Testament, while *Matthew* adds a further twenty-eight. In other words, this emphasis on typology is stated, in the most definite terms, to go back to Jesus himself.

The Christian God, Peter was said to have declared, was the God of Abraham, Isaac, Jacob and Moses.[49] Besides, Jesus was concerned with later Old Testament personages as well, employing David, Solomon, Elijah, Elisha or Jonah as prototypes of himself, and of John the Baptist, in a manner which is thoroughly alien to modern ways of thinking.

Moreover, the same applies to the relevance of ancient Hebrew institutions. Jesus is reported as seeing the Covenant and the priesthood, for example, as models and prototypes of what he himself was doing. Indeed, he is presented as interpreting the entire past history of Israel in this light. The hopes of the earlier Israelites, he believed, were being brought to fulfilment by himself and his disciples. When Israel, in ancient days, was delivered by God, he discerns in this a foreshadowing of the greater deliverance that he himself is bringing; and when the country had been struck by earlier disasters, because of its failure to have faith, that seems to him to prefigure the punishment which will be visited upon the persons who reject his own mission.

Wicked Gentiles are not excluded from this threatened punishment, but it is with the Jews that Jesus is primarily concerned, and the whole destiny of Israel.

The Scriptures, then, were the primary means of revelation in Jesus's world, and the New Testament writers were right in believing that Jesus himself had wholeheartedly adopted the same conception.

So this was the reverential attitude to the Old Testament upon which Peter, inevitably, established his own twofold career, first as the principal apostle of Jesus, and second as the leader of his followers after his death. Indeed, he was said to have declared to the assembled multitude, in the Temple porch, the categorical message, 'You are the heirs of the Prophets; you are within the Covenant which God made with your fathers.'[50]And *1 Peter* alone, purporting to be a letter which Peter himself had written, is made to contain as many as sixty Old Testament quotations.

Moreover, we are told that Paul, too, confirmed that this attitude continued to prevail. The Letter to the Hebrews attributed to him refers to the same covenant and repeats the same conviction,[51] showing clearly that its author saw the Old Testament not only as furnishing predictions, but even as having granted, in advance, positive information about Jesus and what he would say and do. And the Acts of the Apostles declares that Paul asserted to Agrippa II, Jewish king of the northern regions adjoining Judaea (Ituraea, Abilene, Arcene), 'I assert nothing beyond what was foretold by the Prophets and by Moses.'[52] True, not everything that *Acts* records is historical truth. Yet the inclusion of such a statement in the book shows clearly the spirit that inspired Paul and Peter and their contemporaries, just as it had animated Jesus and other Jews of previous centuries. The Gospel writers fell readily in with the same attitude, and indeed believed that with Jesus's life the Scriptures had come true.

It is necessary, also, for any historian who aims at an understanding of how people thought to appreciate that this attachment to typology persisted long after New Testament times. For example, Justin Martyr, in the second century AD, was still devoted to the idea, and produced a long list of scriptural predictions and foreshadowings that he believed had been fulfilled. They include some comparisons that are unconvincing and needed a good deal of distortion. Nevertheless, Justin felt able to assert, about activities in which he himself had participated, 'We do this because with our own eyes we see these things having happened and happening as was prophesied.'[53]

As for Augustine, he was aware that a weakness of this argument lay in the fact that Jesus had not been actually mentioned, and that his doings, therefore, had not been specifically foretold, in so many words, in the Old Testament. Nevertheless, Augustine felt able to add that Jesus had obviously been *meant*.[54] Indeed, the idea was now carried to its ultimate extremity, when it came to be vigorously pronounced not merely that the references to Jesus in the Old Testament were implicit or indirect or secondary, but that the entire collection of its books did not possess any meaning or significance whatsoever except in their allusions to Christ, whose life fulfilled every single prediction and prefiguration that had appeared in the pages of the Old Testament writers.

All the same, it is as well to appreciate – as Peter and others who worked with him must have appreciated – that Jesus, despite his wholehearted adherence to typology, did not by any means leave this matter just where it had been. Certainly, it was said that he denied that he had come to *abolish* the Law and the prophets.[55] Nevertheless, he and his apostles handled Scripture not altogether uncritically, and believed that they themselves had contributed a big, additional development to this typological sort of interpretation.[56] They were convinced that the Kingdom of God which was coming into being, and which was about to introduce the end of the world, fulfilled the Old Testament – but it fulfilled it in a new way of its own. In other words, the role of the Old Testament, if not restricted, had been more sharply defined, with innovations added: Jesus saw it not as dominant but as subsidiary to his mission.[57]

One legitimate way of expressing this attitude is to say that, while closely following and deeply honouring the Old Testament, Jesus interpreted it not as his master but as his servant. The Old Testament was rarely employed by Jesus and Peter and the rest to *create* events, although I believe that Jesus's entry into Jerusalem, directly guided by the Scriptures, may have been an exception – as, in the Gospels, was the place of his birth. Rarely, too, did the Scriptures actually lead the way in which Jesus's thoughts ran. However, the Old

Testament could add punch to his arguments, and could supplement his meanings by its rich background of allusions.

It could also provide edifying *contrasts*, which were, indeed, greater than the similarities. To take one example, Elisha, when he was recruited, asked Elijah for permission to say farewell to his parents; whereas, when Jesus called his disciples, there was no room for anything of the kind.[58]

So Jesus only accepted typology on his own conditions. But he did accept it, and so therefore did Peter – who could be seen as the new Abraham, head of a new people – and so did Paul, neither of whom can even begin to be understood unless we appreciate the typological factor in their thought and behaviour.

Here, then, is the second unfamiliar element in the attitudes of the day which the modern historian has to confront. The first was the ancient readiness to believe in miracles and visions. And this second element is the ancient determination to see everything that was said and that happened in terms of the Old Testament. Both attitudes will need to be borne in mind in this study of Peter, just as they have to be borne in mind in studies of Jesus and Paul.

These are serious obstacles, nowadays, to attaining an objective view. Indeed, in dealing with Peter they are particularly serious because of the deficiency of sources presenting any other kind of picture. More will be said elsewhere about the supposedly miraculous element in our record of Peter. Less, perhaps, will be stated explicitly about the typological aspect, but it must not be forgotten that it was always there, pervading people's minds. It remained, that is to say, very dominant and powerful. If Peter said or did anything, or if anything happened to him, it is a reasonable assumption that an Old Testament precedent could be, and was, quoted – despite the new twist that Jesus had given to this type of interpretation, a twist which Peter acknowledged and retained.

Here, then, are three of the difficulties that any historian attempting to find out the truth about Peter (as about Jesus and Paul) has to contend with: miracles, visions and typology. He or she must thread a way through these hazards and allurements, and try to find out what happenings lie behind them.

Bibliographical note

For references to Peter in the New Testament, see G. Lüdemann, *Early Christianity According to the Traditions in Acts* (1989), p. 1; R. Pesch, *Simon-Petrus* (1980), pp. 160f.

On exorcisms, healings and 'Thaumaturgy', see M. Smith, *Jesus the Magician* (1978), pp. 8, 159, 191, 196; cf. G. Vermes, *Jesus the Jew* (1973), index ss.vv.; C. F. Evans, *The Beginning of the Gospel* (1968), pp. 30f., 43.

On Jewish curative powers, see G. Vermes, op. cit., index ss.vvi. Hanina, healing, Honi; A. E. Harvey, *Companion to the Gospels*, p. 218; D. Tiede, *Jesus and the Future* (1990), p. 46.

Peter's miraculous escape from prison is the subject of a poem by Charles Wesley, in E. P. Clowney, *The Message of I Peter*, p. 98. Another of Peter's 'miracles' was the striking dead of the dishonest Ananias and Sapphira, *Acts* 5.5, 10.

For divergent early Christian opinions about miracles, see Mark 6.51–2; *John* 6.24ff.; H. Hendrickz, *Resurrection Narratives* (1978), pp. 39ff.

Definitions of ecstasy are given in A. Schweitzer, *The Quest of the Historical Jesus* (1906), pp. 177f., 301 note, 302 note.

It is doubtful whether Moses and Elijah in the Transfiguration are intended to stand for the Law and the prophets: see J. A. Fitzmyer, *The Gospel According to Luke* (1981).

Chapter 2

THE SOURCES

The non-canonical Gospels can tell us little about Peter: for example, the Gospel of Thomas deserves a certain amount of attention. However, the principal source is, of course, the New Testament. It is the despair of those who seek plain historical truth. And yet it remains indispensable to the historian.[1]

It is also indispensable for whatever information we are able to acquire about Peter as Jesus's principal helper, and as the subsequent leader of his followers. It is only through the New Testament that we are in a position to get anywhere near the real Peter at all. And yet to employ these books for such a purpose is exceedingly difficult all the same, because as sources of factual information they are ludicrously insufficient and need to be examined with the utmost care before any reliable evidence can be derived from them.

For historical documents are by no means what they set out to be. Actual events, as such, are not what they are primarily interested in. Certainly, such facts can be found in these books, if one looks carefully enough. However, they do not appear for their own sake, but rather for reasons that are *religious*. The books of the New Testament are religious, not historical, documents. Their authors wrote them not to record and repeat happenings and sayings, but to arouse and extend faith in Jesus Christ as risen Lord and Saviour; they are perfectly explicit on this point.[2] As some like to put it, therefore, the Gospels cannot be described as history at all, but rather as *salvation-history*.

The most important, and initial, part of the New Testament comprises the four Gospels, and these are the principal sources for the first part of Peter's career.

Unfortunately, however, their composition was not contemporary with his lifetime (although some recent research tries to bring them, or the authorities on which they depend, closer in date to the events they describe).[3] They are also an extraordinary jumble of contradictions, puzzles, selectivities and hints that are left in the air. They are not history, and yet they do not fit into any other recognized literary genre either.

Nor is there even any certainty about the language in which they were first written. They have come down to us in Greek, yet according to one theory their original language was Aramaic. This is a view that has not won general acceptance. Nevertheless, it is quite widely believed that there existed Aramaic or Hebrew documents, now lost, on which the Gospels were partly based.

Regrettably, we are unaware of who the writers of the four Gospels were. They are, of course, ascribed to Jesus's apostles Matthew and John, and to Mark (John Mark) and Luke, who were companions of Paul. Yet each of these attributions is clouded by serious and convincing doubts. It was a common phenomenon, in the ancient world, to write something and then to attribute it to some eminent figure in the past, in order to give greater weight to what had been written, and in order to do honour to the man to whom it was attributed; and that is what has happened here.

The Gospels were written to proclaim *euangelion* or 'good news': the news that Jesus was the Messiah and Son of God, whose Kingdom he was inaugurating, with Peter as his principal helper. That is why they are 'ultimately poetic and devotional texts, and do not even purport to be chronicles'.[4] Like the writers of other parts of the New Testament, the authors of the Gospels were primarily interested in *edification*. And it was the edification of their own readers that they had principally in mind. 'Each evangelist was concerned with the particular questions, problems and difficulties which affected his own community.'[5] This meant, inevitably, that their books are often anachronistic, 'updating' the significance of what their writers believed had happened and had been said in the past. And they diverge from one another sharply in their versions of those events and sayings. It is a waste of time to try to harmonize these versions and pretend that they do not really differ from one another: the fact that there were four of them shows how open the tradition was.

There have been a great many arguments about the dating and sequence of the Gospels – upon which we have to rely in order to learn about Peter's early career during Jesus's lifetime.

Although some contest this – and have done so very recently – there is a fair measure of agreement that the earliest version available to us appears in the Gospel of Mark. Quite early dates have been suggested: the 60s AD when the First Jewish Revolt was imminent, or even earlier – for example, Clement of Alexandria believed, against modern opinion, that Saint Mark himself, the companion of Paul, was the author of the book.[6] But what looks more convincing is the fact that this writer attributes to Jesus certain sayings which can best be interpreted as 'prophecies' of that revolt uttered *after it had taken place*. One thinks particularly of the passage which begins: 'When you see "the abomination of desolation" usurping a place which is not his (let the reader understand), then those who are in Judaea must take to the hills.'[7] Certainly the 'abomination' created by the Roman capture of Jerusalem in AD 70 was an invitation to take to the hills, and when the Gospel writes of 'the tearing of the Temple's curtain in two',[8] ascribed to the time of the Crucifixion, it is difficult not to suppose that its writer has the Romans' destruction of the Temple in the same year 70 in mind. This seems more probable than the supposition that the passages in question were written *before* the revolt, prophesying, with suspicious accuracy, that it was going to occur.

Yet the situation may not be quite as simple as all that. There remains the possibility, much strengthened by the discovery of a fragment of the Gospel in Cave 7 at Qumran, that the first version of the Gospel of Mark had indeed been written before the rebellion, and that additions were made to it after the revolt was over. However, the whole apocalyptic tone of various sections in the Gospel does leave a strong impression that the entire work was composed, in its final form, at this later stage – after the uprising had been suppressed.

Since it cannot nowadays be seriously maintained, despite arguments to the contrary, that any of the other Gospels are older than *Mark*,[9] we are left with the conclusion that this earliest surviving account of Jesus's life, and of Peter's career while Jesus was still alive, was written down between thirty and forty years after the Crucifixion. This need not be a reason for total despair about the reliability of the tradition. By way of comparison, we do pay quite a lot of attention to Livy (or at least to his historical sections) and Tacitus, although they were writing about things that had happened a good many years before their own lifetimes.

Mark offers a view of Jesus's life which, despite its careful selectiveness, is a great deal more many-sided and complete than the incidental allusions offered, at an earlier date, by the Letters of Paul – although the writer of *Mark*, like Paul, does not seem to know very much about the substance of Jesus's teaching. Reference has been made to the probability that *Mark* was written in the aftermath of the First Jewish Revolt; and it does not seem fortuitous that the book detaches itself from the cause of the Jews, attacking them with direct and unmistakable ferocity, while also, though less directly, offering a by no means favourable view of the Jewish Christians.[10]

And this opinion of the Jews may well be responsible for one of the most enigmatic and peculiar features of this Gospel, the *Messianic Secret*: the author's repeated record of Jesus's insistence that his proclamation of the Kingdom of God, and the miracles allegedly accompanying this proclamation, should be kept a secret, and not given any degree of wide circulation. The reasons for this injunction (which was contradicted, one might think, by the crowds that flocked to Jesus's teaching) have been disputed. But the fact evidently was that the author of *Mark*, so conscious of the Old Testament,[11] felt disconcerted – like many others – because Jesus's message had not been accepted by his fellow-Jews; and so he endeavoured to brush aside or explain away this rejection on the grounds that *Jesus himself* had not desired that his proclamation should become widely known or should be given any degree of publicity. It was not a very plausible supposition on the part of the author of *Mark*, but he did the best that could be done with it. An alternative suggestion – and this might conceivably have been Jesus's own idea – is that the secrecy was stressed because Peter and others seemed to have shown such a disastrous failure to understand the nature of Jesus's mission.

The author of this Gospel of Mark was a man of no mean talent. He knew well how to build up mounting tension, and he wrote in a fast-moving, concise, idiomatic, fresh and circumstantial manner. Fast-moving indeed: almost unremittingly breathless. The man who wrote this Gospel possessed an individual and vigorous mind. And he understood how to tell a dramatic story, sometimes not without ironic implications.

It has been suggested, as we have seen, that the Gospels, and *Mark* in particular, are translations from the Aramaic. Yet *Mark*'s style looks too idiosyncratic and lively to represent anything that an ancient translator was capable of producing. Reference has also been made to the theory that the text which we possess might be a revision of an earlier version, now lost. This does not seem particularly probable; the thesis of a lost original, in whatever language, can scarcely be sustained. However, the author of *Mark* did make use of traditional material, notably in the last surviving verses of the Gospel. It would be interesting to know where this work came into being. Was it written in Rome, or Alexandria, or Galilee? Or at Antioch, where after Jesus's death the Christian Church managed to establish itself? We cannot tell. All we can say is that it is one of the most surprising and original works that have ever been written.

Moreover, *Mark* is vital to our knowledge of Peter. Papias, writing in c.AD, indicated – after 'listening' to John, who is not John the apostle but a later John, 'the Elder'[12] – that Saint Mark himself, the John Mark whom *Acts* mentions as a companion of Paul, not only wrote the Gospel that bore his name, but was close to Peter, who, even if he does not play an altogether outstanding part, figures quite extensively in this Gospel. This is what Papias, according to Eusebius, said:[13]

> Mark, having become Peter's interpreter, wrote down accurately every-thing that he remembered, without however recording in order what was either said or done by the Lord.
>
> For he neither heard the Lord, nor followed him, but subsequently attached himself to Peter, who used to frame his teachings to the needs of his hearers, but had no design of giving a connected account of the Lord's discourses.
>
> So Mark made no mistake, while he thus wrote down some things as he remembered them. For he made it his own care not to omit anything that he heard, or to set down any false statement therein.

It has been suggested that this link between Mark and Peter, if it existed, cannot have been as close as all that, since the author of *Mark* is very ignorant of Palestinian geography. There is an opposite argument, that the largely derogatory picture of Peter which the Gospel presents must necessarily go back to information obtained from Peter himself. The picture is indeed distinctly critical, although it shows Peter asking Jesus a good many questions. But the argument is not impressive because people are not necessarily or habitually derogatory about themselves.

On balance, however, even if we cannot accept that the Gospel was written by Paul's companion Mark, it seems too sweeping and arbitrary to reject Papias altogether, and to believe that he had just got hold of entirely wrong information when he linked the author of the Gospel directly with Peter. The probability that the Gospel is early tends to favour what Papias said, even if he is wrong about the identity of its author. It therefore seems reasonable to suppose, as most of the Fathers did, that Papias had a core of reliable fact at his disposal when he offered the opinion that the author of *Mark*, whoever he was, had more extensive and reliable information to offer about Peter than any other Gospel.

When Papias refers to Mark as Peter's 'interpreter', it is uncertain whether he means the 'interpreter' of Peter's role (according to the judgement of the Gentile Church), or 'translator' (from Aramaic), or 'explainer'. The last view would fit in with the fact that Peter lacked a rabbinical higher education, so that Mark could usefully polish his written style or convert his oral communications into a literary form. The conclusion of the Gospel, however, is missing: did it, perhaps, describe a post-Resurrection Appearance of Jesus to Peter?

Matthew and *Luke* were written after *Mark*, at some period during the last three decades of the first century AD: perhaps between 75 and 85. They employed not only, in all probability, *Mark* (with several kinds of alteration), but also certain sources that the author of *Mark* had not used, or probably even known about. The information derived from these sources added up to something like two hundred verses (nearly a third of the total quantity of *Mark*); and *Matthew* and *Luke* make virtually identical use of that information, often to the point of exact verbal correspondence.

The two hundred verses in question, generally described as products of Q (from the German *Quelle*, source), consist principally of sayings of Jesus. There are at least three different opinions of this Q material. One maintains that it originally consisted of a document, perhaps written initially in Aramaic and subsequently in Greek. The second view, pointing out that there are no traces of any such document today, denies that it ever existed, and argues that the Q material reached *Matthew* and *Luke* through purely oral channels. The third view about Q is that both these above-mentioned theories contain an element of truth, and that the material which goes by this name was derived from sources that had been handed down partly in writing and partly by word of mouth.

But this compromise is not really very satisfactory, since the Q

material, whether handed down orally or in writing, contains certain
consistent, homogeneous features which deny that it was cobbled
together in this twofold way. For instance, it places a constant and
uniform emphasis on the moral instruction attributed to Jesus, and
stresses the prophetic element in his utterances with equal con-
sistency. Moreover, Q invariably insists that Jesus is *already* establishing the Kingdom of God upon the earth. This material shows a
deep consciousness that a crisis is already under way; and that
history is entering upon its final and ultimate process. Such, then,
is the process in which Peter played such a leading part – and *Mark's*
depreciation of him is largely avoided by the inclusion of additional
pro-Petrine material, though the shortcomings that disciples found
it so easy to display are not ignored.[14]

It was suggested that *Mark* might have originated at Antioch in
Syria. And the same suggestion has been made about Q. We cannot
tell if this is right or not. For, after all, we have never seen the Q
material, and efforts to ferret it out and reconstruct it are rarely
indisputable. Nor can we identify even the approximate date when
the material came into existence. One suggestion is that the Q
passages go back to a date not far removed from AD 50, or even
earlier – in which case they might even precede, chronologically, the
Letters of Paul. But this remains uncertain.

Nevertheless, *Matthew* is of great importance to our present study,
because Peter's prominence is greater there than in *Mark*, even if he
does not play much of a part in the Gospel until chapter 14. And
Mark's adverse remarks about him, as we saw earlier, are mostly
avoided.

Moreover, *Matthew* uniquely records Peter's Confession and his
Commissioning by Jesus. That is one conspicuous example of this
Gospel's expansion of *Mark*. True, *Matthew* reproduces more than
six hundred of *Mark's* 661 verses, in language that is often changed
only a little, if at all. But *Matthew*, all the same, may well be
more primitive in parts, and its expansions and enrichments and
adaptations of the Marcan material are conspicuous.[15]

The addition of the Q material has already been mentioned. But over and above this material, *Matthew* also derives a whole lot of information, amounting to some four hundred verses, from a different source altogether. This category of information is customarily classified as M. The extent to which it represents a unity, however, is controversial. It may be described as a unity in the sense that a single theme runs through it: there is constant emphasis upon the practical needs and requirements of daily life, so that M presents a design for living. And it displays signs of quite other tendencies as well, notably instruction, and especially emphatic citations from the Old Testament, and, in addition, a special interest in narrative, so that the M material must be seen as displaying a mixed and multiple character. Once again, as was the case with Q, we cannot tell whether the M tradition came from written documentary sources (now lost) or was handed down orally.

This composite Gospel of Matthew is notable for its parallelisms, especially in triad form (passages displaying a pattern of threefold phraseology). And it is notable, also, for its personal metaphors. It is replete, too, with judgements and warnings. And it has been used to justify the modern theory that the Gospels are founded on the contents of liturgical ceremonial.

Matthew was preferred to *Mark* in ancient times, as its position in the New Testament as the first of the Gospels confirms. It was preferred for a variety of reasons. One was the belief that it had been written by one of Jesus's apostles. Another was its marked veneration for the divine, sacred person of Christ. And yet another reason why *Matthew* was preferred was its inclusion of lengthy, monumental set pieces of discourse. The superior literary style of the book was a further attraction, and the new stories which it included added richness and fascination. Nor can one ignore the fact that it was this Gospel which provided the passage which formed the foundation of the Primacy of Peter, and was therefore the principal basis of the claims of Roman Catholicism. Whatever the truth of such claims, it seems probable that this evangelist saw Peter as the principal link between Jesus and the Christian community of his own day.

We do not know the place where *Matthew*, any more than *Mark*, was composed. Among numerous guesses, perhaps Alexandria and Antioch are particularly plausible, and especially Antioch. But whatever may be the answer to that problem, it remains evident that *Matthew* is the most emphatically Jewish of all the four Gospels. Parts of the book are based on Semitic originals, and Semitic word-plays occur. Moreover, *Matthew* stresses the authority of the Jewish law. This Gospel sees Jesus as the new Moses. And it is careful to note, as we have seen, how Jesus's career and death fulfilled Old Testament prophecies. No doubt there were Gentile Christians among the readership of the work, as there were among the reader-ship of the other Gospels as well. But *Matthew* was also, very definitely, writing for the *Jewish* Christians – of whom there were, at that time, many throughout the eastern provinces of the Roman empire.

In the light of all this, it may at first sight seem strange that the Gospel of Matthew goes out of its way to emphasize the crimes for which the Jews had been responsible, stressing that they had rejected the mission of Jesus, who had directed his appeal to them, and that they had then been the direct cause of his death. *Matthew*, like *Mark*, was eager to demonstrate to the pagan world that the Christians, whether of Jewish or Gentile origin, should be distanced, and exon-erated, from any participation in the First Jewish Revolt against the Romans. Indeed, *Matthew* goes so far as to interpret the destruction of the Jewish Temple by the Romans in AD 70 as the punishment inflicted upon the Jews by God himself – because they had crucified his Son.

As for the third Gospel, which bears the name of *Luke*, it does, in its opening words, suggest that history is one of its primary concerns – although, as we have seen, this is not really true of any of the Gospels. It also changes *Mark*'s picture of Peter, more than *Matthew* does, by rearrangement and deletion, omitting any derogatory allusions to him or the other apostles.

It is disputed whether *Luke* was composed before or after *Matthew*; and the mystery remains, although the author of the book does sound like a second- or third-generation Christian. In any case, however, it does not seem likely that either Gospel derived anything from the other, although both drew upon Q. They differ from one another in that *Luke*, while depending on *Mark*, only reproduces about half of his material, whereas *Matthew* includes more. What is particularly significant, however, is that *Luke* makes use of a special source of his own. And it is by no means the same as the M source employed by *Matthew* (which *Luke* does not employ). *Luke*'s special source, described as L, occupies five hundred verses, no less than half of the Gospel, arousing the conjecture that there may have been a Proto-Luke (L + Q), now lost. As in the case of M, we cannot tell whether L was handed down in documentary form or by oral transmission. But in any case this special source of *Luke* contains all that is most characteristic of this Gospel: the most distinctive and notable stories and sayings in the book.

The original Saint Luke was described by Paul as a doctor.[16] According to tradition, he remained unmarried, and died in Boeotia at the age of eighty-four. Once again, however, he does not seem to have been the author of the Gospel that bears his name. As in the case of *Matthew*, it has been suggested that the Gospel of *Luke* may have originated at Syrian Antioch, although, as in the case of the other work, this must remain uncertain (Pisidian Antioch (Yalvaç),Caesarea Philippi (Banyas), Cyrene (Shahhat) and Lucania have also been suggested).

Unlike *Matthew*, however, this Gospel is not partly addressed to Jewish Christians. On the contrary, it is written exclusively for those of Gentile origin, from whose ranks its author himself may have come, although it has been suggested that he was not a Greek but a non-Jewish Semite.[17] Looking towards the Gentiles, this Gospel does seem to want to attract some of them to become missionaries for the faith. The unidentified Theophilus, the object of *Luke*'s dedication, can scarcely be dismissed as non-existent and symbolic, and was presumably a personage of some standing. He is usually thought to have been a Christian, although it is also possible that he was pagan.[18]

Despite Semitisms, *Luke* is more Hellenistic in manner and approach than the other Gospels. The book is also written in a superior sort of language – it is the only Gospel in literary Hellenistic Greek: displaying three versions of the style. The author reveals an ingenious capacity for arrangement and meaningful simplification. Indeed, the character of the work has been greatly admired and described as 'sunlit'. We seem almost to see a poet writing prose, as in the opening series of legends surrounding Jesus's birth.

Such qualities make for vagueness and impressionism, and detract from *Luke*'s value as a source of historical fact. So does the author's penchant for anachronisms, adjusted to the requirements of the Church at the time of composition, and resulting in distortions of earlier accounts. One example is presented by the parables attributed to Jesus: previous versions are often altered and adjusted in a radical fashion, to suit the taste of the author's contemporaries.

Luke is also determinedly universalist. Its focus on Gentile interests produces alterations in the picture of Jesus, whose proclamation of the Kingdom of God is endowed with a significance for all the world that Jesus, as far as we can tell, seems never to have intended it to possess, since he had directed his mission almost exclusively towards the Jews.[19] And *Luke*'s universalism is closely allied with the same Gospel's special concern for the underprivileged – poor people and sinners, as well as little children (Chapter 5, note 8). Certainly, Jesus himself had felt sympathy with such people. But his sympathy was based on his overriding desire to complete the creation of the Kingdom of God, from which no one was humble enough to be excluded, whereas *Luke* plays much more strongly on the note of compassionate mercifulness, which has earned the Gospel so much popular fame throughout subsequent ages.

As for Peter, *Luke* singled him out and idealized him – or at any rate felt an esteem for him, inherited no doubt from a favourable tradition, which caused him to go easy on his alleged faults. It is possible that the author of the Gospel had the text of *1 Peter* in front of him when he wrote.[20]

John, too, is very important for its contributions to our study of Peter, but the work is totally different from the other three Gospels.

Its writer may well have read them; indeed, it is highly likely that he had read *Mark*, since there are notable coincidences between the two works. It has been suggested that the author of *John* was familiar with *Luke* too, but this has been contested.[21] However, it is by no means impossible that he knew the Gospel of Matthew. And he relied on other sources as well. Yet, whatever material was available to the author of *John*, the book clearly underwent very substantial divergences and re-editings before achieving its final form. Moreover, the process of composition of *John* involved, perhaps, no fewer than five successive stages and processes.

Anyway, in the end product, *John's* conception of Jesus differed fundamentally from those of the other three Gospels. In particular, the kind of selective biography which they had attempted has been abandoned. Instead, narrative material that had appeared in the tradition has been rearranged (possibly between one stage of *John* and another); and we have a sort of intense religious drama, carried through by elaborate theological thought and the employment of complex symbolism.

Nevertheless, the Gospel of John is vital to our consideration of Peter, and must therefore be given further consideration. Certainly, it is a quasi-poetic work, like the Wisdom Literature of the Jews. Moreover, it has been customary to regard *John* as having been written a good deal later than the other three Gospels. But that view is now subject to a good deal of qualification, since some of the material that appears in the work seems of primitive appearance and is nowadays assigned a date as early as anything else in the New Testament – indeed, its author, it has been argued, may even have seen the Empty Tomb himself.[22]

Such an opinion would carry with it the assumption that the Gospel was written by Jesus's apostle John, the son of Zebedee (who survived his executed brother James), and this is an attribution which, although it has its advocates, is not generally accepted.[23] The writer of the book has always been called 'John', and a much later man of the same name, John the Elder, seems a more plausible choice than the apostle for its authorship.[24] However, nothing can be said for certain, and there have been numerous theories, including a conjecture that there might have been more than one author of the work. (The Gospel's own assertion that its writer was the Beloved Disciple[25] remains less than probable.)

In view of all this uncertainty, the dating of the work still remains elusive. One suggestion is that the latest possible date is AD 100–10, but a first edition may have been produced in 75–85. The author has employed his powerful, independent gifts to adapt his sources, but what those sources were and when they came into existence is impossible to determine. In consideration of the other Gospels, we have become accustomed to regard not only their date but also the place of their composition as uncertain. And the same is true of *John*. The book has been variously ascribed to Antioch, Alexandria, Ephesus (Selçuk) and elsewhere in Asia Minor.

What we can say, at least, is that this Gospel seems to emanate from some group that stood apart from the central doctrines of the Christian church – a second branch, as it were, of Christianity,[26] although its members accepted the principle of apostolic authority. Moreover, the writer of *John* was also familiar with certain branches of Judaism. In particular, he differs from the other evangelists in that he seems to have had contacts with the Qumran (Dead Sea) Jewish community – another indication, perhaps, that some of his material is early (even if the book, in the form in which we have it, is not), since that community had ceased to exist in the First Jewish Revolt (AD 66–73).

Yet if *John* has firm Palestinian connections, the work remains basically hostile to the Jews, and its Hellenistic links are stronger, since its writer at times seems to share the conceptions and attitudes of Greco-Jewish authors such as Philo of Alexandria (*c*.30 BC–AD 45). These Greco-Jewish analogies have caused some to suppose that the readership intended for *John* did not comprise members of the Christian community at all, but Jews who spoke Greek. Nevertheless, it still remains more probable that the work was written partly for Christians of Jewish origin, but principally for Gentile Christians. Possibly the resulting book may not have pleased the Romans, owing to its insistence that there was a supreme authority to which the government was irrelevant, and it may there-fore at first have been circulated secretly.

Despite its poetical character and theological preoccupations, *John* is keen to make it clear that its material is based on eye-witness accounts, and the rearrangements to which reference has been made do not prevent the work from adhering carefully to a narrative framework. As regards Jesus himself, *John* displays a certain con-tradiction. On the one hand, guarding against the Docetic view that Jesus's career among humankind was a mere illusion, its author is fully conscious of the actual events of his career upon earth. For instance, he goes even further than the other evangelists in exoner-ating Pilate from responsibility for Jesus's death, and ascribing this to the Jews. And yet, on the other hand, *John* also makes it clear that it scarcely sees Jesus as an incarnate human being at all. When Pilate is made to say, 'Behold the Man',[27] the writer wishes to convey a profound irony, since he does not really seem to believe that Jesus was a 'man' at all. For him, Jesus is divine and pre-existent. And *John* endows his words with an ethereal, all-knowing character that seems at odds with our other information about his manner of speaking.

The most peculiar and mysterious feature of the Gospel of *John*, however, is its treatment of Peter. He has a certain prominence as the apostles' spokesman, but he is not, in this Gospel, the first whom Jesus called, for the work records that his brother Andrew was called before him.[28] And Peter is invariably, some say with a derogatory purpose, bracketed with the mysterious figure described as the 'Beloved Disciple' – to the advantage, moreover, of the latter, since, although Peter seems to be held in honour and even deliberately rehabilitated (though this is sometimes disputed),[29] the Beloved Disciple is especially competitively singled out as possessing even greater distinction.

The point comes out clearly when, according to *John*, Mary Magdalene discovered that Jesus's tomb was empty.[30]

She ran to Simon Peter, and the other disciple, the one whom Jesus loved. 'They have taken the Lord out of the tomb' she said, 'and we do not know where they have laid him.' So Peter and the other disciple set out and made their way to the tomb.

They ran together, but the other disciple ran faster than Peter and reached the tomb first. He peered in and saw the linen wrappings there, but he did not enter. Then Simon Peter caught up with him and went into the tomb. He saw the linen wrappings lying there, and the napkin which had been round his head, not with the wrappings but rolled up in a place by itself.

Then the disciple who had reached the tomb first also went in, and he saw and believed; until then they had not understood the scriptures which showed that he must rise from the dead.

Here is an enigmatic quality, in which, however, the Beloved Disciple fares the better of the two. This is typical of the whole Gospel, in which both Peter and the Beloved Disciple occupy central positions, with a slight but perceptible leaning towards the second, who may even have been intended to appear as a sort of intermediary between Jesus and Peter.

Exactly the same phenomenon is apparent when the risen Lord appears to the apostles beside the Sea of Galilee, and grants them a miraculously vast haul of fish:[31]

Morning came, and Jesus was standing on the beach, but the disciples did not know it was Jesus ... Then the disciple whom Jesus loved said to Peter, 'It is the Lord!' As soon as Simon Peter heard him say 'it is the Lord', he fastened his coat about him (for he had stripped) and plunged into the sea. The rest of them came on in the boat, towing the net full of fish ...

Peter has taken vigorous action, but it had been the Beloved Disciple who first recognized the risen Jesus. A similar impression is given by a poignant scene just before the arrest of Jesus. This was at the Last Supper, where, we are told, Jesus said that one of those present would betray him. 'One of them, the disciple he loved, was reclining close beside Jesus. Simon Peter signalled to him to find out which one he meant.'[32] Then, on the next day,[33]

Peter looked round, and saw the disciple whom Jesus loved following –

the one who at supper had leant back close to him to ask the question, 'Lord, who is it that will betray you?' When he saw him, Peter asked, 'Lord, what about him?' Jesus said, 'If it should be my will that he stay until I come, what is it to you? Follow me.'

That saying of Jesus became current among his followers and was taken to mean that that disciple would not die. He only said, 'If it should be my will that he stay until I come, what is it to you?'

Three questions come to mind, and it must be concluded that the answers to none of them are wholly satisfactory or decisive. Who is the Beloved Disciple? What is the meaning and explanation of the extraordinary scene that has just been described? And why is there this uncomfortable, not wholly balanced, bracketing of Peter and the Beloved Disciple in *John's* Gospel?

First, who is the Beloved Disciple? The Gospel of John identifies him definitely with its own author, but, as we have seen, that is not accurate. It has been suggested that the Beloved Disciple might be merely a symbol, standing for an 'idealized form of discipleship', or for a 'typical Christian', or for Gentile Christianity, while Peter is meant to stand for the Jewish Christian faith. But none of those theories is convincing, since the Gospel evidently intends the Beloved Disciple to be a historical person, visiting, for example, the Empty Tomb.[34] It has been believed, therefore, that the Beloved Disciple, while not the man (perhaps John the Elder) who wrote the Gospel, is another, much earlier John, the apostle John, the son of Zebedee (who did not actually write the Gospel, but was depicted by Renaissance artists as sitting next to Jesus, and leaning on him, at the Last Supper). The reason behind the Gospel's curious speculation about the Beloved Disciple's death, denying that Jesus had said that the Disciple would not die, was probably that he *was* dead when the work was written, although some of his followers had speculated that he would never die.

Yet – and now we come to the third question – the contrast between Jewish and Gentile Christianity may not be entirely baseless, even if unacceptable in just that form. For this bracketing and balancing of Peter with the Beloved Disciple requires further comment. Does it imply deference to Peter, or aim at providing a

dramatic climax in favour of the Beloved Disciple – possibly granting the latter primacy of love and sensitivity in recognizing Jesus,
while leaving Peter first place in the apostolic ministry?[35] Or does
Peter, here, represent the apostolic communities outside the central
Church? All this remains conjectural. The juxtaposition of the two
men certainly reflects a difference, at the time when the Gospel was
written, between two forms of Christian community. Perhaps they
should not, however, be identified too readily and simply with the
Jewish and Gentile sections of that community, but rather with an
apostolic (Petrine) group and a more liberal (Johannine) community – although it still remains possible that, with overlaps, these
do roughly correspond with people of Jewish and Gentile origins
respectively.

The last chapter of *John*, which appears to have been (in whole
or part) the work of another hand,[36] may have been added with an
eye to this controversial contrast and crisis of authority, not only in
order to clear up the problem raised by the fact that the Beloved
Disciple was no longer alive, and was therefore not immortal, but
also to establish that both he and Peter were unique in their different
ways, and essential to the faith.

Our principal source of information about Peter's career after Jesus's
Crucifixion – though by no means always a reliable one – is the
book known as the Acts of the Apostles.

Described as 'one of the great storm-centres of New Testament
scholarship',[37] this work provides the first attempt at a Christian
history, although, like the Gospels, its principal aim is not so much
history as edification: to show, in laudatory terms, how the Christian
faith spread until it reached the centre of the empire.

What history it does present is therefore highly selective. There
is no knowing, for certain, when it was written – any more than we
know the exact date of the Gospels. Perhaps there were two stages
of composition. Probably *Acts* was completed in the late 60s, 70s or
80s AD; a fragment found at Qumran seems previous to 68.[38] It was
believed as early as the later second century that the author of the
book was Saint Luke, who was said to have intended it as the sequel

to his Gospel. The evidence for his authorship of *Acts* is strong, and seems to be confirmed by the 'we passages', in which the writer – employing the same style as is used in the rest of the book – describes Paul and his comrades (who included a certain John Mark) as 'us' rather than 'him' or 'them'.[39] And Acts is dedicated, just as Luke's Gospel is dedicated, to a certain Theophilus.[40] This tends to confirm that the two works were written by the same man.

The first half of Acts deals with the very earliest stages of the story of the Christians who survived Jesus's death, in which Peter is especially prominent. The second half contains chosen scenes from Paul's missionary journeys, up to the time of his arrival in Rome. Acts of the Apostles is a misleading title because these two principals stride through it, in juxtaposition, one after the other, and the other apostles only play a secondary part.

Acts is a skilful, purposeful and emotionally sincere composition. Yet, as has already been suggested, it is scarcely history. Instead, intended perhaps to reinforce or substantiate earlier lost writings, it sets out to present an idealized, general picture of what the earliest Church had been or ought to have been like, growing and pursuing the Way of Salvation and spreading the word of God.

Our accurate knowledge of Peter is a particular sufferer from this method. First, the juxtaposition with Paul is deliberate, too facile and not very accurate, leading to a climax that leaves Peter unmentioned after chapter 15. The accounts, in Acts, of the so-called Apostolic Council and Decree are gravely suspect, and the book's keenness on Church harmony and one-mindedness means that the conflict with Paul, so sharply apparent in his own Letter to the Galatians, is completely played down. 'Harmony' with Rome is also an ideal, and Acts is concerned to show that Christianity is a recognized faith (*religio licita*), no less than Judaism.[41]

Besides, as we shall see later, Peter certainly did not deliver his speeches in the words indicated in Acts. He was no doubt the spokesman of the Church, but surely his orations on the theme were not reported accurately enough for the words with which he is credited to be acceptable. Moreover, his career after Jesus's Crucifixion is supposedly encumbered by various miraculous events of which it is not possible to take any factual cognizance. Some of these 'miracles' are linked to the alleged conversion of the Roman centurion Cornelius, itself very probably fictitious, exemplifying a mission by Peter to the Gentiles which is questionable.

Although the Acts provide by far our best account, indeed at most points our *only* account, of Peter's career in the years following the death of Jesus, nevertheless it is far from satisfactory. In particular, the gentler treatment of Peter by Acts is partly motivated by the desire to equate him with Paul – and to show how similar, really, the two men were, which they probably were not. Peter is continuously displayed as the same brand of apostle as Paul, and in many ways his authentic predecessor as the most prominent Christian leader and missionary. It is one of the book's main preoccupations to tone down and eliminate the differences between these two principal personages of the dawning Church. And one way in which that is done is by moving the actions, characteristics and sayings of one to the other, so as to stress, once again, their similarities.

This method tended to operate against Peter. The author of Acts, although he remained aware that some of his readers belonged to groups more inclined to revere the traditions associated with Peter, was motivated by a certain predilection for Paul. This meant that he tended to diminish the role of Peter in order to accentuate that of Paul; he was robbing Peter to pay Paul. Of course Paul, out of a not unnatural egotism, did the same in his Letters, but Acts proceeded with greater delicacy and tact. However, the net result, as intended, was to cut down the status of Peter, as representative of the Church at Jerusalem, and to raise, correspondingly, the standing of Paul's Church of the Gentiles. When one begins to read Acts the initial chapters do not make this entirely clear, but it becomes obvious enough as Paul begins to monopolize the later part of the book.

Coming to the two so-called Letters of Peter in the New Testament, we are once again on uncertain and potentially treacherous ground, for neither Letter was probably written by Peter at all. Such pseudonymous writings were intended not to deceive, but to pay homage to the memory of the fictitious, revered author.

Taking the first letter, we cannot employ it as safe evidence of what Peter wrote and thought because, despite unanimous early tradition to the contrary (which earned the Epistle a place in the New Testament), most scholars believe that Peter was not its author. Determined attempts have been made to show that this is wrong,[42] but the reattribution to Peter himself is not altogether convincing, even if this First Letter does reflect his thought and experience.

The Letter is written to 'God's scattered people who lodge for a while in Pontus, Galatia, Cappadocia, Asia, and Bithynia'.[43] They may have had to suffer 'trials (*pathemata*) of many kinds'.[44] Does this refer to the persecutions of Nero? If so, Peter could have composed the Letter during the last year or two of his life: although this is not likely. It was written, we are told, at the sister church at 'Babylon',[45] which is generally believed to stand for the great wicked city of Rome, in which, therefore, it is presupposed that Peter was residing at the time when the Letter was written. Its author sends greetings from 'my son Mark',[46] the word 'son' presumably being metaphorical; we have seen that the Gospel of *Mark* was believed to have been derived from Peter, although Mark was never said to have been Peter's son.

The author of this First Letter of Peter also indicates that its author is writing it 'through Silvanus, whom I know to be a trustworthy colleague'[47]: perhaps he is Silas, who appears in *Acts*.[48] Just as Peter might have used the services of Mark to polish up the Gospel attributed to the latter, so, too, he could have employed Silvanus (Silas?) to endow his First Letter with literary style – if indeed we attribute the substance of the Letter to Peter at all, which, as we have seen, is more than doubtful, even though much of it may be based on his thinking.

As for the contents of the First Letter, it warns the recipients that 'your minds must be stripped for action and fully alert',[49] awaiting the last days without despairing. The Church, in this Letter, has an embryonic role (with its own officers),[50] and Rome ('Babylon') too has an incipient pastoral status for these Asian readers. Obedience to the state is inculcated,[51] since it was evidently now possible to suffer state persecution for being a Christian. What is particularly important, however, if Peter was indeed the inspirer of the Letter, though not necessarily its author, is that he has finally come to understand the significance of the suffering Messiah (which the Gospels make it clear that Peter himself had not at first comprehended), and to comprehend its believed relevance to the rest of humanity:[52] and this Epistle passes on the message unambiguously.

1 Peter was evidently used as a homily in the early Church; and it was known to the author of *2 Peter*, although the two works are very different. About *2 Peter* less will be said here, because efforts to demonstrate its authenticity, and to give the Letter a date as early as the 60s AD, have not gained general acceptance[53] – although there was a time, long ago, when they did, because this composition, too, was accepted as part of the New Testament. Perhaps it was written *c.*125 or *c.*150. *2 Peter*'s main message is a warning against false and ungodly teachers, and doctrinal and moral error and confusion.

It warns against myths or 'tales artfully spun'[54] and it is interesting that, although Paul's Letters are regarded as inspired with wisdom by God, they are also said, by *2 Peter*, to include 'some obscure passages, which the ignorant and unstable misinterpret to their own ruin, as they do the other scriptures'.[55] Much is also said about the Last Days, and the judgement of the wicked that they will bring. The author also predicts, retrospectively, the martyrdom of Peter himself.[56]

Bibliographical note

On the non-canonical gospels, including the Gospel of Thomas (sayings, with a few brief scenes), see M. W. Meyer, *The Secret Teachings of Jesus* (1986); M. W. Meyer and H. Bloom, *The Gospel of Thomas: The Hidden Sayings of Jesus* (1992); W. Schneemelcher, *The New Testament Apocrypha* (1992); W. D. Stroker, *Extra-Canonical Sayings of Jesus* (1989); H. Koester, *Harvard Theological Review*, LXXIII, 1980, pp. 105–30; I. Wilson, *Are These the Words of Jesus?*; J. A. Fitzmyer, *The Gospel According to Luke*

(1981), pp. 85ff.; R. Cameron, *The Other Gospels* (1982). W. A. Guillaumont, H. A. Puech *et al.* translated the Gospel of Thomas in 1959, and W. D. Davies and D. C. Allison, *The Gospel According to Saint Matthew*, Vol. I (1988), pp. 441f., comment on its ten Beatitudes. The Gospel According to the Hebrews (or of the Nazarenes), written in Aramaic in Egypt in the second century AD, is of occasional importance; it is not extant but was quoted by Clement of Alexandria and Jerome. The Gospel of Peter, which claimed to be based on direct eyewitness accounts, was occasionally added to the canonical Gospels. See also J. M. Robinson and H. Koester, *Trajectories through Early Christianity* (1971).

On pagan pseudonymous literature, see H. J. Rose, *Oxford Classical Dictionary* (2nd edn, 1970), p. 894. For Christian pseudonymous literature, see D. G. Meade, *Pseudonymity and Canon* (1986); R. Lane Fox, *The Unauthorised Version: Truth and Fiction in the Bible* (1991); H. Koester, *Ancient Christian Gospels* (1990); J. K. Elliott, *Questioning Christian Origins* (1982), p. 126; cf. also C. Gill and T. Wiseman (eds), *Lies and Fiction in the Ancient World* (1992).

On the Synoptic Gospels, see W. F. Farmer, *The Synoptic Problem* (1964); C. F. D. Moule, *The Birth of the New Testament* (3rd edn, 1981) *Excursus* IV (G. M. Styler); E. P. Sanders and M. Davies, *Studying the Synoptic Gospels* (1989); S. D. Moore, *Mark and Luke in Post-Structuralist Perspectives* (1992); G. Theissen, *The Gospels in Context: Social and Political History in the Synoptic Tradition* (1992); J. Wenham, *Redating Matthew, Mark and Luke: A Fresh Assault on the Synoptic Problem* (1991); W. F. Farmer, *The Synoptic Problem* (1964); F. Neirynk, in R. E. Brown, J. A. Fitzmyer and R. E. Murphy (eds), *The New Jerome Biblical Commentary* (1990), pp. 587ff., cf. pp. 596–721. On the early Qumran fragment of Mark, see C. P. Thiede, *The Earliest Gospel Manuscript?* (1992); B. Mayer (ed.), *Christen und Christliches in Qumran?* (1992).

On *Mark*, see M. Hooker, *The Message of Mark* (1983); M. Hengel, *Studies in the Gospel of Mark* (1985); V. K. Robbins, *Jesus the Teacher: A Socio-Rhetorical Interpretation of Mark* (1991); J. C. Anderson and J. D. Moore, *Mark and Method* (1992), A. Y. Collins, *The Beginning of the Gospel* (1993); D. B. Taylor, *Mark's Gospel as Literature and History* (1992); C. Bryan, *A Preface to Mark* (1993).

For the Marcan Secret, see W. Wrede, *The Messianic Secret* (1971); cf. A. Schweitzer, *The Quest of the Historical Jesus* (1910), pp. 339, 342; R. E. Brown, K P. Donfried and L. Reumann (eds), *Peter in the New Testament*

(1973), p. 66, n. 150; H. Räisänen, *The Messianic Secret in Mark's Gospel* (1990). For the crowds that seemed to contradict this, see *Luke 9.11, 5.15, 5.17.*

A. D. Jacobson, *The First Gospel: An Introduction to Q* (1991); J. S. Kluppenburg, *The Shape of Q* (1993); D. Lührmann, *An Itinerary for New Testament Study* (1991), p 47.

On Papias, see J. Kortner, *Papias von Hierapolis* (1983); J. Kurzinger, *Papias von Hierapolis in den Evangelien des Neuen Testaments* (1989); Davies and Allison, op cit., vol I, pp. 12ff.

On the end of Mark's Gospel see O. Cullmann, *Peter: Disciple, Apostle, Martyr* (1962), p. 63; J. Lowe, *Saint Peter* (1956), p. 11; Hooker, op. cit., pp. 118–21; C. P. Thiede, *Simon Peter: From Galilee to Rome* (1986) pp. 231f., n. 157; P. L. Danove, *The End of Mark's Story* (1993).

Discussion of authorship and place in Matthew's Gospel can be found in Davies and Allison, op. cit., vol I, pp. 1–138; D. Patte, *The Gospel According to Matthew* (1987); J. Meier, *The Vision of Matthew* (1991); J. A. Overman, *Matthew's Gospel and Formative Judaism* (1993).

On *Luke*, see the Bibliography in Fitzmyer, op. cit., pp. 29ff., 59ff., 97ff; B. L. Mack, *The Last Gospel* (1993); D. Catchpole, *Quest for Q* (1993); F. W. Danker, *Jesus and the New Age* (1987); C. A. Evans and J. A. Sandeis, *Luke and Scripture* (1993).

Recent books on the Gospel of *John* (other than commentaries) include J. A. T. Robinson, *The Priority of John* (1985); M. Hengel, *The Johannine Question* (1990); D. E. Smith, *Johannine Christianity* (1987); R. F. Collins, *John and his Witness* (1991); J. Painter, *The Quest for the Messiah* (1991); J. Ashton, *Understanding the Fourth Gospel* (1991); P. Perkins, in R. E. Brown *et al.*, *The New Jerome Biblical Commentary*, op. cit., pp. 945–85; J. W. Pryor, *John: Evangelist of the Covenant People* (1992); C. H. Talbert, *Reading John* (1992); M. W. G. Stibbe, *John as Storyteller* (1992); D. Moody Smith, *John Among the Gospels* (1991); V. Schnelle, *Anti-Docetic Christology in the Gospel of John* (1992); R. E. Brown, *John* (bibliography), pp. clxv. f. For the question of Gnostic influence on John, and on who the Gnostics were, see R. E. Brown, *The Gospel According to John*; K. Rudolph, *Gnosis* (1983); B. Layton, *The Gnostic Scriptures* (1987); P. Perkins, *Gnosticism and the New Testament* (1993).

On the Beloved Disciple, see R. E. Brown, *The Community of the Beloved Disciple* (1979); A. H. Maynard, *New Testament Studies*, XXX, 1984, pp. 533ff. (references); K. B. Quast, *Journal for the Study of the New*

Testament, Suppl. 32 (1989) 'Peter and the Beloved Disciple'; Thiede, op. cit., p. 97 argues that despite their different ideas, the followers of Peter must not be impeded. See also Brown, op. cit., p. 147, on the 'second form' of discipleship.

Recent books on the Acts of the Apostles include J. Kremer (ed.), *Les Actes des Apôtres* (1978); M. Hengel, *Acts and the History of Early Christianity* (1979); J. Crowe, *The Acts* (1979); I. H. Marshall, *The Acts of the Apostles* (1992); W. Neill, *The Acts of the Apostles* (1981); L. J. Ogilvie, *Acts* (1983); J. T. Sanders, *The Jews in Luke–Acts* (1987); F. F. Bruce, *The Book of Acts* (rev. edn, 1988); C. J. Hewer, *The Book of Acts in the Setting of Hellenistic History* (1989); G. Lüdemann, *Early Christianity According to the Traditions in Acts* (1989); R. E. Brown *et al.*, *The New Jerome Biblical Commentary*, op. cit., pp. 722–67; B. Reicke, *The Epistles of James, Peter and Jude* (1964).

Thiede, op. cit., pp. 109f., 236, n. 178, eager to ascribe the Letters of Peter to Peter himself, argues that their style is consistent with that of Peter's speeches in *Acts*. There are Docetic tendencies in both these letters (see note after Chapter 3).

On *1 Peter*, see F. Neugebauer, *New Testament Studies*, XXVI, (1980), pp. 61–86; A. W. Wainwright, *A Guide to the New Testament* (1965), p. 253; E. P. Clowney, *The Message of 1 Peter* (1988), especially pp. 19f., 231; J. R. Michaels, *1 Peter* (1988); J. L. McKenzie, *Dictionary of the Bible*, p. 667; W. G. Kümmel, *An Introduction to the New Testament* (1975), pp. 426–9; W. Munro, *Authority in Paul and Peter: The Identification of a Pastoral Stratum in the Pauline Corpus and 1 Peter* (1981); W. J. Dalton, in R. E. Brown *et al. The New Jerome Biblical Commentary*, op. cit., pp. 905f.

On *2 Peter*, see R. E. Brown *et al.*, *Peter in the New Testament*, op. cit., p. 17; Kümmel, op. cit., pp. 429–34; T. Fornberg, *An Early Church in a Pluralistic Society: A Study of Peter 2* (1977); H. Neyrey, in R. E. Brown *et al.*, *The New Jerome Biblical Commentary*, op cit., pp. 1017f.

Part II

WHILE JESUS WAS ALIVE

Chapter 3

THE CALLING OF PETER

This is how the Gospel of Mark tells the story of Simon Peter's calling:[1]

> Jesus was walking by the Sea of Galilee when he saw Simon [Peter] and his brother Andrew at work casting nets in the lake; for they were fishermen. Jesus said to them, 'Come, follow me, and I will make you fishers of men.' At once they left their nets and followed him.

Luke has a more elaborate account, introducing a miracle:[2]

> One day as he [Jesus] stood by the Lake of Gennesaret [Sea of Galilee], with people crowding in on him to listen to the word of God, he noticed two boats lying at the water's edge; the fishermen had come ashore and were washing their nets. He got into one of the boats, which belonged to Simon Peter, and asked him to put out a little way from the shore; then he went on teaching the crowds as he sat in the boat.
>
> When he had finished speaking, he said to Simon, 'Put out into deep water and let down your nets for a catch.' Simon answered, 'Master, we were hard at work all night and caught nothing; but if you say so, I will let down the nets.' They did so and made such a huge catch of fish that

their nets began to split. So they signalled to their partners in the other boat to come and help them. They came, and loaded both boats to the point of sinking.

When Simon saw what had happened he fell at Jesus's knees and said, 'Go, Lord, leave me, sinner that I am!' For he and all his companions were amazed at the catch they had made; so too were his partners James and John, Zebedee's sons. 'Do not be afraid,' said Jesus to Simon; 'from now on you will be catching people.' As soon as they had brought the boats to land, they left everything and followed him.

John's Gospel has picked up a different tradition, in which Peter no longer has the priority:[3]

John [the Baptist] was standing with two of his disciples when Jesus passed by. John looked towards him and said, 'There is the Lamb of God!' When the two disciples heard what he said, they followed Jesus. He turned and saw them following. 'What are you looking for?' he asked. They said, 'Rabbi (which means 'Teacher'), where are you staying?' 'Come and see,' he replied. So they went and saw where he was staying, and spent the rest of the day with him. It was about four in the afternoon.

One of the two who followed Jesus after hearing what John said was Andrew, Simon Peter's brother. The first thing he did was to find his brother Simon and say to him, 'We have found the Messiah' (which is the Hebrew for Christ). He brought Simon to Jesus.

Leaving aside the 'miracle' in *Luke*, which is paralleled in rabbinical texts[4] and bears a curious similarity to Jesus's Miraculous Draught of Fishes, it is impossible to say which version of Peter's calling is correct.

'They left everything and followed me': so the demand was even more imperative and holier than Elijah's call of Elisha to discipleship.[5] But it is tempting to believe that Jesus did in fact say that he would make the two fishermen-brothers fishers of men – perhaps as a metaphor for the healing of the sick[6] – though it may not have been at the moment of their calling that he made the observation. The Gospel of John indicated that Peter's brother was 'called' before him, which may be true, although it could also be due to an undercurrent of the Christian tradition tending to depreciate the role that Peter had played. It is reasonable enough to accept the assertion that Peter had up to that time been a disciple of John the Baptist, as Jesus was himself; this became an important qualification after Jesus's death.[7] Jesus had evidently known Peter before he 'called' him.[8]

Peter's name was Symeon, a Hebrew patriarch's name (Shim'on, the most common Jewish name in Palestine), easily translatable as Simon, a Greek name which had already figured in a play by Aristophanes. A good deal of discussion has been undertaken by theologians about the varying uses of these names in the Gospels. Peter's father was said to have been called Jonah or Johannes[9] (perhaps a typological interpretation was read into this, since the Old Testament hero Jonah had defied death; or does the insertion of the name only mean that Peter had followed John the Baptist?) Peter's father was a fisherman, who had his own boat and hired assistants. He came from Bethsaida, on the north bank of the Sea of Galilee.

Although Jewish, Bethsaida was partly Greek-speaking, and stood in Gentile surroundings, helping to justify the phrase 'Galilee of the Gentiles (or nations)'.[10] The place had been raised to city status by the tetrarch Philip, son of Herod the Great, in 4/2 BC, when it was given the name of Julias after the emperor Augustus's daughter. And Jesus was said to have spoken of the town in uncomplimentary terms.[11] It may not have reacted favourably to his mission.

Besides, discontent was high among the peasants of rural, agrarian Galilee, who bore an oppressive tax burden[12] (relevant to Jesus's parables which were largely agricultural in character). Nevertheless, the name 'Bethsaida' means 'house of fishing', and this was a flourishing activity there. Moreover, the town was on one of the most important trade routes of the Near East, the Via Maris. All in all, the tradition that Peter was poor and humble, cherished by St John Chrysostom, seems mistaken.

This is rather typical of the New Testament, which tends to stress, indeed to overstress, the low social status of the apostles. Thus the writers of these books, and their Church, liked to portray Peter as a rough-hewn type whom God had selected to carry out his loftier aims. It was therefore essential to show that he originated from an unprivileged stratum of society and received an unprivileged education, although to carry out his missions he must have been bilingual, if not orally trilingual.[13] The corollary was that it was a truly wonderful thing for such a simple man to have been chosen by Jesus for his high purposes.

In fact, however, although Peter spoke with a Galilean accent, his economic situation, and that of men like him, must have been far from unfavourable. What lay behind this was salt, a commodity that Jesus himself was not averse to introducing into his teaching.[14] The geographer Strabo alludes to the successful fish-pickling centres at Taricheae (Magdala) on the Sea of Galilee.[15] These activities were in considerable demand, not only from the inhabitants of the region, and the fish-shops of Jerusalem, but also from the Roman army of occupation, and the commerce of the Roman empire outside Palestine. With all these potential purchasers, it is not surprising that Zebedee and his sons, James and John, engaged additional labour for their fishing business.

All this being so, it is not easy, at first sight, to see what persuaded Jesus's future disciples in Galilee to accept his call and become his followers. It is only possible to conjecture, first, that his magnetism proved superior to any other factor, and second that, even though Zebedee and his sons were successful, even success had its unattractive aspects, such as back-breaking hard work and harsh competitiveness, which may have helped to induce Peter and the others to seek this exciting new way of life.[16]

Later, Peter moved to Capernaum (Tell Hum), perhaps because his mother-in-law was there. This was the town where Jesus, who was said to have healed the mother-in-law's high fever, stayed at his and his brother's house[17] (perhaps later a house-church), probably making it the centre of his Galilean mission, although the town disappointed him in this connection.[18] Claims have now been made that the house has been identified, near the synagogue,[19] and this is not out of the question. Peter had a wife whom he later took on his missions,[20] though the stories of her martyrdom[21] are legendary. So are the tales about the healing of her paralysis, and that of their daughter (or adopted daughter?) Petronilla;[22] and there was another story that they had a son.

Peter and Andrew were the first of six pairs of men to be called by Jesus as his apostles, and despite the deviation from this tradition in John's Gospel, Peter was generally believed to have been the first to have been granted this call. Moreover, as we shall see later, he was the first not only in point of time, but in importance and privilege as well.

Matthew asserts (and we may assume that the passage is not a later addition to the Gospel) that it was Jesus who gave him the name Peter, *Petros*, akin to *petra*, which means 'rock' or 'stone'. John's Gospel repeats the story,[23] although it records that this happened more than halfway through Jesus's ministry, while *Matthew* ascribes the event to its start. The name Peter, *Petros*, is the Greek equivalent of the Aramaic *Kefa*, rendered in the New Testament as Cephas. It had not been the apostle's name at birth (which was Simon), but Jesus named him Peter instead.

There has been endless controversy about this, partly because the name-giving is associated with other alleged statements about Peter which will be considered later (see Chapter 7). But it does seem not unlikely that Jesus himself called Peter by this name.

Despite arguments on the subject, *Petros* seems to refer to the person of Peter himself, as a compliment to his zeal or humanity, or both, and not just to something he said or taught or stood for (although the distinction between the two theories is sometimes hard to discern). Giving a name was a traditional prophetic act. And there was nothing novel about calling someone a 'rock'. To Jews the rock at the base of the Temple at Jerusalem was the centre of the world, 'a precious corner-stone for a firm foundation'.[24] Besides, it was apparently quite a frequent custom, when appointing someone to a responsible position, to stress the rock-like permanence of the appointment (no doubt because the tenure of such jobs was often precarious).

However, it is quite possible that Jesus did not intend to call Peter a 'rock', or 'man of rock', at all. *Kefa* could also, perhaps originally, mean 'stone', and what Jesus might perhaps have meant is that Peter was going to be the *foundation stone* of the new movement. There were precedents, for not only was God said to have declared, in Isaiah, 'I am laying a stone in Zion, a block of granite, a precious corner-stone for a firm foundation', but later, in the *Community Rule* of the Qumran sect, the Council of that community is called 'that tried wall, that precious corner-stone'.[25] Jesus, when he was first believed to have made the statement quoted in *Matthew*, might have been credited with an Aramaic pun between two similar words, one meaning 'stone' (*bn*) and the other meaning 'I shall build' (*ybny*).[26] Peter himself was said to have described Jesus as the corner-stone.[27]

The idea that Jesus also intended the word to represent a 'stumbling block' echoing another passage of Isaiah, can be rejected.[28] And so can the theory that Jesus was not referring to the apostle at all, but to someone else.[29] He was referring to Peter, and 'in true Hebrew fashion the full significance of the name is worked out, giving its bearer an apparently unique role to play in the subsequent history of the church'.[30]

Peter was not the only apostle to whom Jesus gave a special name, nickname or honorary title, because he also called James and John, the relatively well-off sons of Zebedee, 'Boanerges'.[31] This is translated as 'sons of thunder', but 'Boanerges' is not the natural Hebrew version of this phrase, and it is possible that the name instead means 'sons of anger', since the two men were excitable and quick-tempered. However, the designation may also have possessed some theological or prophetic significance, of which we have lost sight.[32]

To rename people in this way, for some specific purpose, was far from new, since Abraham had been renamed Abram,[33] and it is a new Abraham that Peter is called to be, the leader of a renovated people.

So these were Jesus's chosen, renamed Three: Peter, James and John. They formed the inner circle of helpers whom Jesus needed; and he took them with him to the top of a mountain, we are told, to witness his Transfiguration.[34] He was accompanied by them, it was said, when he miraculously raised the President of the Synagogue from the dead,[35] and he also sent two of them, Peter and John, to prepare the Passover dinner (Last Supper).[36] The new names of the Three may well have been intended as signs of their recipients' changed identities as Jesus's closest associates. The precise juncture at which he gave any of them their new designations is disputed, however, and has been the subject of much discussion.

There is no doubt that Peter was pre-eminent among the Three, and uniquely 'favoured' as Jesus's principal disciple.[37] The tradition of the Synoptic Gospels and Acts makes this clear, and it is not enough to say that Peter came first, but was not necessarily the chief, or that he was only the 'mouthpiece' or spokesman, or a typical and 'representative disciple', or that his special position was undefined.

Granted that the evangelists enjoyed the benefit of hindsight, the idea that this conception of Peter's pre-eminence was only retrojected from the period after Jesus's death is nevertheless unacceptable, since the evidence demonstrating his leading role during Jesus's lifetime is sufficiently strong to admit no contradiction. True, the Gospel of John seeks to bracket Peter with the mysterious Beloved Disciple, and to contradict the general tradition that he was the first to be called, but Jesus's reliance on Peter as his principal apostle cannot be questioned. Peter speaks and answers for the whole group, *as their leader*, and when they start arguing about who is the greatest of the disciples,[38] we know what the answer must be: it is Peter who is the greatest.

The wider circle of the Twelve may be identified with the apostles, and although the matter is much debated, and even the lists of the Twelve show divergences, it must be assumed that they had already existed in this form in Jesus's lifetime and had been selected by him, as the Gospels declared: 'have I not chosen you, all Twelve?'[39] They were not, that is to say, merely a retrospective creation by the later Church. Their number, if, as we may suppose, it was authentic, recalls other groups of Twelve in Jewish documents,[40] and implies a claim to supersede the twelve tribes of Israel whom, at the end of the world, the twelve apostles will sit on twelve thrones to judge.[41] Their number also reflected the twelve gates, twelve angels and twelve foundation stones named in the Book of Revelation of John.[42]

There were Jewish precedents for such groups of disciples, since Jewish teachers too (at least at a later date, and perhaps earlier too) attracted teams of followers who learnt from their master what instruction he had to give, and handed it out themselves as his delegates. This operated, for instance, in the enrolment of proselytes.[43]

In this way, Jesus, as he so often did, was following a Jewish custom when he, too, enrolled a group of apostles, with Peter as their leader. He was said to have declared: 'to receive you is to receive me'; and 'whoever rejects you rejects me'.[44] Yet, as was likewise his habit, Jesus also enlarged the Jewish custom, and in the process altered its character. The disciples of a Jewish teacher were attached not only to himself but, through him, to the Torah. Whereas the apostles of Jesus were bound only to him, by an intensely personal tie involving devotion to himself as their master.

So Jesus was not alone among Jewish teachers in surrounding himself with disciples. But his disciples not only possessed this especially close personal link with him, but also bore an exceptional responsibility. They did not serve because they had chosen to. They served, on the contrary, because Jesus had selected them and ordered them to follow him. Moreover, their task was as unique as their personal connection with their Master. The disciples of other Jewish sages spent most of their time interpreting the Torah to their teacher's listeners, in accordance with the instructions he offered. But Jesus's disciples were called upon to help him actively in the mighty task in which he was engaged: the bringing about of God's Kingdom.[45] That was what made them unique, and uniquely privileged, and engaged in a unique task. And Peter was the first among them, and their leader whom Jesus himself had appointed. It was Peter who was required to play the leading role when Jesus sent them to proclaim the Kingdom of God, and to this overwhelming cause they, like him, must be prepared to devote their entire lives.[46]

According to one version of what happened, the disciples, augmented to a total of seventy or seventy-two (perhaps a fictitious figure), proclaimed the cause with considerable success.[47] Above all else, they found that they had great gifts of healing. We may not share the ancient belief that sick people were inhabited by devils. But the word went round, at the time, that the disciples succeeded in driving them out, and, indeed, they were widely credited with cures (performed by anointing with oil). They themselves believed this, for it was the seventy or seventy-two themselves who were said to have proudly reported their successes to Jesus.

However, it was the Twelve, led by Peter, who played the leading parts. It is a curious and surprising fact that, alongside the reports of their successes, there was an alternative and concurrent tradition that the apostles were not successful at all. For example, it was explicitly stated that some of their attempts to expel devils from the sick proved a failure.[48] Moreover, on many occasions and in many respects, the apostles are presented as deplorable, bemused figures, at a loss to know what was happening, bewildered, and alarmed, almost like the friends of Job in the Old Testament.[49] Jesus, we are told, addressed them frequently, but they had not the slightest idea what he meant. And after Jesus had been arrested, their confusion and perplexity were intensified. They were, of course, very sad about what had happened, but their principal reactions were consternation and despondency.

This adverse tradition about the apostles appears at its sharpest in the Letter of Barnabas, which actually goes so far as to describe them as 'ruffians of the deepest dye'.[50] But the same note had already been struck by the Gospels. It had been emphasized by *Mark*, which tells a revealing story about Jesus's supposed miraculous feeding of the five or four thousand. This event, it informs us, the apostles completely failed to comprehend or appreciate, so that Jesus was said to have rounded on them in no uncertain terms:

> Have you no inkling yet? Do you still not understand? Are your minds closed? You have eyes: can you not see? You have ears: can you not hear? Have you forgotten?[51]

Here is the clearest possible indication that the evangelist who wrote

Mark wished to brand the apostles as hopelessly inferior. At other junctures, too, he deliberately conveys the same message – for instance, asserting that they deserted Jesus and ran away.[52] True, *Matthew*, although quoting Jesus to the effect that the apostles were cowards of little faith,[53] sometimes makes an attempt to give them rather more credit, but *Luke*, despite similar endeavours, returns to the attack. From the pages of Luke's Gospel we learn that the apostles were intolerant egoists of feeble faith and utterly inadequate mentality and understanding. In one single chapter the writer makes this point no fewer than four times.

This ferocious depreciation of the disciples and apostles, and their leader, Peter, who comes in for his full share of the attacks, seems strange, but it is possible to see why it happened. First, their denigration is intended to highlight Jesus's superior power: their human weakness was only sustained by his vitalizing presence. Second, at the time when the Gospels were being written, there had been a breach between the Jewish Christian Church at Jerusalem and the Gentile Church which existed elsewhere. The breach had been created, in the first place, by Paul's fierce support of the Gentile Christians against those of Jewish origin; it had been sharpened and deepened by the First Jewish Revolt against the Romans, in which (although there were some who tried to dissent from this view) the Jewish Christians but not the Gentile Christians were regarded as having been involved on the defeated Jewish side.

This breach was extended to the attitudes adopted towards those who had been the apostles of Jesus. The Jewish Christians venerated the apostles as their forerunners, whereas the writers of the Gospels, reflecting the Gentile Christian approach, wanted to express hostility towards them. This desire was intensified by the fact that Jesus's mission to the Jews, among whom the Jewish Christians obviously originated, had ended in disaster. But now the blame for this rejection could be shifted from Jesus to the disciples. Certainly, his attempt to convert the Jews had failed – but it had failed, the evangelists were now able to imply, not because of any defects on Jesus's own part, but because his disciples, entrusted by him with this mission, had failed to carry it out, owing to the flaws in their own personalities.

The apostles could not be described as *totally* unsuccessful: the rival tradition proclaiming what they had achieved could not be wholly ignored. However, their supposed successes are presented in a grudging and perfunctory fashion. We are told about what they achieved, but only in vague, general and sketchy terms. Indeed, this sketchiness is rather convincing. It seems quite possible, or even probable, that despite the unmistakable gifts of Jesus himself, his apostles did not achieve anything very substantial at all. This criticism obviously reflects once again, on Peter, who was their leader.

Yet it was Peter whom Jesus had *chosen* to exercise this leadership. So he must have been a man of outstanding gifts, even if, as yet, he could not deploy them very effectively – which was perhaps because, like the rest of the apostles, he was overshadowed by the phenomenal personality of Jesus himself.

Bibliographical note

The following offer à variety of different views about the name of Peter's father: B. F. Robinson, *Journal for the Study of the New Testament*, XXI (1984); C. P. Thiede, *Simon Peter: From Galilee to Rome* (1986) p. 219, n. 249; H. Marshall in C. P. Thiede (ed.), *Das Petrusbild in der neueren Forschung* (1987) p. 200; C. S. C. Williams, *The Acts of the Apostles* (1957), pp. 152f.; O. Cullmann, *Peter: Disciple, Apostle, Martyr* (1962) p. 25, n. 34. For his father's boat, see J. Lowe, *Saint Peter*, p. 4, and for the fishing trade see G. H. R. Horsley, *New Documents Illustrating Early Christianity*, Vol V (1989), pp. 107, 110f. On Peter's Galilean accent, see Horsley, op. cit., p. 31. See also E. M. Meyers *et al.*, *Sepphoris* (1992).

On the idea of Peter 'the Rock', see Thiede, op. cit., p. 38; G. Maier in Thiede (ed.), op. cit., pp. 182, 184; D. E. Nineham, *Saint Mark* (1963; 1967 ed.) p. 116; G. H. Box, *The Gospel of Saint Matthew* (1922) p. 261; *Matthew 7.24*; *Peter 2.4*; R. E. Brown, K. P. Donfried and L. Reumann (eds), *Peter in the New Testament* (1973), p. 90; B. P. Robinson, *Journal for the Study of the New Testament*, XXI, 1984, pp. 90f., 99, 101, n. 26, 102, n. 35, 103, n. 41; cf. *The Shepherd of Hermas*; C. C. Caragounis, *Peter and the Rock* (1990), pp. 102f; G. Lüdemann, *Early Christianity According to the Tra-*

ditions in Acts (1989) p. 110; J. Lowe, *Saint Peter* (1956), p. 56; Box, op cit., pp. 260f. J. C. Fenton, *Saint Matthew*, p. 269. For Peter's names in general, see R. E. Brown *et al.*, op cit., p. 52, n. 114, 58, n. 129, 76 n. 172, 111 n. 244, 116 n. 253, 129 n. 275; see also Cullman, op cit., p. 20. Peter's brother had a Greek name, Andrew. The issue of whether the 'rock' story comes from a post-Resurrection appearance is considered by R. E. Brown *et al.*, op. cit., pp. 79, 97; H. Conzelmann, *History of Primitive Christianity* (1973), pp. 40f. For a bibliography of this whole passage, see W. D. Davies and D. C. Allison, *The Gospel According to Saint Matthew*, Vol II (1991) pp. 643–8. Cf. also J. M. Hull, *Touching the Rock* (1990). For the date at which Peter was called 'Rock', see R. E. Brown, *et al*, op. cit., pp. 79, 97, 161; R. Pesch, *Simon-Petrus* (1980), pp. 25, 27f.; Cullmann, op cit., pp. 21, 23, 188, 191; A. W. Wainwright, *A Guide to the New Testament* (1965), p. 134; Lüdemann, op. cit., pp. 7f; F. J. Cwiekowski, *The Beginnings of the Church* (1988), p. 49.

On Peter's leadership, see S. Brown, op. cit., p. 147; Thiede, op. cit., pp. 30f.; Pesch, op. cit., pp.22f., 48, 63; R. E. Brown *et al*, op. cit., pp. 105, 107; H. Hendrickx, *Resurrection Narratives* (1978), p. 33; Cullmann, op. cit., p.31.

For discussion of the Twelve, see Hendrickx, op. cit., pp. 47f., 51; P. Lang, *The Footprints of Jesus's Twelve in Early Christian Tradition* (1985). For their condemnation, see A. Schweitzer, *The Quest for the Historical Jesus*, p. 146; H. Küng, *Theology Digest*, XXII, 2, 1975, p. 139.

Chapter 4

PETER'S WEAKNESSES AND STRENGTHS

According to The Gospel of Matthew, at Caesarea Philippi Peter, asked by Jesus 'Who do *you* say that I am?', recognized him as 'the Messiah, the Son of the Living God'.[1] Caesarea Philippi, formerly Panion, since 4 BC in the territory of Philip the tetrarch – a 'client' of the Romans like his father Herod the Great – is an unexpected location, which has caused some to conclude that the incident must be genuine. On the other hand, this was an area where revelations were reported from other sources,[2] so that the argument for genuineness is not particularly strong.

Indeed, the authenticity of this whole incident has been questioned. The Gospel of Mark had said much the same as *Matthew*, although limiting itself to Peter's alleged assertion that Jesus was the Messiah.[3] These terms 'Messiah' and 'Son of God', as is recorded elsewhere, had various meanings to Jews at the time. But the continuation of the passage of *Matthew* contains a number of arresting features, which may be an expanded version of *Mark*, or could be based on older material (possibly in Aramaic):[4]

> He [Jesus] then gave his disciples strict orders not to tell anyone that he was the Messiah.

From that time Jesus began to make it clear to his disciples that he had to go to Jerusalem, and endure great suffering at the hands of the elders, chief priests, and scribes; to be put to death, and to be raised again on the third day.

At this Peter took hold of him and began to rebuke him. 'Heaven forbid!' he said. 'No, Lord, this shall never happen to you.' Then Jesus turned and said to Peter, 'Out of my sight, Satan; you are a stumbling-block to me. You think as man thinks, not as God thinks.'

This was one of Jesus's supposed predictions of the execution he was going to suffer. The sharpness of his rebuke to Peter has once again been offered as an argument for authenticity, but here, too, the argument is not conclusive.

The 'secrecy' on which Jesus is said to have insisted, repeated by *Luke*,[5] has been discussed in connection with Mark's Gospel (see Chapter 2). The passage also contains one of a number of predictions by Jesus of the Crucifixion he was going to suffer. True, we need not believe that Jesus offered the precise and detailed forecast which the Gospels record of the sufferings and fate that he was about to endure. But he was steeped in the Old Testament concept of the Suffering Servant:[6] although some regarded suffering as contrary to the will of God, the righteous often suffered in Jewish tradition.[7] It seems by no means improbable that Jesus came to realize that death was in store for him.

Despite the Old Testament, this was a horrifying and unacceptable thought for all his followers, who believed, like the rest of the Jewish people of the time, that under the oppressive rule of the Romans the expected Messiah was to be a great worldly conqueror who would annihilate the mighty of the earth, rule in Jerusalem and make Israel a dominant power.[8] Quite clearly, too, this is what we are told that Peter believed: the idea of a suffering Messiah was foreign to him, and that is why he was said to have been so harshly reprimanded for this 'Satanic' mistake.[9]

This was a strong term because Satan, the Devil (whose kingdom was taken for granted), was the supreme tempter and Jesus's grave enemy:[10] he sought after the disciples to lure them under his control, as he had likewise tried to ensnare Job.[11] But Jesus was said to have used this vigorous language of rebuttal because he was utterly opposed to becoming an earthly Messiah of this kind, or to letting it be understood that this was his intention; and if even his leading disciple Peter could not understand that this was his view, and in that case surely the other apostles could not either, then sharp words, according to the Gospels, were needed.

We have seen that Peter was the leading apostle. Yet here he is showing a wretched lack of comprehension. In fact the Gospels in general, unkind to the other disciples as they are, display Peter in a particularly unfavourable light – as painfully typical of the failings of the rest of them. Despite his exalted position, he emerges from the Gospels as essentially a weak and inadequate personage. He is censured by Paul as having misunderstood what Jesus has said and was trying to do.[12] And, according to this passage in *Mark*, he is deliberately rebuked by Jesus with the cruel term of Satan. And much else too.

The Gospels offer repeated evidence of their writers' view of Peter as a rather feeble character. True, this is partly in order to attack the Jewish Christians, and partly, too, because Peter is taken to represent the other apostles, and their failures to live up to their call, and the lessons they provide regarding the severe demands of discipleship. Moreover, Peter's weakness also serves to show up, by way of contrast, the perfection of Jesus.

Thus Peter is made to appear, personally, as an unsatisfactory figure. In the miraculous Transfiguration scene, he makes the somewhat fatuous suggestion: 'Shall we make three shelters [tents of honour], one for you, one for Moses and one for Elijah?'[13] This reveals that he fails to realize that Jesus was in quite a different category from the two Old Testament prophets. They had miraculously appeared on the scene, it is true. But they were not the equals of Jesus.

'But Peter', *Luke* adds, 'spoke without knowing what he was saying.'[14] And he is explicitly described as perplexed, as well as terrified (like his companions).[15] And then again, when Peter failed to understand a parable, Jesus said, 'are you still as dull as the rest?'[16] Moreover, Peter's attempt to walk on water, like Jesus, failed because it was accompanied by insufficient faith.[17] When Jesus was praying at Gethsemane, Peter, like the other disciples, fell asleep. Jesus came back and saw this, and is reported to have said, 'Asleep, Simon? Could you not stay awake for one hour?'[18] And when men came to arrest Jesus, Peter drew his sword and cut off the right ear of the high priest's servant, Malchus. Jesus, however, reputedly disapproved of this hasty action, which could be of no use and might provoke official retribution. He miraculously restored the ear, with the injunction, 'Stop! No more of that!'[19]

Then there is the terrible story of the Denials, told with such eloquence by the evangelists, although they differ over their timing and location of Peter's disastrous utterances. These had been duly predicted, we are told, by Jesus himself.[20]

> Jesus said to them, 'You will all lose faith; for it is written, "I will strike the shepherd and the sheep will be scattered"' ...
>
> Peter answered, 'Everyone else may lose faith, but I will not.' Jesus said to him, 'Truly I tell you: today, this very night, before the cock crows twice, you yourself will disown me three times.' But Peter answered, 'Even if I have to die with you, I will never disown you.' And they all said the same ...

Peter has been credited with courage for this utterance, but it did not last. For he had not rightly estimated his own weakness, or the difficulty of following Jesus. Thus, after Jesus's arrest and condemnation:[21]

> Peter was still below in the courtyard. One of the high priest's serving-maids came by and saw him there warming himself. She looked closely at him and said, 'You were with this man from Nazareth, this Jesus.' But he denied it: 'I know nothing,' he said; 'I have no idea what you are talking about,' and he went out into the forecourt. The servant-girl saw him there and began to say again to the bystanders, 'He is one of them'; and again he denied it.
>
> Again, a little later, the bystanders said to Peter, 'You must be one of them; you are a Galilean.' At this he started to curse, and declared with an oath, 'I do not know this man you are talking about.' At that moment the cock crowed for the second time; and Peter remembered how Jesus

had said to him, 'Before the cock crows twice you will disown me three times.' And he burst into tears.

Many scholars have concluded that the story is untrue, invented, perhaps, out of hostility towards the Jewish Christian apostles, or as a fulfilment of the Scriptures; some say that it stands for a general denial of Jesus in which all the frightened apostles took part, and that it may have been superimposed, fictitiously, upon a record that had no knowledge of any such tale. But others regard Peter's Denials as genuine – too unflattering to be invented.[22] In any case the story, whether true or not, sets out to show how human and fallible Peter was, like the rest of us, but unlike Jesus. (It will be seen, too, that 'he started to *curse*': presumably not against Jesus, but to protest that he himself was telling the truth.)

However, another important feature of the story of the Denials is Peter's subsequent repentance. He burst into tears, we are told by all the Synoptic Gospels, when he remembered how Jesus had foretold his lamentable utterances,[23] and he went down in theological history as the very model of the repentant sinner. For even if he had denied his Lord, he was sorry about it afterwards – and for this he was rehabilitated. His rehabilitation was illustrated and exemplified by the Appearance of the risen Jesus to him. For in spite of Peter's poor behaviour, Jesus saved him from sinking in the waters of the Sea of Galilee.[24] That is to say, the unworthy but repentant apostle became a direct recipient of Jesus's bounty, which, fortified by a prayer uttered by Jesus himself, made him a special source of strength to the Church, and a keynote of its very existence. Peter's imperfections have magnified his greatness.

When we try to sum up the character of Peter – from the obviously inadequate material at our disposal – we must put aside, I have suggested earlier, the idea that he necessarily, or even probably, came from a poor family.

This has a bearing on his education as well. Misunderstandings have been prompted by his description, in *Acts*, as an 'uneducated layman' (*agrammatos idiotes*).[25] This merely signifies that Peter lacked the formal training of a scribe, priest or rabbi. It does not mean that he was wholly uncultured, even though people in Jerusalem might note, or mock, his Galilean accent.[26] Nor need this lack of specialist training have prevented him from earning respect as a leader, or an incisive speaker. Yet we have already been shown a list of Peter's alleged weaknesses, of which he was said to have been painfully conscious: 'Go, Lord, leave me, sinner that I am!'[27] He was described as slow to understand, but eager, hasty, vehement, exuberant, spontaneous and impulsive. He also, we are told, leapt rapidly from one extreme to the other, as *John* tells us in the following story (whether authentic or not):[28]

> He [Jesus] poured water into a basin, and began to wash his disciples' feet and to wipe them with the towel.
>
> When he came to Simon Peter, Peter said to him, 'You, Lord, washing my feet?' Jesus replied, 'You do not understand now what I am doing, but one day you will.' Peter said: 'I will never let you wash my feet.' 'If I do not wash you,' Jesus replied, 'you have no part with me.' 'Then, Lord,' said Simon Peter, 'not my feet only; wash my hands and head as well!'

The paradoxical blend of human weaknesses and strengths ascribed to Peter has struck and fascinated many, from Origen and St Augustine onwards.[29] But why did Jesus choose him, from among everyone else, as his chief apostle, the leader of the apostolic group? Because, surely, of his devotion and his faith. Jesus was frequently on record as stressing the indispensability and all-powerfulness of faith, without which, indeed, his mission would come to nothing: 'everything is possible to one who believes'.[30] Peter's faith sometimes failed him, at least temporarily, as we know. Yet 'we have left everything to follow you,' he declared.[31] Peter 'accepts the privileged position of Jesus, and, with characteristic eagerness, wants a share in it'. And at the end, when Jesus was doomed and his disciples were leaving him:[32]

> Jesus asked the Twelve, 'Do you also want to leave?' Simon Peter answered him, 'Lord, to whom shall we go? Your words are words of eternal life. We believe and know that you are God's Holy One.'

Peter had nowhere else to turn, and there was nowhere else where he wanted to turn. Despite his human deficiencies and setbacks, among which the Denials are recorded as being so painfully prominent, Peter was, in the last resort, as loyal and faithful to Jesus as human nature permitted him to be. In Jesus, and in his message and mission, Peter's belief was unqualified and unlimited. That is why Jesus chose him and set him apart. And that is why Peter, next to his leader, was the greatest Christian of all time.

Bibliographical note

On whether Peter's Confession was post-Resurrection, or of various dates, see R. E. Brown, K. P. Donfried and L. Reumann (eds), *Peter in the New Testament* (1973), pp. 12, 85; cf. also pp. 107 n. 42, 182, 214 n. 2. On the translation from Aramaic, see C. P. Thiede, *Simon Peter: From Galilee to Rome* (1986) p. 33. The Confession in John, 6.68–9, seems to be separate (ibid. pp. 43f.).

On suffering, see C. S. C. Williams, *The Acts of the Apostles* (2nd ed. 1964), p. 79; C. L. Mitton, *Jesus: The Fact Behind the Faith* (1973) p. 37.

For discussion of Satan, see J. B. Russell, *Satan: the Early Christian Tradition* (1981).

On the failings of Peter, see R. E. Brown, *et al.*, op. cit., p. 62; N. Forsyth, *The Old Enemy: Satan and the Combat Myth* (1987).

Shelters (*skenai*) are discussed in R. E. Brown *et al.*, op. cit., p. 63; Mitton, op. cit., p. 131; C. C. Caragounis, *Peter and the Rock* (1990), p. 97. Thiede, op. cit., p. 222 n. 77, discounts a supposed link with the Feast of the Tabernacles, but W. D. Davies and D. C. Allison, *The Gospel According to Saint Matthew*, Vol II (1991), pp. 609f., find a link with the Old Testament 'tent of meeting'.

On the Denials, see R. E. Brown *et al.*, op. cit., p. 63 n. 139; Caragounis, op. cit., pp. 99f.; C. Kahler, *New Testament Studies*, XXIII, 1976/7, pp. 42f.; R. Pesch, *Simon-Petrus* (1980), pp. 43f., 144 and n. 7; O. Cullmann, *Peter: Disciple, Apostle, Martyr* (1962), p. 190 n. 93. Does *Luke* 22. 31–2 reflect an earlier tradition in which there were no denials? The threefold 'do you love me?' in *John* (21.15–17)may reflect Peter's threefold Denial (13.38, the cock was to crow once, not twice), *cf.*R. E. Brown, *The Gospel According to John* (1966) pp. 1111f., and may signalize his rehabilitation.

The first Denial was in rabbinical legal form: W. L. Cane, *The Gospel According to Mark* (1974), p. 542; Thiede, op. cit., p. 230 n. 148. A. Robertson, *A Harmony of the Gospels* (H. H. Hobbs, *The Gospel of Mark*, p. 68), places the Denials before the Last Supper.

On Peter's culture, see Thiede, op. cit., p. 122; J. Lowe, *Saint Peter* (1956), p. 3. For Peter's character, see G. Turner, *Theology*, XIII, 1926, p. 77; Hobbs, op. cit., p. 26.

Chapter 5

PETER AND JESUS

One of the few things that is certain about Jesus is that Peter was his principal apostle, disciple and helper. And it was in that capacity that Peter became known to the later world. It is therefore of the utmost importance to this study to discover who Jesus was.

This is exceedingly difficult, however, because the sources just do not provide us with the information that we want. For this reason Jesus has been interpreted in an enormous number of different ways – so enormous that one cannot begin to enumerate them, and indeed it is not necessary to do so here, since what we are concerned with, in this book, is his relationship with Peter.

There are, of course, non-canonical Gospels which preserve alleged sayings of Jesus, and a few of them, such as the *Gospel of Thomas*, may contain authentic passages,[1] and may therefore be genuine additions to the received picture. But this remains dubious, and the truth still is that we have to rely almost entirely upon the four canonical Gospels that were included in the New Testament, bearing the names of Jesus's apostles, Matthew and John (the son of Zebedee), and of Paul's companions, Mark and Luke. Something has already been said of these Gospels: and here it may be repeated that these men were almost certainly not the authors of the works in question. We call them the 'evangelists', the bearers of good news (*euangelion*). But we do not know who they were, or when or where they lived. As was suggested earlier, however, the Gospels apparently reached their final form between thirty-five and sixty years after the Crucifixion of Jesus.

So when we try to reconstruct Jesus's life, our first problem is that the writings which tell us about it date, in the form which has come down to us, from one, two or three generations after his death. This raises queries about the true nature and activity not only of Jesus but of the subject of the present study, Peter, the foremost of his helpers. What we have to do, therefore, in order to reconstruct the careers of Jesus and his leading disciple Peter is to examine the Gospels, and endeavour to make a distinction between those portions of them which seem to bear the mark of the Christian Church as it existed after the time of Jesus, and other passages which, on the contrary, look as if they might go back to the lifetime of Jesus himself.

And about this process we need not be as pessimistic as some modern commentators are. It does in the end, after careful examination, seem possible to reconstruct the main features of Jesus's life, thought and teaching: to reconstruct, that is to say, something of his career and personality, which were so close to Peter's that Peter became his principal apostle.

Let us see how this works out in greater detail. First of all, we can abandon AD 1 as the year of Jesus's birth. The date was only adopted because someone, in the Middle Ages, made a miscalculation. Instead, Jesus was born at some time during the final years of what Christians call 'BC'.

The time when Jesus and Peter grew up was a gloomy epoch for Judaism and for Palestine. The country had fallen far from its pristine glories. A millennium earlier, it had been a mighty power under the rule of David and Solomon, and that grandeur had not been forgotten. Subsequently, the land had been split into two kingdoms, Israel and Judah, which had in due course, as the Old Testament relates, succumbed to the great empires of the Middle East, Assyria and Babylonia respectively. Then later again the Persians, and subsequently the Seleucid Greeks, had annexed the whole territory. However, in the second century BC things had looked better for a time, when the nationalist movement of the Hasmonaeans (Maccabees) asserted the country's independence from the Seleucids.

However, they lost their power to the Romans, and it was in a Palestine dominated by Rome that the families of Jesus and Peter were obliged to exist. The Romans had established a Jewish client king, Herod the Great, but ten years after his death in 4 BC the nucleus of the country was annexed and enrolled as a province of the Roman empire named Judaea, under whose prefect it was conceded a measure of internal self-government directed by an obedient Jewish High-Priest and his Council (Sanhedrin). On the northern and eastern peripheries of this new province, however, consisting of the territories of Galilee and Peraea, one of Herod the Great's sons, Herod Antipas (a half-brother of Philip who ruled further to the north) was permitted by the Romans to reign as a puppet prince or tetrarch.

The Jews were nevertheless inspired by their religion to seek explanations and solutions which ignored, and tried to rise above, Roman control and suzerainty.

And it was in the desert wastes of the borderlands of Judaea and Peraea, in about the year AD 28 or 29, that there began to be news of an impressive Jewish preacher who turned his listeners' ears away from the worldly realities of Rome's domination. He was John the Baptist, and his preaching, seen as a revival of the teaching of Elijah,[2] consisted of a proclamation of the imminent dawning of God's Kingdom, or Kingship, upon the earth. This message was not unprecedented, because the Jews had for many centuries been told, and had believed, that their tribulations would one day come to an end when this Kingship of God would come into effect throughout the world, whereupon everything would become perfect, at least for themselves. However, although John the Baptist's message was not, therefore, entirely unfamiliar, it made an apposite arrival at a time of seething Jewish discontent, and attracted widespread attention and expectation.

A necessity urged by this preaching was that everyone should repent of his or her sins. That, too, was not novel, since Jewish theologians had urged repentance before, but John's insistence once again struck an opportune note. Its thoroughgoing, all-out imperative was striking, since he emphasized that the repentance which was needed must be *total*: must be accompanied, that is to say, by a complete and utter change of heart. If only this could be achieved, John maintained, all sins would then be forgiven.

He provided a practical means by which the process could take place and be signalized and facilitated. That means was baptism, which would set a seal on every good intention. The Jews were accustomed to periodical ritual ablutions, but John, using the waters of the Jordan, transformed such proceedings into a once-and-for-all, uniquely significant happening, which was believed to change its recipients for evermore and to make them into new, transformed persons.

One of those who received this baptism from John, we are told, was Jesus. This, it appears, was a genuine historical event. It must be regarded as such because the early Christian Church, after Jesus's death, would have very much liked to pretend that it had never happened. Jesus, in their view, was and had always been sinless, so that his baptism, which indicated a remission of his sins, was out of place. Nevertheless, Jesus's baptism by John passed into the record books, and the fact that it did so, despite the reluctance of the Church, is proof of its authenticity.

It was, and is, stated that Jesus was born at Bethlehem, but that was only said in order to fulfil an Old Testament prophecy[3] and is probably not true at all. It is more likely that he came from Galilee, and indeed it was as 'a Galilean' that he was often known. His birthplace may have been Nazareth, and he was also described as 'the Nazarene'. Galilee had produced imposing holy men before, in considerable numbers, but this was only in the fairly recent past, since the conversion of its people to Judaism was not an old phenomenon. The people of Jerusalem looked down on the Galileans with a certain measure of contempt, regarding them as country bumpkins who did not understand religion very well and got it wrong.

When Jesus, in later times, began to attract widespread veneration, various attempts were made to glorify his origins. For one thing, the difficult doctrine of the Virgin Birth came into existence, so that it could be asserted that his mother Mary – the subject of such great reverence throughout the centuries – had been made pregnant not by her husband Joseph, but by God himself. But then, on a more worldly basis, the evangelists seemed, after all, not to be denying Joseph's paternity of Jesus when, in order to satisfy the belief that the expected Messiah would be a descendant of King David, they credited Joseph with just such a descent.

So Jesus was baptized in the River Jordan by John the Baptist. Not long afterwards, however, John was arrested by Herod Antipas as potentially seditious. It was hardly surprising that the king regarded him in this light, since John's preaching of the imminent Kingdom of God implied that Antipas's own kingship would be eclipsed and superseded: in fact, it would cease to exist. So Antipas, at a location and in circumstances which have been disputed,[4] had this potentially disruptive and revolutionary personage put to death.

After John the Baptist had been arrested, Jesus was told that he, too, was on Antipas's death list.[5] But he went back to Galilee and inaugurated his mission there. This mission presented considerable similarities to John's – and Jesus acknowledged those debts[6] – but there was one notable innovation. John, and other Jews, had pronounced that the Kingdom of God upon earth was imminent. But Jesus declared that, even if it had not yet come into *full* realization, *it had already begun to arrive*: that he himself was, here and now, bringing it into being, having been commanded to do so by God. True, he was indebted to John the Baptist for the whole idea. Yet, all the same, his own new declaration superseded what the Baptist had proclaimed, as the Gospels make clear.[7] Jesus's spectacular and sensational pronouncement was the keynote of his entire programme. It wholly pervaded everything that he thought and did, and everything that he taught, and every moral and social aim that he sought to inculcate.

This can be seen, for example, from his parables. Every one of them originates from, and implies, the single-minded belief that the Kingdom of God was actually being installed, and that he himself was installing it, since that is what God had ordered him to do. The same was true of his supposed miracles. Something has been said elsewhere about what these stories of miracles meant at the time. Here it must only be added that, whenever Jesus claimed, or seemed, to have performed a miraculous action, it was to illustrate and symbolize the fact that he was bringing the Kingdom of God into existence. Jesus, as we have seen, was evidently a powerful healer – a gift that the ancients omitted to distinguish from miraculous powers, but one which Jesus himself, when he performed such cures, deliberately and explicitly related to his leading part in the actual introduction, here and now, of the Kingdom of God upon the earth. He associated these healings with the repentance and forgiveness of sins which were the accompaniments of that already dawning kingdom.

Many Jews thought that this talk of forgiveness of sins was all too easy, and, indeed, provided an encouragement to sinners, who felt comfortably that they might go ahead with wrongdoing since their earlier sins could be wiped out (no doubt they had felt the same when they heard of John the Baptist's preaching on the subject). Jesus emphasized, however, that forgiveness would come as a result of repentance, and what that meant now, to him, was not only the complete change of heart which it had meant to John, but a change of heart which carried with it a specific acceptance of his conviction that the Kingdom of God was already actually coming into effect, and that it was he who was bringing it into effect, according to God's command.

This was an idea that the Jews particularly disliked, because it seemed to them a usurpation of God's free gift and an infringement and denial of the monotheism in which they so passionately believed: they felt that, by claiming to act in this way, and by citing divine authority for what he said he was doing, Jesus was setting himself up as a second God, and thus was seeking to undermine the essential doctrine that there could only be one, single deity.

Jesus's insistence on the forgiveness of sins, in which he enlisted Peter as his principal helper, contributed greatly to the fame of his outstanding compassion: a quality on which the evangelists later dwelt, especially Luke. But it was also pointed out that sins could only be forgiven, and compassion duly exercised, because of the vast change that was taking place: the introduction, by Jesus's initiative, of the Kingdom of God. For the same reason Jesus paid special attention to the poor – because *all* Jews were embraced by the dawning kingship, and the poor, possessing no material resources of their own, had no one but God to whom they could turn. They were therefore entirely willing and able to participate in the dawning kingdom. Moreover, exactly the same applied to those who had sinned, since their repentance would readily secure them enrolment in that kingdom. Indeed this would be easier for them than for anyone else because no complacency, such as enveloped the consciously virtuous, stood in their way. It was with this urgently arriving kingdom in mind that Jesus taught that people should forgive even their enemy and turn the other cheek (an injunction which, although not wholly unheard-of before, seemed to many Jews quite impracticable, and therefore not worth saying). According to this teaching, what purpose could petty worldly enmities conceivably serve when set against the vast opportunity of all entering the Kingdom of God together?

'Suffer little children to come unto me' Jesus was reported to have said.[8] Modern, sentimental interpretations of this request are, however, wholly out of place. The reason why Jesus favoured little children was because they were *tabulae rasae*; the simple, unspoilt, receptive innocence of these smallest and humblest members of human society was precisely the quality needed to greet his difficult message with whole-hearted, unreserved acceptance. Furthermore, Jesus, despite an anti-feminist comment of dubious significance and authenticity at the end (Ch. 114) of the *Gospel of Thomas* (intended by its author to mollify the Jews), was totally lacking in prejudices against women, and indeed welcomed the presence of women close beside him. It would have been misguided to suppose that the kingdom which he was introducing could exist for men only, and not for the women who were the other half of the Jewish and human race.

Such were the feelings and attitudes which Jesus inculcated in his principal helpers, and notably in Peter. But he could not expect these views to be shared by the Jewish teachers of the time, the scribes – who were, for example, by no means surrounded by women. Moreover, in addition to their specific objections to his doctrines, they also rejected Jesus's whole approach, especially his willingness to go outside the synagogues and preach to a more widespread public than their own. Jesus did this because the Jews in the synagogues did not respond sufficiently to his message, but it was not a policy likely to appeal to the rabbis. In this way, although Jesus was a teacher and preacher of outstanding gifts, he was unorthodox, and this, as always happens, made him many enemies.

On the other hand, like John the Baptist, and despite the Gospels' apparently contradictory suggestion that he wished to keep his message 'secret', Jesus was seen and welcomed by many others among his listeners as a direct successor of the revered line of Hebrew prophets. There were some who already, like millions in subsequent ages, saw him as the Messiah: Peter was said to have hailed him by that title, although Jesus himself viewed it, or at least its traditional connotations, with some reluctance.[9] The Messiah was the anointed one, the Greek Christos, who was a descendant of the royal house of David, and was expected, eventually, to arrive upon the earth and raise up Israel out of the misery and foreign oppression into which it had fallen – and to do so with the help of superhuman and supernatural authority.

Another title which was widely attached to the person of Jesus was 'the Son of Man' (or 'the Man'). This was a mysterious and ambiguous appellation, which is hard for us to understand, our range of language being so different from that of the ancient Jews. For they, unlike ourselves, had long been accustomed and dedicated to the employment of corporate communal concepts, and when they said 'the Son of Man' they had very often been thinking in corporate terms, using the phrase to denote the whole of Israel and its hoped-for liberation. However, in epochs closer to the lifetime of Jesus, 'the Son of Man' may well have gained a novel and more specific, and therefore more revolutionary, connotation, referring to an awaited *individual* who would take the lead in bringing about this salvation. It was also possible to call Jesus 'the Son of God', as he has frequently been designated in later times. However, it must be remembered that pious Jews could use this term about each and every one of their people. And indeed the phrase, which had a long previous history in the Near East, could have various different significances which would not necessarily include the belief that a man so described need be regarded as God's actual son.

Matthew's Gospel brought all these terms together.[10] But which of them did Jesus's loyal followers, such as Peter, apply to him? We have no idea: perhaps all of them. But perhaps, also, since the apostles were not expert theologians, such questions scarcely arose. One might hazard the guess that the devoted Peter accepted Jesus with such completeness that he would not have refused him the titles of Messiah, Son of Man, and Son of God, in their most extreme significances. As for Jesus himself, it appears likely that he did not believe that any of these titles were really appropriate to him, since he envisaged his position and mission as unique, so that attempts to define them in traditional terms scarcely applied. Earlier Galilean sages had claimed a direct, personal intimacy with God, and Jesus made a similar claim in unprecedentedly imperative language.

This, again, could scarcely fail to disturb and disgust the Jews. In particular, it brought Jesus into forcible confrontation with the most powerful section of the Jewish leadership, the Pharisees. In the face of this adamant opposition, and despite all the assistance that he received from Peter and his other followers, Jesus's mission in Galilee terminated in failure as he himself freely admitted; by attacking the Galilean towns for their non-belief.[11] King Herod Antipas of Galilee and Peraea was waiting and watching how things would turn out, and when he noted that Jesus's mission was foundering and his cause dwindling, he saw an opportunity to get rid of this implicitly subversive preacher – the man who told of a kingdom of which Herod Antipas was not the ruler – and he therefore got rid of him, as he had got rid of John the Baptist. However, he felt it would have been imprudent to use the same methods of arrest and execution. So instead what Antipas did was to force Jesus to leave his country. Or, at any rate, Jesus left, and Herod Antipas probably did all he could to hasten his departure.

Jesus departed with Peter and his other disciples, and made his way, by gradual stages, to Jerusalem. This was a purposeful and suicidal act. He was moving straight into the home of the central Jewish establishment, to which the Romans gave a free hand in internal religious matters, and he must have known that it would receive him with hostility. In other words, even granting that his forecasts of his end were probably less explicit than the predictions found in the Gospels,[12] Jesus must have known that his move to Jerusalem would mean his arrest and death.

During this period, typology was much in Jesus's mind. Typology, as has been explained, was the belief, widely held and deeply believed among the Jews, that their Bible, what we call the Old Testament, was full of predictions and prefigurations which were, or would be, fulfilled in the lives of their own people, very often with their own deliberate assistance. Jesus had fully absorbed these ideas, and kept them in mind when he, Peter and the other disciples entered Jerusalem. Their entrance was meticulously arranged, in direct accordance with prophetic Old Testament texts, to demonstrate that Jesus was a king, but that his kingship was not of this world but of the Kingdom of God.

It can be assumed, as we have seen, that Jesus's mission in Galilee had already greatly irritated the Pharisees. But there was also a second important Jewish group, the Sadducees, centred upon the figure of the high priest. Jesus, it was said, now deliberately set these against himself as well, by driving the traders out of the Temple[13] – a violent action which makes nonsense of the rival tradition, preserved by Victorian stained-glass windows and a famous hymn, that he was gentle, meek and mild.

Before long, one of Jesus's own apostles, Judas Iscariot, turned against him. Probably he was disillusioned by Jesus's rejection of an earthly kingship for himself. Then, guided by Judas, the Sadducees placed Jesus under arrest. Peter's discreditable denials of his association with the arrested man have been described elsewhere.

Jesus was accused, first, of threatening to destroy the Jewish Temple, and second, of claiming, blasphemously, to be the Messiah and the Son of God. His answer seemed unsatisfactory, since he neither accepted nor rejected the charges, because whatever he answered would have failed to impress or enlighten his unsympathetic accusers.

The Jewish authorities handed him over to the Roman prefect of the province of Judaea, Pontius Pilate, who gave orders for his Crucifixion. Controversy has raged, and still rages, as to whether it was the Jews or the Romans who were responsible for his death. But the dispute has been continually overlaid by later preoccupations, according to which it has seemed desirable to blame or, conversely, to exonerate the Jews for such an anti-Christian act. In the course of this argument, the historical situation in Judaea at the time has often been forgotten or neglected. The fact was, as we have seen, that it constituted a Roman province, in which the Jewish authorities were subordinates to whom the Romans allowed autonomy in religious matters. What they did on this occasion was to pass Jesus over to Pilate to carry out the death sentence. And so, whatever may have been his own feelings – he could well have been reluctant, foreseeing future trouble – Pilate arranged for the Crucifixion of Jesus. And that is how Jesus died: we can ignore the numerous theories that he somehow succeeded in surviving.

This was when, as we will see, Peter began to have his moment of supreme influence and power. It was he who took the lead when, three days after the Crucifixion, Jesus's few surviving followers became convinced that they had seen him resurrected in front of them. This conviction initiated the long process by which the unsuccessful mission of Jesus's lifetime was transformed into triumph after death. It was indeed a revolution kept tenuously alive, largely through the endeavours of Peter. And it has been almost the only revolution in the history of the world that has taken permanent effect. One reason why this Christian revolution has proved so arresting and lasting is that it gave Judaism an entirely new life by attaching it to one single figure and person. This person, in contrast to the divinities of pagan mystery religions, had made his appearance upon earth and had lived there, which is why it is permissible and desirable to try to write his biography and that of his principal follower, Peter. This actual existence of Jesus among humankind was one of the principal factors which made it possible for Christianity, throughout the centuries which lay ahead, to become a far larger religion, in terms of numbers, than the Judaism from which it sprang.

Thus Peter, by playing such a major part in Jesus's mission, and then by assuming the Christian leadership after Jesus's death, was highly prominent in a process which transformed the thoughts and perceptions of a major part of the human race, and still governs the lives of many millions of believers today. What many of them find eternally uplifting about Jesus is this. In order to pursue his overriding aim, he was uncompromising in his refusal to give way to all those, including people of power and authority, who failed to share that aim and endeavoured to silence him. His belief was unremittingly absolute, and he attached no real importance to anything else. Values today are often relative and shifting. And in our own epoch of compromises Jesus's standard still remains plain and urgent, so that it will survive all the sliding ideals that emerge and seek, vainly, to take its place from time to time.

Reference has been made to Peter's role in this revolutionary movement. It was not, as we have seen, entirely or invariably creditable. Certainly he had received an exceptional call from Jesus, and it was he who guided Jesus's other disciples. But he had not fully understood that the man whom he, no doubt, regarded as the Messiah was destined to suffer and die, and with tragic human weakness he denied all association with him after Jesus's traumatic arrest. Yet he was forgiven, and thereafter it was he who believed and declared that he had seen, with his own eyes, the risen Lord.

1. Pentecost (from Greek fiftieth): first celebrated on the 50th day after the Resurrection of Jesus (Whitsunday) when the Holy Spirit was believed to have descended upon Peter (whose speech to the polyglot audience is reported in Acts 2 14ff) and the other disciples. The occasion is adapted from the Jewish Feast of Weeks (Shavuoth). From the Missal of Abbot Berthold of Weingarten, 13th Century. J. Pierpont Morgan Library

2. *Jesus and the Twelve Apostles*, Pala d'Oro, San Marco, Venice.

3. *'Launch Out into the Deep'*, the call of Jesus to Peter, Luke 5.4. From a 13th Century German psalter

4. *Jesus giving the Keys to Peter.*
Painting by Perugino (1446–
1523), Sistine Chapel, Vatican

5. *Peter holding the Keys of the
Kingdom.* Sculpture at Moissac,
France. 12th century

6. *One of Peter's Denials of Jesus*, Catacombs of St. Domitilla (or Sts. Nereus and Achilleus), Rome, 4th century

7. *Peter and Malchus.* Peter has cut off Malchus' right ear with a sword, John 18.10; but Jesus restores it. From a 15th-century French ivory of the betrayal of Jesus

8. *Martyrdom of St. Peter*, alabaster relief of Nottingham School. 15th century, Victoria and Albert Museum, London

9. *Below* Alabaster panels of St. Peter and St. Paul. English, c. 1400

10. *Martyrdoms of St. Peter and St. Paul*, 15th-century manuscript in Biblioteca Laurenziana, Florence

11. *Martyrdom of St. Peter*, from the Bronze Doors of St Peter's Basilica, Rome, redecorated by Antonio Filarete, 1439–1445

12. Marble statue of St. Peter, Vatican, 13th and 14th centuries; and

13. *Peter enthroned*, central panel of altarpiece; school of Guido da Siena, 13th century

Above 14. *Healing of Lame Man by Peter and John at the Beautiful Gate of the Temple*, Raphael *Cartoon* (1483–1520). Victoria and Albert Museum, London

15. Peter's (adopted?) daughter Petronilla admitting Veneranda to heaven. Catacombs of Domitilla, Rome, 4th century

17. Old St. Peter's: exterior with Vatican palace from a drawing by Maarten van Heemskerk, 1533

Bibliographical note

On John the Baptist and Jesus, see W. D. Davies and D. C. Allison, *The Gospel According to Saint Matthew*, Vol I (1988), pp. 285–349. Centres of John the Baptist's teaching and baptising were Bethany and Aenon (near Salim), John 1.28, 3.23, et 10–40; R. E. Brown, *The Gospel According to St John* I–XII, p. 54.

I have attempted to study Jesus elsewhere: see M. Grant, *Jesus* (1977), published as *Jesus: An Historian's View of the Gospels* in the USA. There is also, of course, a constant flow of literature on the subject. Recent books, offering various arresting points of view, include A. N. Wilson, *Jesus* (1992); J. D. Crossan, *The Historical Jesus* (1991); J. P. Meier, *A Marginal Jew* (1992); K.-J. Kuschel, *Born Before All Time? The Dispute Over Christ's Origin* (1992); G. Vidal, *Live from Golgotha* (1992); B. Thiering, *Jesus the Man* (1992); W. Marxsen, *Jesus and the Church*; J. Macquarrie, *Jesus Christ in Modern Thought*; J. H. Charlesworth (ed.), *Jesus' Jewishness*; C. S. Song, *Jesus and the Reign of God*; N. A. Dahl, *Jesus the Christ*; A. R. Eckardt, *Reclaiming the Jesus of History*; B. Witherington III, *The Christology of Jesus*; G. Vermes, *The Religion of Jesus the Jew*; B. H. Fuller, *Christ and Christianity*.

The treacherous role of Judas is denied by H. Maccoby, *Judas Iscariot and the Myth of Jewish Evil* (1992). *John* 18.10 is our source for the report that, at the time of the arrest, Peter cut off the ear of the high priest's servant Malchus. But his name was omitted by the three synoptic evangelists, to avoid specific mention of violent resistance to the authorities. See also bibliography (Other Books) for some earlier publications.

Part III

AFTER JESUS'S DEATH

Chapter 6

PETER AND THE RESURRECTION

'Christ's conquest of death, enshrined in the solemnities of Easter week, has overwhelmed human hearts for so many centuries.'[1] His Resurrection, that is to say, is an indispensable and undetachable part of the Christian religion. It was the proof of life after death.

This has always seemed to be the case, from the very moment at which the event was first believed to have occurred. If they had not been fortified by this conviction, the small group of those who had been the personal associates of Jesus, and who then scattered in despair and depression, would have died out, just as other Messianic sects had faded away when their leaders had vanished. What kept the former followers of Jesus and their faith going, and converted them from terrified and despondent men and women, at the time when Jesus was crucified, into the founders and missionaries of a mighty Church, was their belief that their master had risen from the dead.

Indeed, without the Resurrection, according to Paul, the Christian religion could not exist: 'If Christ was not raised, then our gospel is null and void, and so too is your faith.'[2] Christianity stands or falls by Jesus's Resurrection. 'You cannot take the Resurrection away from Christianity without radically altering its character and destroying its very identity.'[3] Paul went so far as to say that Jesus was only 'proclaimed the Son of God' at his Resurrection.[4] Be that as it may, the Resurrection was the irreplaceable, solid foundation of the apostles' faith, and the chief ingredient and origin of their message and Church. It was an event, claimed as a historical fact to which eyewitnesses could testify, that turned the faint-hearted disciples into followers who were ready to die for the belief that this new understanding had given them.

The most important point was that the Resurrection of Jesus was held to mean that all human beings, too, or all who believe in him, shall likewise be granted resurrection from the dead. 'In his great mercy', we read in *1 Peter*,[5] 'by the Resurrection of Jesus Christ from the dead, God gave *us* new birth into a living hope, the hope of an inheritance, reserved in heaven for you, which nothing can destroy or spoil or wither.' 'O Death, where is your sting?'[6] Indeed, the process had perhaps already begun. According to Paul, just as people had all died at Jesus's death, so too they have *already*, in a sense, risen, like him, from the dead – they are *in union with* the risen Christ.[7]

In the process of allegedly witnessing, and asserting and reporting, this Resurrection of Jesus, not only Paul, but at an earlier stage Peter, played an altogether central part.

Like most other New Testament events and reported events (see Chapter 1) the Resurrection of Jesus was 'according to the Scriptures' (that is to say, the Old Testament), as Jesus himself was believed to have emphasized.[8]

Indeed it could be said to have been prefigured by 'proofs' consisting of the alleged rising from the dead, in various forms, of a number of Old Testament personages – Abraham, Enoch, Moses, Isaac, Jacob, Elijah – although none of the resurrection stories created a persistent Jewish belief in individual resurrection, or seemed to Paul a complete or satisfactory precedent for Jesus.

It was Daniel, faced with suffering and martyrdom, who had, for the first time (as far as we know), clearly expressed the belief in a *general* resurrection, dreaming of the day when the masses of the dead would rise again, as Mark's Gospel appreciated.[9] And later Hebrew thought, embodied, for example, in *The Wisdom of Solomon, Jubilees* and *2 Esdras*, pressed the point home: because the Jews always felt a deep religious conviction that man is made for fellowship with God. From the second century BC the Pharisees accepted the idea that physical resurrection was a possibility, and would take place.

This Jewish concept of rising from the dead maintained that the soul of every man and woman would necessarily be *united with the body* in resurrection at the end of time. The Hebrews did not make our distinction between body and soul, and the Greek doctrine of immortality of the soul was alien to them. Granted that a few exceptional individuals such as Moses had experienced some sort of personal resurrection, its ultimate coming to the world was at first regarded by these Jewish believers as a corporate, communal affair.

But who would this group be: who would earn such a reward? Ever since the earliest days of Hebrew thinking there had been discussions about the definition and identity of those who would, eventually, enjoy such a corporeal resurrection. Was it to be a 'remnant' of all deserving Jews? Or all Jews that there were, without selection or qualification? Or even the whole of humankind, as some of the more recent holy books suggested?[10] Whatever the conclusion, the Jewish insistence on the *corporate* character of the community was at first maintained. In one or other of the senses proposed, the ultimate resurrection of the dead would be corporate and communal.

Opinions were changing, however, and under the influence of the stories about Moses and the others, the idea of *individual* resurrection began to assume a greater prominence. The influence of Hellenism on this growing point of view was paradoxical. On the one hand, there was no doubt that such attitudes were strengthened by Hellenistic thinking, but at the same time many pagans found the conception shocking:[11] the Athenians, for example, were quite uncomprehending about the concept, and so perhaps were the people of Corinth.[12]

Nevertheless, more positive speculations on the subject became intensified among the Jews by the belief that John the Baptist had actually risen from the dead in precisely this bodily manner.[13] Thus, by the time of Jesus, the belief that individuals of great magnitude and quality might rise corporeally from the dead, in advance of the general, communal resurrection, was no longer as unfamiliar or suspect an idea as it had been earlier.

Jesus was crucified some time between AD 30 and 36, and it seems unlikely that this event was entirely fictitious. Whether it was mainly the act of the Jews or Romans, as we have seen, has been passionately argued ever since. In any case it was a horrifying disaster, but Christians tried to assert that it was in accordance with the will of God, all the same.[14]

Then, three days later, Jesus was said to have risen from the dead. This supposed Resurrection was not recounted by any of the four canonical Gospels (only by the apocryphal *Gospel of Peter*)[15] and was not stated to have been witnessed by anyone, despite later paintings, notably by Piero della Francesca. Jesus was said (with doubtful reliability, at least about the details) to have predicted no fewer than three times that it would happen: but his predictions were received with perplexity.[16]

However, the reality of the Resurrection was alleged to have been proved by the subsequent Appearances of the risen Christ upon earth, on eight, or nine, or twenty occasions (are one, two or more traditions fused?).[17] Much of the vocabulary employed to describe these Appearances was taken, in accordance with typological custom, from the Old Testament.[18]

At first there was probably just a list of those to whom Jesus had supposedly appeared,[19] but the earliest surviving record of these Appearances was offered by Paul, writing to the Christians at Corinth:[20]

> First and foremost, I handed on to you the tradition I had received: that Christ died for our sins, in accordance with the Scriptures; that he was buried; that he was raised to life on the Third Day, in accordance with the scriptures; and that he appeared to Cephas [Peter], and afterwards to the Twelve.

Then he appeared to over five hundred of our brothers at once, most of whom are still alive, though some have died. Then he appeared to James, and afterwards to all the apostles. Last of all he appeared to me too; it was like a sudden, abnormal birth.

So Peter was ascribed the first of these Appearances of the dead Jesus. And Luke's Gospel too, credits him with the same privilege.

These Appearances are found in various other, quite different and contradictory forms in the Gospels (sometimes giving prominence to women, although their evidence had no legal validity,[21] and their initial silence was mysterious).

The Appearances are outside the limits of mortal space and time, and faith is needed to believe in them. Paul, although he knew that this faith was the basic *sine qua non* of his religion, realized that, like the Crucifixion itself,[22] the Appearances that softened its blow were a real stumbling block. For belief in them demanded an utter suspension of reason, since they contradict the human rationality which says that a corpse cannot come to life again.

However, this was an age when miracles and visions were believed in. Appearances were therefore only to be expected, whether or not Jesus, in his lifetime, had hinted that they would take place after his death. We can consider the Appearances either as illusions or as symbolical. 'One can well imagine that a story about Jesus that symbolised a spiritual truth about the believer's relation to the risen Christ would the more readily be accepted as having a basis in history.'[23] Moreover, the apostles were only too ready to accept such manifestations, after the terrible trauma of the Crucifixion. So they were 'chosen' to see the risen Jesus:[24] Peter first of all, according to Paul.

We can say, then, that the Appearances were wishful or metaphorical thinking, unless one prefers to regard them as hallucinations. (This term can hardly be applied to a *mass affair*, recorded in the suggestion that Jesus once appeared to 'more than five hundred'.)[25] Subjective, intuitive, visionary experiences – even doubted at the time[26] – they were characteristic of the epoch, responding to the terrible event of Jesus's death, and attributable to the apostles' uniquely close personal association with him.

The term *ophthe*, 'he was seen', is employed in the Scriptures to express the perception of a revelation, not the establishment of a fact through rational evidence. When Peter claimed to have 'seen' the risen Jesus, the other stunned and confused apostles followed his lead. It apparently took them some time to do so, and denials of the possibility of such Appearances remained in the air. But Peter's proclaimed faith prevailed, and it was upon this, and ultimately upon the fact that the risen Jesus had appeared to him, that the Church was founded.

The word *ophthe* could not have been used, and could not have enjoyed the wide circulation that it did, unless at least one person could be named to whom it was said that the risen Jesus had appeared. In this connection it is his alleged Appearance to Peter that took first place in the minds of the Gospel writers (other than *Mark* which, in its original text, does not mention Appearances at all). Attention has been centred on the supposed Appearance to Peter, partly because he is the first man, so it was said, to have received this distinction, and partly because a sight of the Empty Tomb is conceded to Peter alone, before an Appearance at Emmaus (S.W. of Jerusalem) to 'two of them'.[27] These two – one of whom was apparently Peter, it has been believed since the time of Origen[28] – it was maintained, subsequently reported what they had seen to the other apostles at Jerusalem, to whom Jesus then made a further Appearance.[29]

The insertion of the reference to Peter alone, before these two other Appearances, is somewhat awkward but evidently deliberate – an intentional assertion of his primacy. When *ophthe* appears again in *1 Corinthians*,[30] it seems to be an earlier echo of the same tradition, relating to those who had seen Jesus after his death. As for Paul, he quite clearly accepts that Jesus's Appearance to himself is a supplementary addition to the Appearances to others of which he had been told: 'Jesus appeared, last of all, to me too: it was like a sudden, abnormal birth.'[31] In fact some of those who are not prepared to regard all the Appearances as fictitious have nevertheless decided to accept that only those to Peter and Paul deserve to be regarded as truly authentic.[32]

The awkwardness of the insertion of Peter's name before the Emmaus Appearance has been mentioned. If one considers the emphasis on Peter's prior, superior role, and Paul's clear statement that the first Appearance was to Peter, it is rather strange that Peter is not recorded as the central figure in most of the Appearance stories in the Gospels, although it does remain possible, even if wholly conjectural, that an Appearance to him was recorded in the original [lost] climax of *Mark*.[33] This silence may well be due to a desire, on the part of certain groups and persons, to diminish Peter's importance. In the light of such a desire, it is understandable that the Gentile Christians who produced the Gospels, at least in their final form, were unwilling to preserve and repeat records of Jesus's initial Appearance to Peter.[34]

And yet, in spite of such suppressions and conflicting accounts, the Appearance to Peter is described by Paul as the first, and takes firm precedence over Appearances to others: indeed, this was one of the principal justifications of Peter's subsequent authority. The locality of this Appearance to Peter remains unclear, but it was believed to have taken place in Galilee, or on the way to that country. It is also possible that this Appearance occurred in Jerusalem.[35] As we shall see, there were comparable disagreements about where the other Appearances had taken place as well.

What remains important, in any case, is not so much whether the Appearances actually happened, which is beyond the scope of rationalistic thinking, or even *where* they supposedly happened, but what took place in the hearts and minds of the men and women who had been Jesus's followers, and who *believed* that the risen Jesus had appeared.

This belief caused them to see Jesus's Crucifixion in an entirely new light. It was not a failure, a humiliation and a disaster, but a triumph, which totally metamorphosed their ways of thinking. They believed that they had *seen* the risen Lord, and this carried with it the conviction that his death was not a catastrophic defeat but a unique victory – a victory won by Jesus on the cross, and through him by the human spirit, and by themselves, who would, they were now convinced, be able to share this supreme glory. Meanwhile they must muster up the moral and spiritual insight to live by his example and by everything Jesus had stood for. He had indeed risen, they believed, and his Resurrection had carried them with him.

So the Easter event, as Jesus's followers now interpreted it, had totally reinforced their faith, to which they felt certain he had called them. When they said 'he is risen', this meant that they were sure he was not dead but alive.

For ourselves, who hope to be students of history, the fact that really matters is not so much whether the Resurrection took place, or whether or where there were subsequent Appearances. What is important is the effect that the *belief* in these events exercised on those who had been followers of Jesus; and on Christians of all later times, who, as a result of the same conviction, have felt impelled to acknowledge a spiritual power in their own lives which they can interpret as that of Jesus displaying, in accordance with his invariable practice, God's wisdom and righteousness.

As has already been suggested, corporeal resurrection is a doctrine which it is nowadays difficult to believe in. However, Luke's Gospel in particular, prompted by a desire to combat Docetism – the doctrine that Jesus possessed no truly human body – is eager to stress the physical, corporeal character of the risen Jesus, who ate and drank.[36] And this despite the fact that Jesus himself, in his lifetime, had apparently not favoured this full-blooded, physical, literalistic idea of resurrections.[37] But *Luke* did, as far as Jesus was concerned, and so, later, did Ignatius for the same reason, in order not to depreciate the humanness of Jesus. So too did Augustine, though in a more casuistical and perplexed fashion.[38]

Anyway, Peter manifestly took the lead, professing that he had seen the risen Lord. His evidence, accorded priority and primacy by Paul, was regarded as a unique distinction, which sufficed, moreover, to convince others – and even to convince the apostles that they, subsequently, were being accorded a similar experience.[39]

One curious point, however, is that the biblical writers continued to differ, as they had differed in respect of the Appearance to Peter, about whether the other Appearances took place in or near Jerusalem, in Galilee, or on the road from one to the other. References in *Mark* and *Matthew*, and most of the allusions in Paul's Letters as well as in the *Gospel of Peter*, point to Galilee. But Jerusalem became the centre of the Christian faith, and so there was a tendency to transfer the Appearances to that neighbourhood. It has been suggested that the reports of them were connected with the movements of pilgrims to and from the Jerusalem festivals.[40]

After the Crucifixion of Jesus, his tomb, although guarded and closed by stones (there are Old Testament precedents for this),[41] was allegedly found to be empty.

This has frequently been doubted as fictitious or a late-injected embellishment. But the Empty Tomb has also frequently been reasserted, if not as a fact then at least as an early tradition, perhaps intended to display that what God creates is not destroyed, but recreated and transformed. In particular, the relationship of the emptiness of the tomb to the Resurrection of Jesus has frequently been discussed. Some have denied any connection, or any suggestion that the Empty Tomb is proof of the Resurrection.[42] Nevertheless, early Christians would have regarded the Resurrection as unconvincing without the Empty Tomb, and the conviction that it was found empty helped to encourage the belief in the subsequent Appearances.

But if the tomb *was* empty, why was it empty? This subject, too, has been endlessly debated. The evangelists were eager to deny that the body had been stolen, a theory that the Gospel of Matthew attributed to the malice of the Jews.[43] Very possibly some friends of Jesus had bribed the guards and taken the body away. Or the local gardener might have removed it, afraid that the crowd of sightseers would damage his lettuces.[44] The theory of an intervention by white-robed angels who spirited the body away – with reference back to

Daniel[45] – can be disregarded. But what had happened to the corpse, if it was removed, we cannot tell. Anyway the word went round that it was no longer there.

This absence of the body must have encouraged the belief that Jesus was about to rise again (after the statutory descent into Hell).[46] After appearing on earth he would then ascend to Heaven[47] (which was believed to be in the sky), although whether this would happen immediately, or after 'forty days', was disputed. This theory of the Ascension could be described as 'merely the use of spatial language to describe exaltation and glorification'.[48] However, those who preferred to take it literally asserted that, having arrived in Heaven, Jesus would sit on the right hand of God, until his Second Coming (*parousia*), which would not be immediate, as some hoped, but would take place at the end of the world, whenever that might be.[49] Some, on the other hand, wondered if there was going to be a *parousia* at all, a doubt inspired by the suggestion that Jesus's coming among humankind may have been the one and only divine visitation that the world would receive.[50]

The Resurrection of Jesus was said to have occurred 'on the third day'. It is difficult to see how this idea came into being. Since nobody actually saw the Resurrection happen, how could it be decided that the event occurred on the third day? There are a number of possible answers to this question. First, because the third day was the day on which the women found the tomb empty; second, because it was, perhaps, on every third day that the Christians of the early Church assembled for worship; third, because it was the day on which the risen Jesus was said to have made his first Appearance; fourth, there were precedents in earlier religious history, and particularly in the Old Testament (although the Old Testament precedents that could be cited were little better than fantastic).[51] Or does the 'third day' only mean the crucial, decisive day? Or perhaps a day after a short interval? Or should one fall back on the fact that the Jews often counted parts of days as wholes? In any case, it came to be agreed that the Resurrection had taken place on the third day.

*

There were several *kinds* of story recounting the Appearances of the Risen Jesus.[52] Paul's idea of the Appearances, to which reference has been made, was different from that of the evangelists because, unlike Peter and the others, Paul could not, or did not, claim to have seen the risen Jesus in the flesh. Rather he saw him, Paul said, in a vision[53] (was he referring to his experience before the Damascus gate or to some other occasion?). Paul therefore goes to some pains to define the Appearance to himself as not wholly physical. It was objective indeed, he maintained, yet impalpable, the stuff of which dream-like visions are made.[54]

There was a contrast, that is to say, between the Appearance of the risen Lord as Paul envisaged him, and, say, the Lazarus whom Jesus had supposedly resuscitated in corporeal form.[55] True, the Lazarus miracle seemed to demonstrate or symbolize the power of the living God to reverse the progress of death. But the personal survival of Jesus, as seen by Paul, was quite different, being not merely a bodily resuscitation (he appreciated that this was a strain on people's credence), but a transformation, glorification and exultation into a new, higher, incorruptible form of spirit-body. This hypothesis deliberately took an independent line and was contested, notably by the Gospels. (Origen followed Paul's hint, and thought in terms of a 'body appropriate to the heavenly environment'.)[56] Nevertheless, the Lazarus miracle remained important, not only because it illustrated the power of God, but also because it meant that an individual resurrection was possible without waiting for the universal rising from the dead on the last day.

It was, however, this final resurrection *of everybody* that Paul was really interested in. It was this, which he once again interpreted in a spiritual light, that the Resurrection of Jesus seemed to Paul directly to foreshadow, as the 'first fruits' of the harvest of the dead.[57] (Yet Paul evidently hoped that he, too, might be individually raised from the dead in advance of the general resurrection.[58])

As for Peter, we do not know exactly what he meant by the Resurrection of Jesus, or what he thought about it. However, he was regarded as having been absolutely in the forefront of the risen Lord's Appearances: of the first of which he himself was declared, by Paul, to have been the object and recipient. It seems to have been

Peter's assurance that he had seen the risen Jesus which prompted so many others to say that they, too, had enjoyed a similar experience. In other words, Peter *did* believe that Jesus had risen from the dead.

Is it really credible that Peter believed in these Appearances, when they were not in the realm of historical happenings? Yes, I believe it is, in the heated atmosphere of the time, alight with miracles and visions, and rendered more emotional still by the apostles' recent loss of their Master. Indeed, Peter's subsequent leadership was largely based on that belief, which he caused others to share. We, for our part, are at liberty to imagine that this Appearance was a delusion, and so, to the rational mind, it has to be. But if so, it was a delusion which nevertheless proved uniquely responsible for creating, in the long run, a world-wide movement of belief, thus influencing the entire subsequent development of history.

Bibliographical note

On the indispensable centrality of the Resurrection of Jesus, see C. Davies, *Theology Digest*, VIII, 2, 1960, p. 100 (among the primitive Christians); G. Bornkamm, *Jesus of Nazareth*, (1973), pp. 181, 186 (Paul); E. M. Blaiklock, *Acts*, p. 49; L. Goppelt, *Apostolic and Post-Apostolic Times* (1970), p. 13 (the apostles in general). See also D. Tiede, *Jesus and the Future* (1990), p. 58; O. O'Donovan, *Resurrection and the Moral Order*, new ed. 1993; Lord Dacre, 'An Agreeable Myth', *Sunday Telegraph*, 11 April 1993.

For the Resurrection of Jesus as general resurrection, see *Rom.* 6.11; Davies loc. cit.; H. Kung, *Theology Digest XXIII, 2, 1975, p. 140*; A. W. Wainwright, *A Guide to the New Testament* (1965), p. 225; M. Brandle, *Theology Digest*, XVI, 1968, pp. 15f.; Tiede, loc. cit.

On Jewish ideas of resurrection, see W. L. Craig, *New Testament Studies*, XXXI, 1985, pp. 61f., n. 16. Jews were disquieted by the transitoriness of life: W. Pannenberg, *Theology Digest*, XXIII, 2, 1975, p. 43. An unpublished fragment of an Ezekiel Apocryphon shows that the doctrine of the physical resurrection was not unknown at Qumran: M. Hengel, *The Hellenization of Judaea* (1989), p. 90 n. 235a.

On the Crucifixion not necessarily being in AD 33, see G. Vermes, *The Times*, 28 December 1989, p.11. Had some Jews taken over the idea of an 'atoning death' from the Greeks? *Pace* Hengel, op. cit., pp. 60, 89n. 230.

On the sharply differing accounts of the appearances of the risen Jesus in the New Testament, see R. E. Brown, K. P. Donfried and L. Reumann (eds), *Peter in the New Testament* (1973), pp. 33ff.; G. A. Wells, *The Jesus of the Early Christians* (1971), pp. 40ff.; H. Hendrickx, *Resurrection Narratives* (1978), pp. 106f.; S. Brown, *The Origins of Christianity* (1984); X. Léon-Dufour, *The Gospels and the Jesus of History*, pp. 257f. E. L. Bode, *The First Easter Morning* (1970), pp. 39, 44, offers five possible explanations for the initial silence of the women who claimed to have seen him. On the Appearance to Mary Magdalene, see A. Stock, *The Bible Today*, XX, 6, 1982, p. 356 (she misunderstood it); Hendrickx, op. cit., pp. 105ff. G. Turner, *New Blackfriars*, LVI, 661, 1975, p. 278, contests R. Bultmann's dismissal of the Appearances as impossible (*New Testament and Mythology: and Other Basic Writings* (1985), pp. 37ff.; *cf.* Wells, op. cit., p. 49). For their 'liberal', i.e. metaphorical interpretation, see Goppelt, op. cit., pp. 18f; W. Marxsen in C. F. D. Moule (ed.), *The Significance of the Message of the Resurrection for Faith in Jesus Christ* (1968), pp. 15–50; M. S. Enslin, *The Prophet from Nazareth*, p. 129; P. Winter, *On the Trial of Jesus* 2nd edn., 1974, p. 149. Against this interpretation, see G. Lohfink, *Theology Digest*, XVII, 2, 1969, pp. 111ff. St Thomas Aquinas, *Summa Theologica*, III, 55, 2 ad. 1, pronounced that the disciples saw the risen Jesus 'with the eyes of faith'; *cf.* A. Stock, *The Bible Today*, XX, 6, 1982, p. 357. For connections of the Appearances with the Eucharist, see Hendrickx, op. cit., pp. 79–85; and with Festivals, ibid., p. 15; C. F. D. Moule, *New Testament Studies*, IV, 1957/8, pp. 58ff.

For Docetism, see Acts of Peter and Gospel of Peter; R. Cameron (ed.), *The Other Gospels* (1982), p. 187; R. Lane Fox, *The Unauthorised Version: Truth and Fiction in the Bible* (1991), pp. 148, 151; J. L. McKenzie, *Dictionary of the Bible*, p. 45; *Oxford Dictionary of the Church* (2nd edn), pp. 1068, 1070; R. E. Brown, *The Gospel According to John* (1966), p. lxxvi; H. Schonfield, *The Pentecost Revolution* (1985), p. 206.

On Jesus's Appearance to Peter, see D. H. Gee, *Journal of Theological Studies*, XL, 1989, p. 488, who believes that Peter, seeing the Risen Jesus, sprang into the sea because he was ashamed to face him.

The Empty Tomb is discussed by J. D. M. Derrett, *The Anastasis* (1987), index, s.v.; W. L. Craig, *New Testament Studies*, XXXI, 1985, pp. 39–67; R. H. Stein, *Journal of the Evangelical Theological Society*, XX, 1977, pp. 23–9; Hendrickx, op. cit., p. 19; S. Neill, *The Interpretation of the New*

Testament 1861–1961 (1966), pp. 287f.; E. C. Hoskyns and N. Davey, *Crucifixion–Resurrection* (1981), p. 355. G. W. H. Lampe, *The Resurrection* (1966), p. 112, doubts whether the tomb *was* empty. For details of Palestinian tombs, see R. E. Brown, op. cit., p. 982; J. A. Fitzmyer, *The Gospel According to Luke* (1981), p. 1544.

On the End of the World (*parousia*, Second Coming), see Acts, 1.7, 1.11, 3.20 (after 'a time of recovery'); Matt. 24.22 ('time of troubles' will be cut short); 1 Cor. 15.24; S. Brown, *The Origins of Christianity* (1984), p. 25; A. W. Wainwright, *A Guide to the New Testament* (1965), p. 162. Although Peter may have believed that the End of the World had arrived already, most people thought it belonged to the future, at some incalculable date. There was a growing awareness that it would not be immediate: 2 Peter, 3.3–10 (though John 17.1–13 seems to regard the Resurrection and the *parousia* as a single event, bringing eternal life now: R. Bultmann, *Glauben und Verstehen*, III, p. 89, IV, p. 155). Jesus was 'our deliverer from the retribution to come': 1 Thessalonians, 1, 10. Joel 2.28–32 was quoted, and there had been other prophets who had similarly vivid expectations: J. Riches, *The World of Jesus* (1991), p. 101. Christianity split seriously when it was recognized that the End would be delayed: J. Muddiman in L. Houlden (ed.), *Judaism and Christianity* (1988), p. 40. The subject was endlessly disputed: Lane Fox, op. cit., p. 346.

On the Ascension, see G. Lohfink, *Theology Digest*, XVII, 2, 1969, p. 111; A. Schweitzer, *The Quest of the Historical Jesus* (1906), p. 346 n. 1; A. R. C. Leaney, *Studia Evangelica*, IV, 1968, p. 417; Fitzmyer, op. cit., pp. 195, 1589 (Acts and Gospels differ). In 1950 the Catholic Church also promulgated the dogma of the Assumption of the Virgin Mary.

Resurrection on 'the third day' is discussed by W. L. Craig, *New Testament Studies*, XXXI, 1985, pp. 42–9; H. von Campenhausen, *Tradition and Life in the Church* (1968) (1968), pp. 42–89.

Chapter 7

THE LEADERSHIP OF PETER

After the Crucifixion, the disciples scattered in dismay, perhaps fleeing back, for the most part, to Galilee. It was when some of them reached Galilee, according to one view, that the Appearances of the dead Jesus began. Peter had come there, and a number of others. According to the Gospel of John, ' "I am going out fishing," said Peter. "We will go with you," said the others. So they set off and got into the boat.'[1] The enormous catch of fishes which the risen Jesus then provided belongs to the realm of miracles, and consequently evades the attention of historians (see Chapter 1). But what they have to note is that the resumption of their former secular activity by Peter and the rest meant that, with the death of Jesus, they at first regarded their discipleship as over. According to the New Testament tradition, however, the risen Lord decisively recalled them, and under Peter (recognized as their chief, not least because of the initial Appearance to him) they led the small band of Christians that survived. And whatever view is taken of the Resurrection, they did take the lead in just that fashion.

According to Matthew's Gospel, Jesus had already prophesied this glorious future for Peter in his lifetime (at Caesarea Philippi).

And whether that is true or not, after Jesus's death Peter indeed assumed the leadership role. It is therefore necessary to take a careful look at the terms in which the evangelist described the Commission that Jesus had supposedly entrusted to him at Caesarea Philippi. In Chapter 3 it was indicated that this might have been the occasion when Simon received his new name Cephas or Peter, the Rock or Foundation Stone; and *Matthew*, ascribing to the same event Peter's Confession of the true superhuman identity of Jesus, indicates that Jesus went on to say:[2]

> I will give you the keys of the Kingdom of Heaven; what you forbid on earth shall be forbidden in heaven, and what you allow on earth shall be allowed in heaven.

The Authorised Version of the New Testament (1611) provided this more literal translation:

> I will give unto thee the keys of the Kingdom of Heaven, and whatsoever thou shalt bind on earth shall be bound in heaven, and whatsoever thou shalt loose on earth shall be loosed in heaven.

This passage has given rise to an immense polemical literature, mirroring differences between the Churches.

John's Gospel quotes the 'Rock' saying to Peter without linking it to this further declaration by Jesus.[3] And despite all the argument on the subject it does seem justifiable to regard the two assertions as separate.[4] The former probably dates back to the lifetime of Jesus, and the second saying was later, of post-Resurrection, Matthean date, or even forming a post-Matthean insertion into the already written *Gospel According to Saint Matthew*. Arguments in favour of such *extreme* lateness are improbable, however, since the passage is couched in Semitic language suggestive of quite early composition.

Now, not only can these sayings, about the Keys and the Binding–Loosing, be separated from the 'Rock' assertion, but it is also probable that the two sayings (about the Keys and the Binding–Loosing) were originally separate *from one another*. The Keys, echoing a passage in Isaiah,[5] were the symbol of power of the administrator, steward or door-keeper of the household. But they are also the signs and symbols of authority in God's Kingdom, meaning that Peter is the human instrument destined to lead God's people there: and he is therefore entitled either to admit people to the mysteries of that kingdom or to exclude them.[6] He will open the door to the kingdom, in contrast to the Pharisees who, Jesus reputedly said, closed it in people's faces.[7]

As for Binding and Loosing (*'sar, serā*), they are closely related to the same passage in *Isaiah* as the saying about the Keys, even though the two assertions ascribed to Jesus were, in all probability, originally separate. 'Binding' and 'Loosing' are rendered in the New English Bible by the terms 'forbidding' and 'allowing' – a rabbinical power, of declaring what is permitted and not permitted, which Jesus was also said to have conferred upon his disciples in general.[8]

That is to say, condemnation and acquittal (valid in the Kingdom of Heaven, and related to withholding and forgiving sins) are in the forefront. Peter is given the authority to decide how much and how little of the Jewish Law shall henceforward require to be observed, and there was understood to be an implication that all Jesus's followers would benefit. In inter-testamental literature, and in ancient magical texts, Binding and Loosing are most frequently associated with exorcism. The Gospel of Matthew, however, in connection with Jesus himself is shifting and broadening the significance of the terms, in their application to Peter.

Having pronounced in this same passage (probably, once again, by conflating two separate utterances) that Jesus had given Simon his new name *Petros*, the Stone or Rock, Matthew's Gospel went on to ascribe to him the further assertion: 'and on this rock I will build my Church, and the powers of death shall never conquer it'.[9] On Peter, that is to say, Jesus will keep building his church as long as there is such a Church on earth. The saying has evoked the passionate and endless controversy to which reference has already been made, since Catholics have usually claimed it as the justification and basis of the supremacy of the Church of Rome and the foundation of the towering fabric of apostolic succession; and Protestants have demurred.

Without entering into this dispute, it may be observed first that there is no evidence that Jesus meant there to be a visible, concentrated, personalized centre of the Church, but second that, although the word *ekklesia* (Church) is very rare in the Gospels, it is common in the Pauline Letters and the *Acts*. There is no reason to reject *ekklesia* as a later, anachronistic insertion into the Gospel: it is a rendering of the already existent Hebrew *gāhāl*, *'ēdah* or *kenishta*, the sacred community, brotherhood or congregation of Israel, and there are Aramaic equivalents as well.[10] The 'Church' is universal, evoking the idea of the people of God as a temple, and embodying the divine Jewish people – the people, now, of Jesus, the new Israel, the eschatological kingdom that has succeeded to the old Israel, which has failed to live up to its calling.

Of this Church, Peter is here declared to be the foundation. Jesus is responding to him, in the second part of a two-part 'pronouncement story', and offering him a very special revelation and also a very special commission. 'Simon, Simon, take heed. Satan has been given leave to sift all of you like wheat. But I have prayed for you, Simon, that your faith may not fail, and when you are restored, give strength to your brothers.'[11] John's Gospel emphatically extracts a triple profession of love for Jesus from Peter, perhaps to balance his earlier threefold Denial. 'Then feed my sheep [or lambs],' Jesus three times concludes.[12]

This is a solemn rehabilitation and command. Perhaps it reflects a longer original narrative. It assumes what in ancient times was regarded as a traditional shape: it can be described, that is to say, as a 'divine Commission'. In no fewer than twenty-seven passages of the Old Testament, a literary form has been found in which there is this sort of delegation of power and a commissioning by God. The formula consists of a regular series of elements: preface, confrontation, reaction, commission, protest, reassurance and conclusion.[13] In the case of Jesus's command, the protest and conclusion are not to be found (at least in the version that has come down to us). But all the other elements in the traditional commissioning are there. This form of utterance appears very frequently not only in the Old Testament, but also in various other parts of the New Testament as well. Indeed, the latter contains no fewer than thirty-seven examples of a comparable sort of commission. Jesus's command, as it has come down to us, is clearly intended to formulate the establishment of a new Church community, which the power of death, *Matthew* tells us, will never conquer.[14]

We have to decide, however, whether these assertions of a special commission accorded to Peter – whatever the dates at which they were written down – relate accurately to something that Jesus said to him before his Crucifixion; or whether, alternatively, they were invented after the Crucifixion to reflect and justify the leadership which Peter at that stage assumed. Although certainty is impossible, and the 'Rock' saying has been attributed, by some, to the earlier period, the latter alternative is the more likely. Peter needed all the authority he could get. Much came from his prime role in the aftermath of Jesus's death, and much more could be derived from the assertion that Jesus had explicitly commissioned him.

In any case, Peter was now establishing his unquestioned leadership of the small group of faithful who, after the Crucifixion, had first dispersed and then returned to Jerusalem. This leadership has been doubted. But the evidence in favour of it should be sufficient to carry conviction. Peter had, at last, recognized how wrong he was to refuse the idea of a suffering Messiah, and he had believed that the Resurrection had taken place and must be preached. When the women, according to one (miraculous) version of the story, went into Jesus's tomb and found an angel there, the angel told them to go and tell the news of his forthcoming Appearances to the disciples and to Peter,[15] who is thus singled out and stressed (it is not enough just to say that he was mentioned because he was near at hand). *Acts*, at the outset, names Peter first among the surviving apostles.[16] And Paul in *Galatians* admits Peter's supremacy,[17] of which apparently even the distant converts he was addressing in that letter were aware. The greatest historical puzzle of the Church's history, it is said, is its origins. But without Peter it could have had no history at all. John's Gospel cryptically and allusively balances the leadership of Peter against the mysterious 'Beloved Disciple', and not alto-gether in Peter's favour, yet the general evidence will admit no rivalry to the leadership of Peter after Jesus's death.

The actuality of this leadership was confirmed by the fact that the authorities three times felt it worthwhile to arrest Peter.[18] On one occasion he was said to have escaped by a miracle, and indeed he was credited with a series of miraculous happenings resembling those ascribed to Jesus (see Chapter 1). These again confirm Peter's primacy, which *Acts* takes pains to equate with the later pre-eminence of Paul. *Acts* also quotes the rising numbers of followers whom Peter enrolled,[19] although the totals are suspect. He had allegedly appointed a twelfth apostle (Matthias) to replace Judas Iscariot.[20] Evidently Peter's position was, to begin with, that of the first of the Twelve – for whom he continued to speak.

The Twelve formed a vital link between Jesus and the early Church. Yet it seems doubtful whether they long survived Jesus's death, or exercised any substantial corporate leadership. Certainly they still appear early in *Acts*. However, the book does not mention many of them by name. And after the execution of James, the son of Zebedee, they seem to have faded away; Jerusalem ceased to be the focal centre of Christianity. Those who came to rule the group of Christians, as it gradually created a structure for itself, were not 'the Twelve', or 'the Seven' whom they appointed to wait at table and distribute food to the widows,[21] but 'the Three': Peter, James the Great (the son of Zebedee, executed by Agrippa I in AD 44, and John (his brother; or John 'the Priest').[22] This vesting of power in 'the Three', as well as in 'the Twelve', was paralleled in Old Testament practice,[23] and also in the contemporary Jewish sect at Qumran, which was ruled by three priests and twelve laymen, 'men of special holiness'. As for the Three who led the followers of the crucified Jesus, Paul says that two of them, Peter and John, seemed to be 'pillars'.[24] Perhaps he is being sarcastic. Or this may be a further reference to 'foundation stones' or 'rocks'. The new threefold leadership does suggest a certain reorganization of the community, perhaps in the direction of democratization, and perhaps not.

*

One of the first problems of the Church had been the crisis caused by Stephen.

A Greek-speaking ('Hellenist') Jewish Christian, a member of 'the Seven', he was credited by *Acts*, like Peter, with 'wonders and signs', and was assigned a long speech outlining the Christian philosophy of history.[25] But he lost some of his Greek-speaking supporters and fell foul of the Jews. Indeed, although he was orthodox rather than liberal, they put him to death, possibly in the winter of 36–7, because of his pronounced and supposedly blasphemous Messianism.[26]

Unfortunately we have no knowledge of what Peter's view was about this. It might be surmised that, whatever he felt about food distributions, he could have regarded Stephen as less than tactful, although no doubt he deplored his death. What we are told, however, is that the violent persecutions which followed caused all the Christians except the apostles to scatter outside Jerusalem.[27] Even the leading apostle Peter, accompanied by John, the son of Zebedee, soon left again, this time not for other countries, but for Samaria immediately adjoining the Jewish homeland.

Bibliographical note

The Keys are discussed by C. P. Thiede, *Simon Peter: From Galilee to Rome* (1986), p. 41; O. Cullmann, *Peter: Disciple, Apostle, Martyr* (1962), pp. 209f. *Cf.* also Revelation 3.7; Isaiah 22.22. Peter was symbolized in art by two crossed keys: D. Attwater, *Dictionary of Saints* (2nd ed., 1983), p. 266.

On Binding and Loosing, see R. Pesch, *Simon-Petrus* (1980), p. 103 n. 36; Thiede, op. cit., p. 41; R. M. Grant, *A Historical Introduction to the New Testament* (1963), p. 404.

For the powers of death (gates of Sheol), see Revelation 1.18, 20.1 (angel's keys): Psalms 9.13, 107.18; R. E. Brown, K. P. Donfried and L. Reumann (eds), *Peter in the New Testament* (1973), p. 92; Cullmann, op. cit., p. 208; A. E. Harvey, *Companion to the Gospels* (1970), p. 68 note (a).

On the *ekklesia*, see G. Bornkamm, *Jesus of Nazareth* (1973), p. 187; Cullman, op. cit., pp. 161, 170, 183ff., 194–7, 222; R. E. Brown *et al.*, op.

cit., p. 92, 100; Thiede, op. cit., pp. 39f., 42; G. Maier in C. P. Thiede (ed.), *Das Petrusbild in der neueren Forschung* (1987), p. 171; Grant, op. cit., p. 396.

According to S. Brown, *The Origins of Christianity* (1984), p. 83, Peter carried out his commission by communicating the Resurrection faith (*cf.* Thiede, op. cit., pp. 93, 103; F. Gils, *Ephemerides Theologicae Lovanienses*, XXXVIII, 1962, p. 5). On the commission as a post-Resurrection concept, see Cullman, op. cit., p. 65; Thiede, op. cit., p. 108; G. O'Collins, *Heythrop Journal*, XXII, 1981, pp. 1, 3, 11.

Peter's leadership is considered by Thiede, op. cit., pp. 93, 103; Maier, op. cit., p. 181, *cf.* p. 187 nn. 75–80.

Chapter 8

THE SPEECHES ATTRIBUTED TO

PETER

In order to keep the shattered early Christians together and increase their numbers, Peter must have been a competent and persuasive speaker – an especially important asset in that ancient epoch, in which little could be achieved without oratory. Indeed, Peter has been described as the great orator and preacher of early Christianity, and this is a justifiable conclusion. It is particularly justifiable because the author of *Acts*, who knew so much about the early Christians, allots Peter no fewer than nine speeches. These alleged speeches have a good deal in common. They stress that Jesus rose from the dead, that he was the Messiah heralded by Old Testament prophecy, and that non-Jews will come into the fold during the Messianic age that was to follow.

In Acts. 1, we are informed that Peter stood up and addressed the brotherhood, which at that time supposedly numbered about 120 persons.[1] He tells of the death of Judas Iscariot, quoting the *Psalms*, of which David was supposedly the author.[2] This serves as a prelude to the appointment, by Peter, of Judas's successor among the Twelve, Matthias. The speech might have been first recorded in Aramaic, and could have come to the writer of *Acts* in an oral rather than a written form.

In Acts. 2, after the miraculous multilinguality (*glossolalia*) of Pentecost, Peter 'stood up with the eleven', and allegedly delivered his message to his 'fellow-Jews', 'all who live in Jerusalem' and the 'men of Israel'.³ He was said to have quoted the prophet Joel about the 'last days', which he saw as arriving, and once again supposedly cited the *Psalms*, referring to the burial of David and to his prophecies of the coming of Jesus:⁴

> For David says of him: 'I foresaw that the Lord would be with me for ever, with him at my right hand I cannot be shaken' ...
>
> He spoke as a prophet who knew that God had sworn to him that one of his own direct descendants should sit on his throne; and when he said he was not abandoned to death, and his flesh never saw corruption, he spoke with foreknowledge of the resurrection of the Messiah.
>
> Now Jesus has been raised by God, and of this we are all witnesses ... Let all Israel then accept as certain that God has made this same Jesus, whom you crucified, both Lord and Messiah.

Although placing Jesus at the centre of everything,⁵ Peter was at the same time recorded in this passage, as formulating a basic missionary text for the new Israel, in which there would be a purified and emancipated Judaism, still respectful of the Temple.⁶ In this spirit, Peter added, it can be seen that a new epoch has dawned. 'Save yourselves', he is made to conclude, 'from this crooked age!'⁷

In Acts. 3 Peter (accompanied by John, the son of Zebedee) is asserted to have addressed the crowd after healing a cripple. He spoke, we are told, of 'the God of Abraham, Isaac and Jacob, the God of our Fathers', alluding to God's Covenant with Abraham, and quoting Moses, Samuel and the prophets as foretelling the Messiahship of Jesus.⁸ He is reported to have referred to Jesus as God's 'servant' (*pais*), but above all his speech was said to have dwelt on the iniquity of the Crucifixion, and the need for repentance which it inspires.⁹

In Acts. 4, Peter, under arrest, is quoted as addressing the principal Jews in the Sanhedrin on similar lines:¹⁰

> This Jesus is the stone, rejected by you the builders, which has become

the corner-stone. There is no salvation through anyone else; in all the world no other name has been granted to mankind by which we can be saved.

Then in Acts. 10, defending the conversion of a Gentile (see Chapter 9), Peter is ascribed what is virtually a credal utterance, a hymn of praise (perhaps from Aramaic sources) about the life, death and Resurrection of Jesus.[11] This speech has been seen by some as the basis of the Gospel of Mark, although its theology has been the subject of a good deal of debate.

It is possible to take two views about the speeches attributed to Peter in *Acts*. They can be described as brief and clear, muscular, vivid and powerful, gems of concentrated evangelism. Or they can be called boringly stereotyped and repetitive. But if that is what they seem to us, it is partly at least because their message is now so familiar. It was not familiar at that time, and we may assume that Peter, if it was he who delivered such a message, did so with fire and skill.

But are the speeches authentically his? Surely not, at least in the form in which they have come down to us. It is a well-known fact that the speeches recorded by the ancients could not possibly be word-for-word reproductions of what the speakers said. For one thing, what was said was not taken down or preserved. Besides, authors liked to offer their own versions of speeches, compatible with their own literary styles. All this applies abundantly to the speeches attributed to Peter in *Acts*.

In other words, the sayings which *Acts* ascribe to Peter are for the most part sayings composed by the writer of the book who, while sometimes trying to imagine what the speaker was likely to have said, is more directly concerned with attributing to him utterances which the writer of *Acts* considers that he *ought* to have made. This meant that this author's conscientious regression to what he regarded as Peter's own views was not continuous or dominant, so that sometimes the phrases he attributed to Peter were phrases to which Peter might even actually have objected; we cannot tell. In any case, the speeches of Peter in *Acts* reflect not so much his own opinions as those of the Church at the time when the book was written. It is impossible to believe that they faithfully reproduced anything that Peter himself had said.

Yet these speeches are extremely valuable records all the same. They reflect what the composer of *Acts*, and no doubt many of his contemporaries, thought about Peter, and about the disciples on whose behalf, as well as his own, Peter was supposed to be speaking. These so-called speeches of Peter are therefore a compendium of the teaching of the early Christian Church at the time when *Acts* was written. This teaching was the *kerygma*, the faith-eliciting 'announcement', founded upon an announcement by God himself of God's eschatological salvation through Christ – a doctrinal assertion based on the Old Testament Scriptures, which the Christology founded on Jesus had endowed with new life.

As far as we can make out, the *kerygma* of these late first-century Christians (blending primitive Palestinian and Hellenistic forms) took a shape that was something like this:[12]

> God promised through the agency of his Prophets that he would, when the time was ripe, move into action and liberate his people from their miseries and oppressions. And he has now fulfilled this promise by sending Jesus into the world: Jesus, who, although he had lived an exemplary and wonderful life, was killed on the cross by evil men. However, he conquered this wretched fate, and conquered death itself, by rising from the dead, and ascending to Heaven where he sits at the right hand of God. From there, he sends down to his followers the gift of the Holy Spirit, and when his father sees that the time has come he will return to the world again to deliver judgement upon all humankind, and to transform every one of its inhabitants in accordance with the will of God. In view of that prospect, men and women should make good their repentance here and now, while there still remains time to do so.

No doubt the contents of this *kerygma*, represented by the speeches ascribed to Peter, were derived from a number of sources. They were surely, it has already been said, not delivered by Peter, at least in the form in which we have them. And yet we cannot reject altogether the role of Peter in their formulation. After all, he was the leader and spokesman of the earliest Christians after Jesus's death, and an eloquent leader and spokesman at that. Moreover, we have found good cause to suppose that Peter believed that the resurrected Jesus had appeared to him. It is therefore a reasonable conclusion that Peter delivered pronouncements of the new Christian faith in a number of orations, and that although these, as they have come down to us, are couched in the language of *Acts*, they may well not be far from Peter's own thought. They do, therefore, in all probability, and despite every objection, give us some idea how Peter's mind worked. We are beginning, that is to say, to come a little closer to what sort of a man Peter really was.

Bibliographical note

On Peter's 'speeches', see G. Turner, *Theology*, XIII, 1926, p. 76; H. N. Ridderbos in C. P. Thiede (ed.), *Das Petrusbild in der neueren Forschung* (1987), pp. 65f.; E. V. Blaiklock, *Acts*, pp. 63f., 65, 72f.; C. P. Thiede, *Simon Peter: From Galilee to Rome* (1986), pp. 115, 121.

For Acts. 2, see E. Kränkl, *Jesus Der Knecht Gottes*, p. 135; R. Pesch, *Simon-Petrus* (1980), p. 56 and n.16; G. Vermes, *The Religion of Jesus the Jew* (1993), p. 150; R. R. Williams, *The Acts of the Apostles*, pp. 43ff.; C. S. C. Williams, *The Acts of the Apostles*, pp. 65ff.

For Acts. 3, see O. Cullmann, *Peter: Disciple, Apostle, Martyr* (1962), pp. 68f.; Vermes, op. cit., pp. 97, 150; R. R. Williams, op. cit., pp. 53ff.; C. S. C. Williams, op. cit., pp. 75ff.

For Acts. 4, see R. R. Williams, op. cit., pp. 53ff.; C. S. C. Williams, op. cit., pp. 82f.

For Acts. 10, see R. R. Williams, op. cit., pp. 92f.; C. S. C. Williams, op. cit., p. 132.

On the style of Peter's speeches, *cf.* 1 and 2 Peter; Thiede, op. cit., pp. 109f., 236 n. 178. On their being seemingly primitive, see C. S. C. Williams, op. cit., pp. 47f.

Chapter 9

CORNELIUS: PETER AND THE
GENTILES

After the martyrdom of Stephen,[1] 'those who had been scattered ... made their way to Phoenicia, Cyprus and Antioch, bringing the message to Jews only and to no others'.[2] One of the principal tasks of Peter, then, as the most prominent figure in this infant Christian community, and of the Jerusalem apostles, was to undertake missionary activity in Jewish lands, as leader of the Jewish Christian mission. (This was also the 'missionary age' of Judaism, Hillel being for attempts to convert the Gentiles, and Shammai against them.)[3]

However, this task, among the small band of former followers of Jesus, was interpreted with a certain degree of broadness. There is good reason to accept the authenticity of the report, in *Acts*, that Peter was sent to Samaria, north of Jerusalem, as part of their missionary activity.[4] Although the Samaritans were Jews, they were Jews of a deviant type. They accepted the Jewish Law, and in Jewish Messianic fashion hoped for a *taleb*, a restorer. But they rejected the Temple at Jerusalem, took no cognizance of the worship practised in that city, and developed their own form of the Bible. That they were, therefore, sharply divided from the Jews, and in consequence unorthodox, the Gospels point out on more than one occasion, when Jesus was said to have concerned himself with them.[5] So now Peter, while not exactly stepping beyond Judaism, was nevertheless, at the apostles' request, moving beyond orthodox Jewry.

According to Acts, one of the Seven, Philip (not the apostle), had been to Samaria first. It was said that he performed miracles and baptisms, and encountered the magician Simon Magus (on whom, however, see Chapter 12).[6] Then Peter, accompanied by John, the son of Zebedee, entered the Samaritan scene – all the more readily, it would seem, because Jerusalem, in the persecutions following the death of Stephen, had become uncomfortable for Christian leaders.

The duty of Peter and John was to have a look at the converts to Christianity, in this country of heterodox and borderline Judaism: to have a look, that is to say, at the men who owed their conversion to Philip.[7]

> When the Apostles in Jerusalem heard that Samaria had accepted the word of God, they sent off Peter and John, who went down there and prayed for the converts [by Philip], asking that they might receive the Holy Spirit.
>
> Until then the Spirit had not come upon any of them; they had been baptised into the name of the Lord Jesus, that and nothing more. So Peter and John laid their hands on them, and they received the Holy Spirit.

When the apostles, as Acts says, 'sent off' Peter and John, that need not mean that Peter was any less the community's leader. However, it looks very much as though the Jerusalem Church had, for some reason, found Philip's conversions inadequate or unsatisfactory, and that its leader, Peter, had been dispatched, with John, to confirm and complete them. This they did, and then 'took the road back to Jerusalem, bringing the good news to many Samaritan villages on the way'.[8]

Peter next carried his missionary activities to Lydda (Lodd) and Joppa (Jaffa),[9] which, in spite of suggestions (probably exaggerated) that he adopted a liberal pro-Gentile position, were strongly, purely, Jewish cities. It was from Joppa, however, that Peter was said to have gone to Caesarea Maritima (Sdot Yam), which was a pagan centre, and thus stood for an altogether new field of missionary activity.

Acts lays enormous stress on Peter's conversion to Christianity, there, of the Roman centurion Cornelius. The event, seen as the classic inauguration of Gentile conversion, is accompanied by various miracles, which the historian has to set aside or discount. The essential feature of the story, however, is that this Gentile duly became a Christian, and that Peter spoke up firmly in favour of the conversion of suitable Gentiles. At first, this caused offence to Christians who were strict observers of the Jewish Law. But they later accepted the idea that the conversion of Cornelius by Peter was a divine sign – a product of the direct intervention by God.[10]

Cornelius was supposedly a centurion in the Italian cohort. We need not, I think, worry too much about whether there *was* an Italian cohort in Israel at the time (see the bibliographical note at the end of this chapter). But whether there was or not, the whole story of Cornelius's conversion bears all the marks of fictitiousness, as a number of theologians have agreed. There are several reasons for concluding that the entire tale is invented – like Peter's alleged assertion at the time: 'I now understand how true it is that God has no favourites.'[11] For one thing, Cornelius's 'Roman character' is carefully, and surely artificially, designed to point the way to Rome's eventual replacement of Jerusalem as the centre of Christian attention. Second, *Acts* takes a good deal of trouble to balance the doings and achievements of Peter against those of Paul, which are narrated later in the book. In this way, Peter's role, as a supposed missionary to at least a few Gentiles, can be seen as a sort of preliminary, invented comparison with Paul.

Furthermore, the Cornelius story bears a disquieting resemblance to a tale told by Jesus himself: *Matthew* and *Luke*'s versions of the story of the servant of the centurion in Capernaum, whom Jesus was supposed to have converted.[12] Matthew's Gospel is content to describe the centurion, on that occasion, as a Gentile who trustfully approaches Jesus and is heard by him. But *Luke*, while not denying that the centurion is a Gentile, emphasizes, in addition, that he loves the Jews and has had a synagogue built for them. (*John* says it was the *son* of this 'officer in the royal service' who was healed – perhaps the 'centurion' was thought of as a mercenary officer of Herod Antipas.[13] What is striking, however, is that *Matthew* and *Luke's* accounts so closely resemble the story of Cornelius in *Acts*, which reports, in very much the same vein, that Cornelius is a Gentile who has given alms to the Jewish people. The Gospels, in their report of the centurion converted by Jesus, and *Acts*, in its story of Cornelius, also coincide in their assertions that both Jesus and Peter are asked to help through the medium of messengers sent to their houses. These resemblances cannot be entirely fortuitous: at some stage, the one tale must have given birth to the other.

These correspondences between Peter's alleged conversion of Cornelius and Jesus's supposed earlier conversion of the servant of the centurion in Capernaum (Tell Hum) are so notable that – although G. Lüdemann, discussing the resemblances, says 'we need not assume a doublet'[14] – that is precisely what the evidence suggests that we do have to assume. In other words, the account in *Acts* is unhistorical. But the conversion ascribed to Jesus by *Luke* was probably unauthentic too. As I have pointed out elsewhere, Jesus's mission was almost entirely directed towards the Jews, and the evangelists had to go to considerable lengths to drag in his conversion of the odd Gentile.[15] (Whether Jesus would have gone on to the Gentiles if he had lived longer must remain conjectural.)

If Jesus's mission, as long as it lasted, had not been more or less limited to the Jews, it would not have created so much of a sensation when Paul later announced, at Pisidian Antioch (Yalvaç) or Corinth or both, that, disappointed by the Jewish response, he was turning to the Gentiles.[16] In order not to ignore this later decision by Paul, those who defend the authenticity of Peter's conversion of Cornelius have to set it apart as a 'special case',[17] his additional reported baptisms only being given, in the New Testament, in vague round numbers.

These two narratives are expressly intended to symbolize Gentile belief, and foreshadow the evangelization of nations. But they have another aim as well. Despite Jewish and Christian hostility towards the presence of the Roman army in Palestine, the centurion mentioned by Luke's Gospel, in connection with Jesus, was described as respected by the Jews, and pious. By the same token, one of the special intentions of *Acts*, in telling of the conversion of Cornelius, was to stress that he enjoyed a particularly high standing, even among the Jews. This was to show not only that the Jews respected him, but also that the Gentile mission of the Christians had *not* started in the lower orders of society (compare the alleged conversion by Philip of an Ethiopian eunuch 'of great authority').[18]

However, the alleged 'acceptance' by the Jewish Christians of the God-given desirability of Cornelius's conversion seems, in *Acts*,[19] all to facile and ready. It is directed against, and intended to correct but at the same time to appease, the Jewish Christians. For they were deeply opposed to the conversion of Gentiles. To them, any suggestion that the tragic Crucifixion of their Lord, and the actions of his followers, should be represented as events intended, under divine guidance, to rescue the Gentiles from the deplorable fates which such people so handsomely merited was nothing short of blasphemous. In their views of a better future, the Gentiles could obviously have no favourable part at all. On the contrary, the restoration of Israel, for which the Jewish Christians, like the Jews, so intensely hoped, must carry with it liberation from Rome – which meant the punishment of the Gentiles. Jesus, to them, was the Messiah of the Israelites, and the Gentile Romans had killed him because he seemed to them to constitute a threat to their rule. His death, therefore, was a martyrdom for Israel, standing for God's sacred purpose on behalf of his chosen people against Gentile Roman oppression. Thus, for Jesus, or Peter, to look favourably upon a Gentile seemed entirely shocking: a theological outrage, and an apostasy.

All this placed the author of *Acts* in a difficult position. Writing for the Gentile Christians, he was eager, like the writer of *Luke*, to drag in a Gentile conversion. Yet at the same time he did not want to cause irreparable offence to the Jewish Christians either. He therefore attempts to have the best of both worlds. He softens his picture of Peter's conversion of Cornelius, by giving the impression that, although this did occur, it was a special case, not on the same systematic scale as those of Paul later on. Then he adds that Cornelius was, in any case, very close to the Jews: 'a good and religious man, acknowledged as such by the whole Jewish nation'.

One reason why Peter was said to have converted a Gentile was because he later adopted a moderate attitude towards the conditions required of those who did join the Christian community, as we shall see in the next chapter. However, what was to follow will confirm the suggestion that, all the same, he himself probably did not try to convert any Gentiles at all.[20]

Bibliographical note

For Peter in Samaria, see C. P. Thiede, *Simon Peter: From Galilee to Rome* (1986), pp. 129f., 133; O. Cullmann, *Peter: Disciple, Apostle, Martyr* (1962), p. 36; R. E. Brown, K. P. Donfried and L. Reumann (eds), *Peter in the New Testament* (1973), p. 412 and n. 93. Peter and John were only 'smuggled into' the story according to E. Schwartz, *Gesammelte Schriften* (1963), p. 144 n. 2 (G.Lüdemann, *Early Christianity According to the Traditions in Acts*, 1989, p. 96).

On the Samaritans, see A. D. Crown (ed.), *The Samaritans* (1989); Cullmann, loc. cit.; H. Schonfield, *The Pentecost Revolution* (1985), p. 94.

On Lydda and Joppa (Jewish), see Lüdemann, op. cit., p. 123; M. Hengel in C. P. Thiede (ed.), *Das Petrusbild in der neueren Forschung* (1987), p. 164.

The Italian cohort is discussed by C. S. C. Williams, *The Acts of the Apostles* (1967), p. 134 (references); R. R. Williams, *The Acts of the Apostles* (1953), p. 91; R. M. Grant, *A Historical Introduction to the New Testament* (1963), p. 145; Thiede, op. cit., pp. 141f., 216 n. 15; R. Pesch, *Simon-Petrus* (1980), pp. 44, 82.

On the fictitious nature of the Cornelius incident, see R. M. Grant, op. cit., pp. 145, 393; M. Dibelius, *Conectanea Neotestamentica*, XI, 1948, pp. 50ff.

Jesus and the Gentiles, see M. Grant, *Jesus* (1977), pp. 121f. Would he have gone on to them if he had been given time? J. L. Houlden, *Times Literary Supplement*, 5 April 1985, p. 391. According to Matt. 28.19, the risen Jesus entrusted this task of Gentile conversion to the disciples.

Chapter 10

THE CLASH WITH PAUL

Paul, in his *Letter to the Galatians*, reports that: 'I did go up to Jerusalem [his first visit as a Christian] to get to know Cephas [Peter], and I stayed two weeks with him. I saw none of the other Apostles, except James, the Lord's brother. What I write is plain truth; God knows I am not lying!'[1]

He says that this happened three years after his conversion, and some therefore date the Jerusalem trip to 35/37 (although this depends, of course, on the date to which we ascribe Jesus's Crucifixion). *Acts* also refers to Paul's visit.[2] Evidently, Peter was the community's recognized leader at this stage, and Paul probably wanted to get information from him about Jesus. But the reason for Paul's somewhat defiant tone, at the end, is mysterious. Presumably there were some troublemakers in Galatia who were misquoting what had happened, and Paul wanted to set the record straight.

Then, according to *Acts*, took place what is usually described as the Apostolic Council at Jerusalem, attributed to the time of Passover, AD 48. Acts. 15 paints a picture of single-minded unanimity (*homothumadon*)[3] – an idealized and inaccurate picture as most now believe. Admittedly there was quite a long debate.[4] Peter, who had previously 'gone off elsewhere'[5] to escape King Agrippa I, but had now evidently come back, agreed with the chosen missionaries to the Gentiles, Paul and Barnabas, that no tiresome restrictions should be imposed on Gentile converts. However, they should obey Jewish dietary rules (abstaining from meat offered to idols, from blood, and from anything that had been strangled), and they should refrain from fornication – the Four Regulations which James ('the Just') the brother of Jesus, *Acts* indicates, had proposed.[6]

The question of the Jewish dietary laws was more significant than it might perhaps seem, for they constituted a not unimportant element in the Jews' perpetual struggle to preserve the separateness of Israel. One aspect of this struggle, emphasized by rabbinical custom, was the demand for a strict segregation from any possibility of defilement by association with Gentiles while eating. One can see that this attitude created awkward questions for Christians, since it raised the problem of whether Jewish and Gentile Christians could take part in ceremonial meals, the 'Lord's Suppers', together.

Peter had already, on other occasions, allegedly displayed a liberal attitude, or willingness to compromise (in the belief that this was the divine will), about applying these regulations in their full strictness to Gentile converts, many of whom may likewise have compromised by meeting the Jewish requirements half-way. But now, at Antioch, where Jewish Christians may have somewhat relaxed the full rigour of the tradition, he expressed willingness (to some extent at least) to give way to the Jews on the point:[7] 'after many hesitations', it has been suggested,[8] which were perhaps overcome by the conviction that Jesus himself had taken a less than strict view on the subject.[9]

But what actually happened at the Apostolic Council? We shall assume for a moment that there was one, ignoring, however, the unsatisfactory nature of such a name, which is likely to produce anachronistic ideas.[10] The Council has been the subject of a host of varying modern interpretations. Probably the predominant view, for which there is a lot to be said – and it leaves open, perhaps uncomfortably open, the question of whether the Council actually took place – is that *Acts* created the story from two fundamental traditions or memories which had been handed down to its writer.

The first tradition was that at Jerusalem the Christian leadership, including Paul, Peter and James the brother of Jesus, came to an agreement that, although Pharisee missionaries to the Gentiles would argue to the contrary, Gentiles could be accepted within the ranks of the Christians without having been circumcised. This was a tradition that seems to be confirmed by Paul. The second tradition was that nevertheless, in certain communities where Jewish and Gentile Christians were mixed, Gentiles were obliged, in order to maintain this association, to fall in with certain other Jewish regulations regarding impurity, and rules relating to food.

As to circumcision, even *Acts*, determined though its writer is to record harmony, admits that there had been 'fierce dissension' on the subject,[11] which it probably does not differentiate sufficiently from the food problems. The book does record what looks like a compromise between Paul and Barnabas, on the one hand, who were against imposing Jewish restrictions on Gentile converts, and Christians such as James who espoused orthodox Jewish practices. In due course this decision was incorporated, we are told, in what is known as the Apostolic Decree, issued allegedly to 'our brothers of Gentile origin' in Antioch, the rest of Syria, and Cilicia.[12]

But to go back to the Apostolic Council, more thought is required about what, precisely, was Peter's role at the meeting, if it occurred. Our sources are unreliable and uninformative on this point. If there was such a meeting, Peter was there and took part in the discussions. It was evidently important to secure his agreement. But it is not at all clear whether his opinion carried supreme weight, so that one might speak of his dominance over his fellow-Christians. Whatever had been said or written on this point before Acts is lost, but Acts 15 does not exactly present Peter as occupying a position of primacy at the alleged Council. What the book does, instead, is to present him as an important element in the general picture of single-minded unanimity that it wanted to display.

However, the trouble is that the Apostolic Council *probably never took place*.[13] It is likely to have been invented by the author of *Acts*, as a tremendous event, an inaugural Church Council, once again in order to illustrate the thesis that the early Christians were single-minded and unanimous, able to produce a decisive, eirenic, ecumenical consensus. The developments that followed will show, as we shall see, that this was by no means the case. All is not being told quite straight.

Others try to get away from the problem by suggesting that Acts 15 is a conflation of *two* Jerusalem meetings. The first of these peacefully aligned Peter with Paul, whose insistence on the Gentiles' freedom from circumcision prevailed, whereas the second confirmed the Four Regulations (which may be fictitious) in the absence of Paul. According to this second hypothesis, Paul never enforced the Decree, either because he did not know about it or because the churches in other provinces were, or could be assumed as being, outside the area to which the Decree was meant to apply. That is possible. But in any case, even if the Apostolic Council did take place, which is more than doubtful, its decisions failed to have any effect, as will shortly become clear.

First let us see how Paul interpreted what had happened in his Letter to the Galatians:[14]

I went again to Jerusalem with Barnabas, taking Titus with us ... But as for the men of high reputation (not that their importance matters to me: God does not recognise these personal distinctions), these men of repute, I say, did not prolong the consultation [or gave me no further instructions], but on the contrary acknowledged that I had been entrusted with the Gospel for Gentiles as surely as Peter had been entrusted with the Gospel for Jews. For God, whose action made Peter an Apostle to the Jews, also made me an Apostle to the Gentiles.

Recognizing, then, the favour thus bestowed on me, those reputed pillars of our society, James, Cephas and John, accepted Barnabas and myself as partners, and shook hands upon it, agreeing that we should go to the Gentiles while they went to the Jews.

This does not sound at all like the Apostolic Council described by Acts. So do the two accounts describe the same occasion? There has been a great deal of discussion on this subject. In fact, the two versions are hopelessly at variance. And indeed the same is true of many comparisons between Acts and Galatians. In Acts, Paul is associated with the activities of the apostles at Jerusalem shortly after his conversion on the road to Damascus. He preaches the Christian message to the Gentiles, after Peter and others have done the same and set the precedent. Subsequently, Paul visits Jerusalem again, in the company of Barnabas, as a starting-point for their journey to Antioch to undertake relief work, bringing supplies during the famine.

After their first missionary journey, they proceed to Jerusalem once more, as representatives of the church at Antioch, in order to consult the apostles and elders about the problem of whether Gentile converts should have to undergo circumcision.

At this 'Apostolic Council', as we have seen, it was decided, on the motion of Peter and James, that Gentile converts did not need to be circumcised, but that they should refrain, all the same, from eating meat that had been sacrificed to pagan images (as well as abstaining from fornication) and, in general, should obey Jewish dietary regulations. Paul and his companions convey this decision to Antioch. And that is the end of the matter, which never comes up again. As for Paul himself, he agrees to conform with the whole of Jewish Law and never denies its correctness in application to Jews. Out of respect for Jewish feeling, and despite the decision that has been taken, he even circumcises Timothy, a convert of mixed Greek and Jewish parentage.[15]

Paul's *Letter to the Galatians*, however, has an entirely different tale to tell. From the moment of his conversion Paul is the apostle to the Gentiles, whereas Peter is the apostle 'of the circumcised'. For the first three years after Paul has become a Christian he makes no contact with the apostles at all. Then for the first time he goes to see Peter, but is in touch with no other apostle 'except James, the brother of the Lord', and is still quite unknown to the churches of Judaea. Later, after an absence extending over fourteen years, he revisits Jerusalem in the company of Barnabas, not as a delegate or representative, but 'by revelation' – in other words, on his own initiative – in order to have private talks with Peter, James the brother of Jesus, and John the son of Zebedee, whom he ironically describes, as we have seen, as 'those reputed pillars of our society.'[16]

His purpose is to communicate to them the Gospel that he had been preaching to the Gentiles.

Galatians lets us know that Paul's listeners recognized this independent mission of his, and that they left him a completely free hand, on the single understanding that the Gentile converts should contribute their share to the relief of the poor at Jerusalem (which Paul said he had already intended to arrange).[17] Of the Apostolic Council or Decree, there is no mention.

Subsequently, at Antioch, according to the same Letter, Paul has a vigorous difference of opinion with Peter, of which *Acts* says nothing at all. This was because Peter, instigated by 'certain persons' (or 'a certain person') sent by James,[18] had terminated his own habit of eating in the company of Gentile converts. Paul takes exception to this change, as representing an endeavour to coerce the Gentiles into adopting Jewish dietary regulations; and he assails the Jewish Law as both valueless and positively harmful. Of the Apostolic ban on the eating of meat that had been sacrificed to pagan images, recorded in *Acts*, there is no mention at all any longer. Nonetheless, this does not deter Paul from claiming equal authority with the very foremost apostles, and he sharply criticizes anyone who interprets the teaching of Jesus in any way different from himself. 'God is not to be fooled: a man reaps what he sows.'[19]

This whole theme somewhat loses its importance, however, if we conclude that the Apostolic Council, as such, did not actually take place. In that case, the meetings between Paul, Peter and the rest must have been more or less private, if they occurred at all.

One thing, however, had nevertheless emerged. *Two* separate Christian missionary areas were now in existence (although *Acts* does not seem willing to accept the division), one for Jews and one for Christians. The former was in the hands of Peter, which again casts doubt on his alleged activity among the Gentiles. But this division, and the agreement to maintain it, was not likely to be workable in practice, because of the inevitable clash of personalities, and, in addition, because in most places the population was mixed, consisting both of Jews and of Gentiles, so that any clear-cut division into two missionary areas was unattainable.

In any case the agreement, if it ever was reached, almost immediately broke down. Paul himself, as we have seen, may well have failed to enforce it.[20] And after this supposed understanding between Peter and Paul at Jerusalem, in which they were allegedly confirmed in their missions to the Jews and Christians respectively, the two men encountered one another, and clashed, at Antioch.

This was the third city of the empire, with a population of half a million inhabitants, and it was there that the followers of Jesus had first been called 'Christians',[21] recognized as a group distinct from the Jews. Quite early on, after Stephen had been put to death for being a Christian,[22] some of the scattered missionaries had made their way to Antioch (before Paul and Peter did the same), where they undertook conversions. Then Paul had certainly gone to the city in AD 45 at the earliest, allegedly for a whole year. He and Barnabas had brought food to the community, which was partly of Gentile and partly of Jewish origin. Peter may also have gone to Antioch after his release from prison. Anyway, both Peter and Paul were at Antioch now – the year might have been AD 49 – and it was there that the disastrous difference of opinion occurred. It is described in uncompromising terms by Paul in his Letter to the Galatians:[23]

When Cephas [Peter] came to Antioch, I opposed him to his face, because he was clearly in the wrong. For until certain persons [or a certain person] came from James, he was taking his meals with Gentile Christians. But after they [or he] came he drew back and began to hold aloof, because he was afraid of the advocates of circumcision. The other Jewish Christians showed the same lack of principle. Even Barnabas was carried away and played false like the rest.

But when I saw that their conduct did not square with [or that they were not making progress towards] the truth of the Gospel, I said to Cephas, before the whole congregation, 'If you, a Jew born and bred, live like a Gentile, and not like a Jew, how can you insist that Gentiles must live like Jews?'

This remarkable assertion mirrors an extremely deep difference between Paul and Peter, which cannot be minimized, as John Chrysostom and Jerome tried to do, or dismissed as a mere 'stage trick'.[24] It is manifest that the period immediately after the Crucifixion of Jesus did *not* witness the harmony among his followers in which *Acts* has tried to induce us to believe, but was instead characterized by sharp rivalry between two mutually hostile groups. One of the groups was that of James the brother of Jesus and his fellow-Jews born in Palestine, who believed in Jesus but were also convinced that this belief entailed the maintenance of traditional Jewish institutions such as circumcision. The other group was led by Paul, and consisted of men whose education had been partly Greek and who were of Gentile origin. They, too, believed in Jesus, and although they may well have respected conformity with many aspects of Jewish Law, they were certain that this faith in him, with all its power and intensity, completely superseded some of the other old regulations of Judaism.

There is little doubt about what happened. James, leader of the faction which believed that Gentile Christians must obey Jewish customs, had not, after all, been prepared to abide by the Jerusalem agreement – if there was one – and had sent men, or a man, to persuade or compel Peter to cease from having meals with Gentile Christians. Peter might have felt relatively liberal about this before – although, as we have seen, his actual conversion of Gentiles is doubtful – but now he gave in to James because, Paul said, he was 'afraid'. This is perhaps an unduly harsh condemnation of the dilemma in which Peter found himself, since what he was really trying to do was to mediate between two extreme positions. And so he paid the penalty which flexible, diplomatic, careful, moderate mediators, compromisers and bridge-men pay. He was said to be frightened (perhaps for the future of his own mission, but not, surely, of freedom-fighters, as has been suggested).[25] Can he be accused of wavering? Yes, he certainly abandoned a position he believed in, but no doubt because he hoped to bridge the gulf which had widened between James and Paul.

And one other thing is clear. First we had heard of Peter as the Christian leader. Then we heard of a joint leadership of Peter, James and John. Now we learn that Peter has bowed to the wishes of

James. The man who will henceforward take the lead among the Jewish Christians of Jerusalem is not Peter; it is James. The leadership of Christianity in its central Palestinian city has passed back to the family of Jesus himself, with whom it will remain for a good many years. That is another penalty that mediators and compromisers pay. They do not manage to retain the leadership.

Nevertheless, despite a remarkable proliferation of sectarian rivals at Antioch,[26] Peter stayed on in the place for something like seven years, perhaps until about AD 56. The tradition of the Fathers that he became the first bishop of Antioch[27] is anachronistic. Yet Peter obviously played a prominent part in the Christian community of the place, and this formed a substantial part of the second half of his missionary activity, following the clash with Paul. But very little is known about this phase, and we cannot even say for certain whether, for the most part, Peter was now trying to proselytize Gentiles as well as, or instead of, Jews.

It seems quite possible that, on leaving Antioch and on his way to Rome, Peter visited various places, including Pontus (where he was credited with the foundation of churches at Amasia [Amasra] and Sinope [Sinop]) and then went to Corinth in Greece. He did not found the church at Corinth, as an ancient belief maintained.[28] However, there was a party there that adopted his name, since Paul, writing to the Corinthian Christians, tells us about its existence. Corinth, it appears, was another city, like Antioch, where there was an abundance of sects, each claiming to be Christian: there were at least two rival groups, or possibly four.[29]

> I have been told, my brothers, by Chloe's people that there are quarrels among you. What I mean is this: each of you is saying, 'I am Paul's man,' or 'I am for Apollos'; 'I follow Cephas [Peter],' or 'I am Christ's.'
> Surely Christ has not been divided among you!

What was this 'Cephas [Peter]' party? There have been various suggestions. One idea is that it might have consisted of men and women who had been baptized by Peter and had subsequently migrated to Corinth. Another conjecture is that it was a Jewish Christian body inspired by Peter's period of leadership after the

Crucifixion of Jesus, which felt itself to represent the original, true Church, in contrast to that of the upstart Paul – although why it has to be distinguished from the 'Jesus party' is undiscoverable. Nor can we determine if Peter's consent had been obtained before his name was used for one of the groups. Indeed, whether Peter went to Corinth at all, on his way to Rome, is uncertain. But there is a slight balance of probability in favour of saying that he did (or that he had perhaps visited Corinth earlier).

Peter's subsequent relations with Paul likewise remain a matter of conjecture. But when Paul sneers at 'sham brothers' and 'super-apostles'[30] he need not necessarily be referring to Peter, and there are some good reasons for believing that, at least superficially and up to a point, the relations between the two men were patched up. As we will see in the next chapter, it seems probable that they coexisted at Rome, presumably on adequate terms with one another. However, it would be an exaggeration to claim, with 2 *Peter*, that Peter had become a devotee of Paul, and even that Letter itself goes on to say that some of what Paul had written was obscure and liable to ruinous misinterpretation.[31]

In any case, Peter's career had suffered decisive setbacks when he ceased to be an active member of the governing Christian Three and clashed with Paul. We shall now see how he apparently rectified this position and achieved lasting fame, at Rome.

Bibliographical note

The contrast between Peter (Jewish Church) and Paul (Gentile Church) was stressed by C. Bauer (1792–1860).

For the importance of circumcision to the Jews, see M. Grant, *History of Ancient Israel* (1984), p. 59. See also R. E. Brown, K. P. Donfried and L. Reumann (eds), *Peter in the New Testament* (1973), pp. 26f.; A. Cole, *Galatians* (1965), p. 75; J. D. G. Dunn, *Unity and Diversity in the New Testament* (2nd ed., 1990), pp. 252f.

Chapter 11

PAUL AND JAMES

Paul

The career of Peter was shown, in Chapter 10, to have been inextricably intertwined with that of Paul, so that it is essential to say something more about who Paul was, and what he said and did.

Paul was born in Cilicia, a portion of south-eastern Asia Minor which formed part of the Roman province of Syria-Cilicia. His birthplace was the autonomous and privileged ('free') city of Tarsus, where he belonged to the substantial community of Jews of the Dispersion. Paul's family, which claimed to be descended from the Jewish tribe of Benjamin, consisted of strict, practising Pharisees. The Acts of the Apostles indicates that Paul pursued his studies at Jerusalem under the leading Pharisee of the day, Gamaliel.[1] But this remains dubious because a passage in his own Letters makes it seem probable that, during his youthful years, he had not yet visited Jerusalem at all: 'I remained unknown by sight', he says, 'to Christ's congregations in Judaea.'[2] It is more likely, therefore, that when he was young he remained in his home town of Tarsus.

His father, in whose house Paul still lived, was a Jew who wove cloth for carpets, tents and shoes from the goat's hair which was a product of the country and consequently bore the name of *cilicium*. His son Paul learnt the same trade, and we may conjecture that he joined his father in its practice while he was young.

The family seems to have been rather well off, and in the future Paul, although not always unwilling to accept monetary contributions from local communities, continued to insist, proudly, that he was not obliged to rely on the proceeds of his preaching in order to maintain himself. Instead, he had two other resources to keep him going. The first was the cash derived from his inherited capital. The second was his skill at operating the craft of weaving he had learnt, for he was always prepared to carry on working at it, wherever he went. To do so was a Jewish custom, and it was a custom which Paul followed.

Tarsus had been thoroughly Hellenized, and was a place where Greek culture flourished. Paul therefore knew Greek very well, and wrote his Letters in that language. But he did not become a member of the Greek citizen body of Tarsus. Certainly, as a Jew, he might have done this: Greek cities of this type included among their citizens certain of the more prominent Jews who were numbered among their residents. But Paul belonged instead to the separate *Jewish* community, which was also a characteristic feature of such cities, and possessed a quasi-autonomous status and other not inconsiderable privileges.

Moreover, Paul and his family also enjoyed another, less customary distinction, for they possessed a non-Jewish citizenship which was not Greek, but Roman. They were, that is to say, Roman citizens. In townships of this kind there were a number of Roman citizens, and a few of them were Jews. When Paul's family had acquired Roman citizenship, and why, we do not know. But it may have been acquired by Paul's father (or grandfather), either as a reward for some service he had rendered to a local Roman governor or commander, or because he had been a slave or a prisoner of war who was granted his freedom. When Paul's mother gave birth to a son, she and her husband gave him the Jewish name of Saul. But at some stage this was replaced by a Roman name, Paul. It seems likely that this new name was selected because it was the Roman name which was closest to what he had originally been called.

So Paul possessed the advantage of belonging to three different worlds at one and the same time: Jewish, Hellenic and Roman. And in the years to come he displayed the capacity to exploit this triple status to a remarkable degree.

However, it was his Jewish origin which weighed most heavily with him. And in this capacity as a young man, Paul was very active and aggressive indeed. He may well have belonged not merely to the community of the Pharisees, like his father, but also to some specialized circle inside that community, of exceptionally devout inclinations. At all events, shortly after the Crucifixion of Jesus, Paul (like other Jews) began to display extreme hostility to the dead man's Jewish disciples, who believed that Jesus had been the Messiah, a claim, of course, which the rest of the Jews strongly rejected.

A few years later one of these disciples, Stephen, was stoned to death by outraged Jews in Jerusalem. The Acts of the Apostles reported that Paul was present and supported the murderers, whose coats he looked after while they performed the deed.[3] That is not a likely story, since, as we have seen, Paul himself suggested that he had not yet visited Jerusalem at the time. Nevertheless, it remains true that he took a vigorous part in the attacks that the Jews and their leaders directed against the followers of the crucified Jesus.

It seems probable that, in so doing, Paul was protected and egged on by the powers of coercion which the Roman authorities delegated to the Jewish Council (Sanhedrin) at Jerusalem, and to its minor counterparts in other parts of the Near East. It was no doubt on behalf of one of these Councils that Paul set out upon the punitive missions against the Christians which he now proceeded to undertake. Since Paul had not yet been to Jerusalem, it may well have been the Jewish Council at his home town of Tarsus that promoted his journeys aimed at exterminating the Christians. Or it might have been the Jewish leadership in the great Syrian city of Antioch. We cannot tell. Nor do we know if whatever Jewish Council directed him had received its instructions from Jerusalem, or was acting independently. No doubt the instructions given to Paul were that he should persuade these dissidents to mend their ways, and his call to order was probably backed by the threat of sanctions, such as ejection from the synagogues.

And so, not very long after Stephen's death, Paul departed – perhaps from Tarsus or Antioch – upon one such disciplinary mission, to Damascus. This was, in some ways, a Syrian equivalent to Tarsus. That is to say, it lay within the boundaries of the Roman province of Syria-Cilicia, within which it enjoyed the autonomy known as 'freedom'. And, once again like Tarsus, it included within its population a Jewish community of considerable dimensions. Among its inhabitants, however, there was also a group of men and women devoted to the memory and teaching of Jesus, and it was these whom Paul was intended to bring back into the Jewish fold.

Things turned out differently, however, as is well known. 'On the road to Damascus', presumably outside one of the city gates, Paul tells us that a vision of Jesus, accompanied by a blinding light, came upon him.[4] The force of the phenomenon, according to this tradition, overwhelmed him and he fell off his horse onto the ground. He was taken into Damascus, and when he got back his senses he was a different man. In particular, his hostile attitude to Jesus and his followers had vanished, and he had become their fanatical supporter instead. It remains doubtful whether Paul's conversion was really quite as dramatically sudden as this story recounts. For we cannot discount the alternate possibility that he had long been plagued by psychological doubts attributing a greater significance to Jesus, which came to a head when he arrived at Damascus. If so, however, such doubts must have been at a curiously secondary level, since Paul, unlike Peter, had never himself been personally acquainted with Jesus at all.

After he had finally and fully experienced this change of heart, Paul declared it openly at Damascus, which so annoyed the city's administration that he was first placed under arrest and then compelled to go elsewhere. Damascus, at this time, belonged to a Roman 'client' (puppet) king, Aretas IV of Nabataean Arabia, and Paul left for other parts of Arabia, travelling around for three years, and no doubt proclaiming his conversion to anyone who would listen.

Thereafter he went back to Judaea, and we have seen in earlier chapters what happened. Essentially there was a conflict between those supporters of the memory of Jesus desirous of restricting the new faith to the people who, like Jesus himself, were Jews or were prepared to embrace Jewish customs to the full, and those who, on the contrary, wanted to do everything possible to convert the Gentiles – that is to say, the Greeks who were the inhabitants of the eastern provinces of the Roman empire.

At Jerusalem, where Jesus had been crucified, the leaders of the former group were Peter, who had been Jesus's closest adherent, and James the Just, who was described as Jesus's brother. It was Peter, for the time being, who led the missionary movement which this recently established group of followers of Jesus was directing towards their fellow-Jews in Judaea and other near-eastern territories. Paul, on the other hand, despite his strongly Jewish origins – and it has been argued that he still remained a practising Jew,[5] although he found the legalism of the Jewish faith too unrealistically perfectionist – began to assume the headship of a mission to the Gentiles. These he saw as included in the entirely new course by which Jesus, the second Adam, had brought all men to life. This was virtually an innovation, since even if there had been Gentile converts to Christianity before, they had never amounted to more than a few individuals. The Gospels make this perfectly clear, stressing Jesus's evidently sparse Gentile contacts and conversions, and *Acts* performs a similar service for Peter.

How soon, and by what stages, Paul embarked on this revolutionary programme remains obscure. We have seen that after expulsion from Damascus he disappeared into Arabia for three years. But thereafter he spent almost a decade as a missionary in Syria and in his home country of Cilicia. Presumably, during that period, he carried out missionary activities on behalf of the Christian cause. And it may be conjectured that, for most of the time, these activities continued to be directed towards his fellow-Jews, who, it was still hoped, would form the nucleus of the future Christian community. At some point, however, Paul turned towards the Gentiles, thus promoting the division between his own proselytization of these non-Jewish people and Peter's already existent mission to the Jews. When, precisely, Paul took this decisive step is one of the many obscurities that confront us. He himself ascribed God's order that the step should be taken to the moment of his conversion. But the Acts of the Apostles attributed the new line to subsequent occasions.[6] At all events, it was not initially envisaged that the Gentiles were to be the *main* body of Christians. They were to be supplementary, so to speak, to the principal Jewish core of the faithful.

This was, in all probability, the thinking behind Paul's first missionary journey, which began c.AD 45 and lasted for several years, comprising tours of Syria, Cyprus and Asia Minor. It appears likely that this journey had the backing (even if it was somewhat cautious) of Peter and James in Jerusalem. The understanding seems to have been that Paul and his fellow-missionaries would preach and teach in Jewish synagogues, even though it was probably conceded that, if appropriate Gentiles presented themselves for conversion, this should not be denied to them.

That, however, is not how matters turned out. The Jews of the Dispersion, for the most part, refused to agree that Jesus had been the Messiah, and felt – like Jews everywhere, as we have seen – that Paul's assertion that Jesus's death had cancelled all sins invalidated God's free forgiveness of the penitents; so they firmly rejected the message that Paul and his companion Barnabas were trying to convey to them. In consequence, the two travellers turned increasingly to the Gentiles. As we have seen elsewhere, however, the question of what concessions the followers of Christ ought to make to the Gentiles – for example, and in particular, whether they should have to undergo circumcision – raised furious disputes back home in Jerusalem. These problems are symbolically brought together in the Acts of the Apostles, which offers, as we saw, a description of a Jerusalem 'Apostolic Council' convened to debate the matters at issue. It seems more than doubtful whether any such dramatic single Council meeting ever took place. But the vigour, tension and bitterness of the discussions of this problem are beyond any doubt, and Peter was deeply involved in them.

It was at this point, perhaps, that an agreement was reached – perhaps tacitly – to the effect that, while Peter should continue to pursue his Jewish mission, Paul should concentrate, henceforward, upon evangelizing the Gentiles.

And so he set out on his second three-year journey, across Asia Minor, Macedonia and Achaea (Greece). In the course of this second journey, he encountered the Roman governor (proconsul) of Achaea, Gallio,[7] whom we know to have held this office c.AD 52. Gallio's capital was at Corinth, where Paul proceeded to spend a year and a half or more. Then he went back to Antioch, and subsequently, perhaps in spring 53, he departed on his third journey, yet another manifestation of his almost incredible feats of missionary travelling. It is probable that this third journey lasted for at least five years, three of which were spent at Ephesus (Selçuk), the important Greek city on the west coast of Asia Minor.

Then, in AD 58, Paul returned to Jerusalem. There is some confusion at this point, because this is the third of his visits to be recorded in his Letters, but the fifth according to the Acts of the Apostles. At all events, Paul was at Jerusalem in 58. Although, according to one view, he still did not break with Jewish Law, the angry Jews threatened to kill him. However, the Roman authorities saved his life by placing him under arrest. The Jews brought charges of blasphemy against him, which were heard by the procurator (governor) of Judaea, Marcus Antonius Felix, at his capital Caesarea Maritima (Sdot Yam). But Felix did not feel able to pronounce a verdict, and in 60 a new governor, Publius Porcius Festus, again postponed making a decision, so that Paul remained in prison at Caesarea for two years.[8]

It was now, however, that his status as a Roman citizen came in useful. Paul, citing this status, and despairing of reconciliation with the Jewish Christian leadership after the execution of a possible intermediary James the Just, in AD 62, appealed that his case should be heard by the emperor's court at Rome;[9] this appeal was duly granted. *Acts* describes Paul's eventful journey to the imperial capital, where he spent two years.

The story that he left Italy for a time in order to go to Spain appears not to be authentic. More probably, he stayed in Rome, at first under some sort of house arrest, and latterly in prison. The Roman authorities, working under the emperor Nero (54–68), put him on trial, as his transfer to their city required. Indeed, there may have been two trials; we cannot be sure. Finally, however, it appears that the imperial law-court condemned Paul to execution, and he was put to death. The date of his death is uncertain. It may have been in AD 64, when Nero had many Christians executed in the hope (largely unfulfilled) of displaying them as scapegoats for the Great Fire of Rome. Or Paul could have been put to death earlier.

His relevance to the present book lies in his inextricable relationship with Peter. From the point of view of this relationship, by far the most important of Paul's Letters is the Epistle to the Galatians, in which the clash between the two men at Antioch is described. However, the whole astonishing collection of Paul's Letters is something that the biographer of Paul cannot do without. Written at various stages of Paul's career, they throw light not only upon his own mental processes, and upon the preaching and teaching which resulted from them, but also upon his relations with Peter and others. He himself has something to say about the motives that lay behind his work. 'I cannot help myself,' he told the Corinthians, 'it would be misery for me not to preach.'[10] 'Proclaim the message,' commanded 2 *Timothy*, 'press it home on all occasions, convenient or inconvenient; use argument, reproof and appeal, with all the patience that the work of teaching requires.'[11] And whether or not Paul himself was the writer of this particular Letter, it may well reflect his sentiments and practice, for his tireless missionary work was of just this character. Such was the man with whom Peter had to contend, and as far as possible get along.

James

Although inadequately described in the New Testament, and accorded especially little justice in *Acts*, James is of importance in this story, because it was he who supplanted Peter as the leader of the Christians after the Crucifixion of Jesus.

The James (Jacob) to whom reference is made, neither the son of Zebedee (James 'the Great', executed by King Agrippa I) nor the son of Alphaeus (James 'the Less'), was 'the Lord's brother' according to Paul in his Letter to the Galatians .[12] The Gospels record brothers of Jesus, including James,[13] and the contexts seem to show that these writers have a blood relationship between Jesus and his brothers in mind. Tertullian (c.AD 160–240) and Clement of Alexandria (c.150–211/216), too, confirm that this was what was believed in the first two centuries AD. Origen (c.184/6–254/5) and others, however, bearing in mind that 'brother' (*adelphos*) can cover a wider range of meanings, suggested that James was a *stepbrother* of Jesus: in other words, that Joseph had been married to another wife before he was married to Mary. A rival theory, sponsored by Jerome (c.348–420), held that Jesus and James were really cousins.[14] These views, contradicting the simple brotherly relationship, came into being because it was increasingly stressed, from the second century onwards, that Mary, the wife of Joseph, was not only a virgin when she gave birth to Jesus, but remained a virgin all her life.

James, it appears, was not very keen on the preaching of Jesus, and may indeed have been positively opposed to it, as long as Jesus was alive.[15] After the Crucifixion, however, he became converted. This, according to Paul, was because he was vouchsafed an Appearance of the risen Christ.[16] Probably this Appearance was needed, and invented, by the tradition, because James's kinship with Jesus (accompanied, as it had been, by a measure of scepticism) was not held to be sufficient to justify the prominent position which James now came to occupy.

For within a short time after Paul's conversion James was a significant leader in the Christian Church, and he became even more important after Agrippa I had the apostle James 'the Great' (the son of Zebedee) executed in AD 44 and Peter fled from Jerusalem. It was then that James 'the brother of Jesus' came to power in Peter's place. He had not been one of the original Twelve, but Paul seems to have regarded him as an apostle all the same.[17]

Although Acts does not, on the whole, do justice to James, the book does make him the chief spokesman for the Jerusalem church at the probably non-existent Apostolic Council, in which he was alleged to have intervened in favour of a measure of Jewish ortho-doxy, indicating that Gentile converts should comply with the Four Regulations:[18]

> In my judgement we should impose no irksome restrictions on those of the Gentiles who are turning to God. Instead we should instruct them by letter to abstain from things polluted by contact with idols, from fornication, from anything that has been strangled, and from blood.

Later tradition maintained that James was called 'the Just' (Zaddik, like the Qumran Teacher of Righteousness), and was noted for his pious fulfilment of Jewish Law. He may have possessed priestly privileges, and it was perhaps because of his influence that the Pharisee Gamaliel urged leniency to Peter and the Christians.[19]

Nevertheless, it does not appear that James was entirely rigorous and conservative. For example, as the quotation deprecating 'irksome restrictions' suggested, he was against those Jewish Christians who wanted Gentile Christians to subject themselves to the *whole* of Jewish Law, including circumcision. What James recommended instead was that they should only adhere to part of the Law. This did not, however, affect his beliefs about what *Jewish* Christians ought to do. It was the conviction of James that these should persist in their observance of Jewish regulations, which is what he did himself.

This dual policy explains how subsequent tradition was able to stress not only James's devoutness, but also the high respect in which he was held among many Jews as well as among Jewish Christians. This respect was demonstrated in AD 62, when the high priest Ananus, while the Roman procurator (governor of the province) was away, arranged for James to be put to death. For other Jews strongly expressed their resentment of this action. Varying accounts of what happened are given by the first-century Jewish historian Josephus and by the late second-century Christian writer Hegesippus.[20] Hegesippus, quoted by Eusebius, claims that James was thrown down from a tower of the Temple by the Pharisees. But Josephus's account is more plausible. His version is that James was stoned to death instead, and that the responsibility for this rested with the Jerusalem party of the Sadducees, whereas the Pharisees had associated themselves with objections to his killing.

James's apparent capacity to establish an active and friendly relationship between the Jews (or some of them) and the Jewish Christians is interesting, and invites further speculation. It can be conjectured, for instance, that the Jewish Christians might to a large extent have shared in the nationalistic hopes and expectations of the Jews, which were to culminate in their First Revolt against the Romans only a few years after James's death; and that James, too, had viewed these ideas with favour.

In any case, James came to have an enormous reputation. In the early Church, according to the passages already referred to in the historian Eusebius, James was believed (wrongly) to have been the first bishop of Jerusalem, and was regarded also as the writer of the Epistle of James which is perhaps, instead, of late first-century or early second-century date. And in the Jewish Christian *Homilies* (Greek) and *Recognitions* (Syriac and Latin), which date from the later fourth century but were attributed to Clement of Rome (c.AD 96), James has become a legendary personage and hero.

After he was put to death, the church at Jerusalem remained under the control of Jesus's family, known as the *desposynoi* (masters), for many years to come. This happened frequently in Jewish sects, which likewise continued to be dominated by the families of their founders.

There do remain, however, certain mysteries and questions about the position that James had held during his lifetime. Evidently he was, for a time, the leader of the Christian community at Jerusalem. But since that was so, since he played such an important part in the early Church and in the events of his epoch, why are we given so little information about him? Why has he been pushed into the position of a shadowy, background figure?[21] The answer seems to be this. Whether he was Jesus's brother or not, James had known him personally, and had been close to him, in a way with which Paul could not hope to compete. This meant that James was nearer to the source of the faith than Paul could ever expect to be. Moreover,

James's aims and interests were by no means those of Paul. On occasion, indeed, they held exactly opposite views.

For Paul, then, James must have been a continual source of disapproval and irritation. And with the subsequent triumph of Pauline Christianity, his significance, even if it could not be expunged from the record completely, was at any rate retroactively lessened. This made James an ambiguous figure, about whom *Acts*, in consequence, is curiously reticent. In fact, however, James had been someone who could even overrule Peter. Some have gone further still and have asserted that, despite the popular tradition that Peter was the first head of the Church, the neglected James had really been its first leader. This seems to go too far. Peter *was* the first leader of the Christians after Jesus's death. But the fact that he was later superseded by James is indicative of the significant setback that his career had suffered.

Bibliographical note

On Paul, see M. Grant, *Saint Paul* (1982). Other recent books include M. Braybrooke, *Christian–Jewish Relations: A New Look*; M. Hengel, *The Pre-Christian Paul* (1993); J. A. Ziesler, *Pauline Christianity*; G. Lüdemann, *Paul: Apostle to the Gentiles*; H. Maccoby, *Paul and Hellenism*; G. Messadie, *The Firebrand: The Life of Saul, Apostle*; E. P. Sanders, *Paul and Palestinian Judaism*, 10. *Paul, the Law and the Jewish People*; A. F. Segal, *Paul the Convert*; N. T. Wright, *The Climax of the Covenant*. Gallio: Lucius Annaeus Gallio Novatus, brother of the philosopher Seneca, adopted by the orator and senator Lucius Junius Gallio.

On James probably being Jesus's brother, see C. L. Mitton, *Jesus: The Fact Behind the Faith* (1973), p. 90 (i.e. not stepbrother or cousin). On his not being the same as James the Less, the son of Alphaeus, see D. Attwater, *Dictionary of Saints* (2nd ed., 1983), p. 179.

For the importance of James, see J. B. Adamson, *James: The Man and his Message* (1989); W. K. Prentice, *Studies in Roman Economic and Social History in Honor of A. C. Johnson* (1951), pp. 144–51. For the Gospel of Thomas, see the bibliographical note, p. 47. The so-called Letter of James dates from the end of the second century AD: W. G. Kümmel, *Introduction to the New Testament* (1975) p. 414. G. Vermes, *Times Literary Supplement*,

4 December 1992, p. 6, points out that R. H. Eisenman and M. Wise, *The Dead Sea Scrolls Uncovered*, are wrong to link the Scrolls with James and his adherents. For the Scrolls see also H. Shanks (ed.), *Understanding the Dead Sea Scrolls* (1993), a matter also discussed by O. Betz and R. Riesner, *Jesus, Qumran and the Vatican* (1994).

Part IV

ROME

Chapter 12

PETER IN ROME

While it is a Catholic conviction that Peter went to Rome and became its bishop, many Protestants have taken the view that he never went there at all. The arguments *against* his residence in Rome can be marshalled in the following way:[1]

(1) Paul's Letter to the Galatians indicates that Peter's activities took place at Jerusalem. There is also a mention of a visit to Antioch, where Peter met with the disapproval of Paul by refusing to associate with Gentile Christians, and even induced Paul's companion Barnabas to adopt a similar procedure.[2] But nothing is said here about Rome.

(2) Paul's Letter to the Romans is addressed to the Christians at Rome. In the whole of this address, however, there is no mention of Peter at all, which seems strange if he was indeed in Rome.

(3) As we have already seen, one of the principal purposes of *Acts* is to institute a comparison between Peter and Paul: whereas Galatians shows them in conflict and confrontation, Acts deliberately displays unanimity. Since the book terminates with Paul preaching in Rome, it is surely to be expected that its author would mention that Peter had preceded him there, or was his companion

there, if any such tradition existed. But there is no mention of any such thing.

(4) The Epistle *1 Clement* (c.AD 96), which purports to have been written by Clement of Rome, on behalf of the church of that city, to the church at Corinth, records Peter's noble past, but has nothing whatever to say about his having been at Rome.[3] Moreover, the aim of the entire passage is to compare him with Paul, and draw a parallel between them. In these circumstances, it is possible to deduce that no tradition of Peter's residence or martyrdom at Rome was known to the writer of the Letter.

(5) When writings of later date do make references to the martyrdom of Peter, they fail to indicate where this took place. If it had taken place at Rome, one would expect this to be specified.

(6) In support of the opposite argument it has been supposed that when Ignatius, who died in about AD 110, said to the Romans, 'I did not request you, as Peter and Paul did',[4] he was implying that Peter, as well as Paul, had preached to their community in the city. However, Justin Martyr, when he was writing in about the middle of the second century, does not make any mention of Peter having been there. About the activities of Simon Magus in the city he has a good deal to say. But on Simon's supposed confrontation with Peter in Rome, which is the theme of so many later stories, Justin remains entirely silent.

(7) The earliest evidence for Peter's alleged residence in Rome that can be dated with any degree of accuracy comes from Dionysius of Corinth. It was during the bishopric of Soter AD 166–74) that Dionysius wrote to the church of Rome, expressing gratitude to its members for their financial assistance. Part of the Letter has been reproduced by Eusebius.[5] In this, Dionysius observes that it is right and proper that the churches of Rome and Corinth should operate in unison, since they had both been founded jointly by Peter and Paul (and this, in the case of Rome, was echoed by Irenaeus).[6]

However, this mention of the role of Peter does not readily invite acceptance. For one thing, what Dionysius stated about Corinth was not true. That is to say, he had seriously distorted the history of his own church. And, since he had been so inaccurate about the church he knew so well, there is no reason to believe what he said about Rome either. Moreover, there are positive reasons for disbelieving what he wrote on the subject. For one thing, his ascription to Paul of a joint role in the foundation of the Roman church does not seem to be correct. On the contrary, Paul observed in *Romans* that he had never met the Christians in Rome,[7] in the foundation of whose Church, therefore, he cannot have played a part. So why believe the statement about Peter either, which goes far beyond anything said by Ignatius or Justin?

(8) Later on, it became customary to report, without any justification, that Peter had resided at Rome for twenty-five years, and to declare that he had been not merely the joint founder but the sole founder of its Church, so that the alleged participation of Paul in its establishment was gradually expunged from the record.

The elimination of one apostle or the other was only to be expected, once it came to be believed that the early Church had already been governed by a *single* episcopal, monarchical personage (even if the idea of any continuous succession, in that role, had never been in Jesus's mind).[8] And when that doctrine became incorporated in the tradition, it was natural that Peter should be preferred to Paul, since the former, but not the latter, had been a close personal associate of Jesus. It could be assumed that Peter had received, at first hand, the true Christian faith, and the belief that he had founded the Church of Rome could become a means of strengthening the authority of that church in its fight against heresies. But it was a belief that was false.

These are all points worth bearing in mind, but they do not add up to anything like a demonstration that Peter never went to Rome. Point 1 refers to Jerusalem as the centre of Peter's activities. But that does not mean that he did not go to Rome afterwards. With reference to the second point, certainly there were Christians at Rome who were in close touch with Paul, but that does not deny that there may have been others who followed Peter. The third point ignores the fact that the second half of *Acts* is intended to concentrate on Paul. The omission of Peter in his favour, in those chapters, need not seem surprising. Points 4–7 are interesting, but not conclusive;

4 and 6 (like 2) suggest the presence of more than one Christian group in Rome. The eighth argument correctly points out that the duration (like the significance) of Peter's residence at Rome was much exaggerated, but that does not mean that he was not there at all.

On the contrary, despite such reasons for scepticism, there is a large measure of agreement that Peter *did* go to Rome. It seems likely that he arrived there some time between 54 and 58, or possibly as late as 63. He might conceivably have been there before, perhaps in 42, and later in 59, although this remains conjectural.

Peter was not, however, the founder of the Roman church, since otherwise Paul would have mentioned his name when he wrote of that foundation. Nor did Paul himself found the Roman church. Nor, therefore, did Peter and Paul establish it jointly. It was apparently established at a previous date, perhaps in the early 40s, by unknown travellers, traders or soldiers.

It was a church that was basically Jewish, adopting a moderately conservative Jewish Christian stance. But it also contained a good many 'God-fearers' (*sebomenoi*, Jewish by sympathy, but not by direct allegiance) and Gentile proselytes.[9]

As for Peter, it has been suggested that he did not lead the Roman church at all, but only went there as a missionary and was, as *1 Peter* says, one elder among others.[10] And that is quite probable. Accepting the assumption that Peter *did* go to Rome, and resided there for a time, there are traditions that he lived with Aquila and his wife Priscilla or Prisca, wealthy tent-makers from Pontus and leaders of the Christian community, of whom he approved.[11] Their house at Rome, a 'house-church', was said to have been on the site of the church of Santa Prisca.[12] But there was also a story that both Peter and Paul stayed in Rome with the senator Pudens and his daughters Praxedis and Pudentiana (both of whom Peter allegedly baptized), at their house on the Vicus Patricius (Via Urbana), the site upon which the church of Santa Pudenziana now stands.

It was said to have been in Rome that Peter (and perhaps Paul as well, if their traditional association in the city is correct) grappled with their powerful, 'heretical' rival Simon Magus, who was later regarded as an originator of the Gnostic heresy. This report is by no means impossible, although *Acts*, bearing in mind that Simon Magus was greatly admired in Samaria, prefers to locate the confrontation there, at a much earlier stage, and to ascribe it both to Peter and (first) to Philip.[13] The pseudonymous *Acts of Peter*, in the later second century AD, attribute the meetings of Simon Magus and Peter to various locations, ending with Rome.

Bibliographical note

The Catholic position is now restated by R. E. Brown, K. P. Donfried and L. Reumann (eds), *Peter in the New Testament* (1973), p. 12 n. 25 (*cf.* pp. 41, 48 n. 114); *cf.* also pp. 186f. n. 3, and p. 215; R. E. Brown, *The Gospel According to John* (1966), p. 1117; and W. D. Davies and D. C. Allison, *The Gospel According to Saint Matthew*, Vol. II (1991), p. 643. On whether we can detect *Frühkatholicismus* in *Acts*, see J. A. Fitzmyer, *The Gospel According to Luke* (1981), pp. 23ff.

Peter's presence in Rome was formerly doubted, later accepted, by O. Cullmann, *Peter: Disciple, Apostle, Martyr* (1962), p. 78; *cf.* F. J. Cwiekowski, *The Beginnings of the Church* (1988), pp. 99, 174, 196. His stay there was believed in England, where Peterborough Abbey Church was founded so that 'just as blessed Peter was present in Rome, so he might also be present in this spot in spirit': J. Lees-Milne, *Saint Peter's* (1967), p. 114. Peter's alleged landing in Italy was celebrated by the foundation of the Church of S. Piero a Grado, not far from Pisa.

On Ignatius, see W. R. Schoedel, *Ignatius of Antioch* (1986).

Simon Magus in Rome is discussed by G. R. S. Mead, *Simon Magus* (1991); C. P. Thiede, *Simon Peter: From Galilee to Rome* (1986), pp. 241f. n. 18; G. A. Wells, *The Jesus of the Early Christians* (1971), p. 189 n. 3; H. Schonfield, *Those Incredible Christians* (1985), p. 120; Fitzmyer, op. cit., p. 11. The legend of Peter's defeat of Simon Magus was particularly widespread in the early fifth century AD: C. Petri, *Roma Cristiana* (1976), pp. 1558–62.

On the topography of Rome, see L. Richardson, *A New Topographical Dictionary of Ancient Rome* (1992); *cf.* A. Rollins, *Rome in the Fourth Century*.

Chapter 13

THE DEATH AND BURIAL-PLACE
OF PETER

The Acts of Peter reported a legend to the effect that, when Nero started persecuting the Christians in AD 64,[1] Peter fled from Rome, but that as he was on his way out of the region the phantom of Jesus appeared to him and said, 'Whither goest thou?' – *Quo Vadis?* This was an echo of Peter's supposed words to Jesus in John's Gospel,[2] and the title of Henryk Sienkiewicz's famous book (1896). Thereupon Peter turned back to the city and to his death. Obviously the story has met with some disbelief. But its testimony to Peter's martyrdom should not be neglected.

There has been a great deal of discussion about the martyrdom of Peter, but on the whole it does seem probable that it took place: that he was executed at Rome during Nero's persecutions, possibly, though not necessarily, dying when the persecution began in AD 64, or at any rate before Nero's death in 68.

An explicit written reference to his martyrdom was made by Clement of Rome, writing perhaps *c.*96 but alternatively as early as 69–70, when Nero's persecution was a fresh memory.[3]

Because of jealousy [*zelos*] and envy, the greatest and justest pillars were persecuted and contended unto death. Let us set before our eyes the good [upright] Apostles: Peter, who because of unjustified jealousy [*zelos*] suffered not one or two, but many, afflictions, and having given witness [*marturesas*] he went to the place of glory which was his due.

The term 'jealousy' appears a number of times in the Bible, although it is sometimes rendered as 'zeal'. Exactly what this jealousy was from which Peter suffered is uncertain. Clement asserts that Peter had to endure it 'many times'. But the jealousy that finally led to his death – for that is what *marturesas* apparently refers to – may well have been displayed by ultra-conservative Jewish Christian missionaries, who insisted on circumcision, disapproved of the more moderate line which Peter had already taken at Antioch, and consequently denounced him to the Roman authorities. Later the Gospel of John (or rather its last chapter, of controversial authorship) retrospectively made Jesus forecast this martyrdom of Peter, whom he was said to have addressed in these terms:[4]

In very truth I tell you. When you were young you fastened your belt about you and walked where you chose. But when you are old you will stretch out your arms, and a stranger will bind you fast, and carry you where you have no wish to go.

He said this to indicate the manner of death by which Peter was to glorify God.

This 'manner of death' was surely martyrdom and crucifixion, and not merely some other form of unnatural death. The Acts of Peter, which did not necessarily adhere to historical fact, later added that Peter insisted on being crucified upside down, so as not to compete with Jesus. In an earlier chapter of *John*, too, there is an implicit reference to Peter's martyrdom:[5]

Simon Peter said to him [Jesus], 'Lord, where are you going?' Jesus replied, 'I am going where you cannot follow me now, but one day you will.'

It had seemed strange that the writer of *Acts* seemed to know nothing about the death of Peter (or Paul), or at least did not want to mention the subject. Various reasons have been suggested. In the end, however, the traditions of Peter's martyrdom, as of Paul's, remained firm.

There had been a shrine of Peter in the Vatican area since at least AD 160–70, and Constantine I the Great (306–37) was so convinced of its authenticity that, in the face of great difficulties, he built his resplendent basilica, St Peter's, over the site.

It had formerly housed a necropolis. Christians, and no doubt others, had occasionally been buried there since the first century AD. But modern excavations have shown that it was in the second century that the necropolis became particularly extensive. This, then, was where the shrine of Peter was erected c.AD 160–70, if not earlier. Whether Peter had actually been buried on that spot, however, remains uncertain. Evidently the builders of the shrine believed that he had. And they might have been right. Or they might not. We cannot tell.

A Roman author named Gaius, writing in about AD 200, indicates his knowledge of this shrine, as well as of a shrine for Paul on the Via Ostiensis: that is, where the Basilica of Saint Paul Outside the Walls (S. Paoli Fuori le Mura) now stands.[6] Mention must also be made of another shrine in Rome, beside the third milestone on the Via Appia. Here both St Peter and St Paul were jointly commemorated on 29 June of every year, as the Calendar of Philocalus (354) records. (This was a date on which a Festival of Romulus had also been celebrated since the beginning of imperial times.)

There has been much discussion about the origin of the shrine on the Via Appia, and about its relation to the two separate shrines of Peter and Paul in the Vatican area and on the Via Ostiensis. In particular, two alternative explanations have been put forward. According to one, the joint shrine on the Via Appia was established to rival and supersede the two separate memorials of the apostles elsewhere. According to the other explanation, however, relics believed to be the bones of the two men were temporarily transferred from their separate receptacles to the joint site on the Via

Appia, probably during the persecution of the Christians by the emperor Valerian in 258. The trouble with this theory, however, is that no such transfer is recorded by any ancient source.

While Damasus I was bishop of Rome or Pope (AD 366–84), the festival for the two apostles on 29 June was marked by a procession from the Basilica of St Peter to the Basilica of St Paul, followed by a culminating celebration at the joint shrine on the Via Appia. Owing to the complication and length of these ceremonies, their final phase, consisting of rites at the shrine on the Via Appia, was abandoned later in the fourth century AD. Then, subsequently, it was found better – for what reason we do not exactly know – to postpone the celebration at the Basilica of St Paul to 30 June.

Throughout this period Rome was taking steps to claim both Peter and Paul as its own – because of the belief that they were martyred in the city. This was expressed by Damasus I, who observed that, 'although the East sent the Apostles, yet because of the merit of their martyrdom Rome has acquired a superior right to claim them as citizens'. And so he spoke deliberately of Rome as 'the Apostolic See', as his immediate predecessor Liberius (352–66) had also done.

Nevertheless, what had really happened to the body of Peter remains mysterious. Were martyrs' bodies just thrown into a common grave, or did Peter originally have at least a simple flat-brick tomb? The strange, late report that he was buried separately by the senator Marcellus[7] can be ignored: it is all too reminiscent of the legends that Jesus was buried by Joseph of Arimathea (N. of Jerusalem). But the tradition that Peter was, in some form or other, buried on the south side of the Vatican, near the place of his execution, is very early. And Gaius mentioned 'monuments', *tropaia*, which were believed to mark the burial-places (or places of execution) of the apostles.

'Archaeology', wrote John Ward-Perkins,[8] 'has not proved and cannot prove that this was the site of Peter's grave.'

On the other hand archaeology has proved that since about the year 160 this spot has been the object of a veneration which early hardened into a firm belief that this was in fact the burial place of the Apostle. Archaeological research has, moreover, shown that the surviving features of the second-century shrine are consistent with, and in several respects most readily explained by, the hypothesis that the shrine marks the site of an actual burial, which was disturbed by the builders of the adjoining mausoleum and which the contemporary Christian community rightly or wrongly identified as that of Peter. Whether, a century after Peter's death, they had good reason for their belief cannot be decided. But that the shrine which they erected became the centre-piece of Constantine's basilica – the earliest great Christian site of the west, of which we can judge the splendid appearance from a late sixteenth-century painting by Domenico Tasseli(?) in the Church of Trinità dei Monti – and that, situated directly beneath the high altar of the present church, it has received continuous veneration for more than eighteen centuries, is a demonstrable historical fact.

What are we to conclude from all this? First of all, Constantine I the Great was evidently convinced that the site at the Vatican, where he built Saint Peter's, was in fact the burial-place of Peter. This was a conviction that graffiti indicate had come down from an earlier date. So sure of this was Constantine that he went to enormous lengths and expense to clear the site for his church – which was difficult not only because part of a hill had to be cut away, but also because the burials from the necropolis that had to be removed were protected by law and religious convention, and yet the graves had to be opened and filled in or destroyed.

Was Constantine right in his conviction? We cannot tell. All we can say is that there had been a monument to Peter there since at least AD 160–70. There is, of course, a gap of nearly a hundred years between the supposed date of the martyrdom of Peter and AD 160–70. Can one assume that the tradition which bridged that gap was correct and reliable? It needs faith, as well as archaeology, to say so. It is certainly possible that Peter was buried under what is now his Basilica. But it cannot be proved.

As to Peter's bones, it is not at all unlikely that the bodies of those who had been executed were all thrown into a common pit. A determined attempt has been made to claim that *his* bones have been found, but this has not met with general acceptance. It is, once again, *possible* that some faithful admirer of Peter succeeded in hunting out his body or his bones, extracted them from the pit and reverently placed them in a casket. But, as before, it cannot be proved. Nor can it even be regarded as very plausible – conceivably the bones that were found are those of some early bishop of Rome. (Nor was it considered desirable or necessary by the early Christians to preserve the relics of martyrs, since the End of the World was believed to be at hand.)

The Roman church, meanwhile, had already acquired its position of leadership and dominance by the second century AD, because of a combination of its activities and its presence in the imperial capital, and Damasus and many others were merely reinforcing this point.

Bibliographical note

On the 'jealousy' or 'zeal' of Peter, see C. P. Thiede, *Simon Peter: From Galilee to Rome* (1986), pp. 239f. n. 205; R. Pesch, *Simon-Petrus* (1980), p. 169; *cf.* Psalms 69.9.

For the martyrdom of Peter, see Pesch, op. cit., pp. 113f.; O. Cullmann, *Peter: Disciple, Apostle, Martyr* (1962), pp. 88f., 114. J. Munck, *Petrus und Paulus in der Offenbarung Johannis* (1950), argued that Revelation 11, 3–12, 'two witnesses', alludes to Peter and Paul. J. Lowe, *Saint Peter* (1956), p. 27, disagrees. One of the 'twelve' in the Ascension of Isaiah, 3.4, is probably Peter: Cullmann, op. cit., p. 112. For some of the vast martyrological literature, see Pesch, op. cit., p. 129; M. Guarducci, *La tomba di San Pietro: una straordinaria vicenda* (1989), pp. 14f. (*cf.* details in her bibliographical note, p. 182). Peter's martyrdom was wrongly ascribed to the site of the Church of S. Pietro in Montorio at Rome, hence the Tempietto there (1502). For Peter's alleged crucifixion upside-down, *cf.* the relief in the shrine of Sixtus IV (1471–84) in Saint Peter's, and Michelangelo's 'Crucifixion of Peter' in the Cappella Paolina of the Vatican.

On the burial-place of Peter, see J. M. C. Toynbee and J. B. Ward-Perkins, *The Shrine of St Peter and the Vatican Excavations* (1956); E. E. Kirschbaum, *The Tombs of St Peter and St Paul* (1959); A. A. de Marco, *The Tomb of St Peter: A Representative Bibliography of the Excavations*

(1964); Guarducci, op. cit. (extensive bibliography, see above); J. Lees-Milne, *Saint Peter's* (1967), pp. 71–7, 79f., 96ff., 142; J. B. Ward-Perkins, *Encyclopaedia Britannica* (1971) edn), Vol. XVIII, p. 735; W. Jordan, *Das Apostelgrab: der sakrale Grundstein der Vatikanischen Basilika* (1990).

On the pagan necropolis beneath St Peter's, see H. Mielsch and H. von Hesberg, *Die heidnische Nekropole unter Sankt Peter*, Vol. I, 1986, Vol. II, 1992/3 (*Memorie della Pontificia Accademia Romana di Archeologia*, ser. III, 16, 1 and 2). A third volume by W. Eck and G. Daltrop is being published.

The San Sebastiano excavations leave many unanswered riddles about the Appian Way: Cullmann, op. cit., pp. 132–5; Lowe, op. cit., p. 40; M. Guarducci, *Mélanges de l'École Française à Rome*, XCVIII, 1986, pp. 811ff.

For how the Festival of Romulus was replaced by a Christian festival, see Lowe, op. cit., p. 36.

On Peter's bones, see Guarducci, *La tomba di San Pietro* (1989), pp. 75ff.; Thiede, op. cit., p. 256 nn. 350 and 351; Pesch, op. cit., p. 132; Lowe, op. cit., p. 45 ('possible'); J. K. Elliott, *Questioning Christian Origins* (1982), p. 127 ('inconclusive'). P. Poupart is now said to have dismissed the find as 'unauthentic' (1991). D. Browder suggested in 1958 that the bones might be those of an early bishop of Rome.

EPILOGUE

While the supposed tomb of Peter at Rome, in the second century AD and later, came to be treated with increasing reverence – leading eventually to the construction of Constantine's massive Basilica – a doctrinal and literary conflict was going on about the relative roles of Peter and Paul in the Christian tradition.

This conflict is already perceptible in the Gospels, where an anti-Petrine element was imperfectly assimilated with pro-Petrine material. In *Acts* an effort was made to reconcile the two points of view, by balancing the alleged deeds of the two men in parallel narratives, without stressing their differences. These had become a subject to be avoided after the opinion that both Peter and Paul had suffered martyrdom became an established belief.

The subsequent career and ultimate end of Peter are not described in the New Testament. This is probably because its books, and even those most inclined to commend him, are dependent on sources influenced from an early period by Paul and his teaching, which viewed Peter with disfavour.

An endeavour was made, at quite an early date, to have another look at what Peter had done, and to rehabilitate him, but by the end of the first century AD this process had not reached completion. There was quite an ample tradition in his favour, but it had been suppressed and never fully came to light again. Subsequent attempts were, indeed, made to resuscitate this pro-Petrine material. But for the most part they proved unsuccessful, and what Peter really achieved was forgotten.

As for Rome, however, the link that the place had claimed with the two greatest apostles was continually restated and emphasized. As was stated at the end of the last chapter, Rome had come to occupy a strong position: it could make more impressive and influential claims than any other city.

Thus, not long after the Gospel of Matthew, Ignatius expounded a fairly developed view of the episcopal office, in relation to Rome and, furthermore, it had an *embarras de richesses* as regards resident apostles' – not one apostle only, but two, were believed to have resided in the city. However, in the long run it was Peter, despite his controversial status in early Christianity, who was rated as the more impressive founder of the Church – which, increasingly, came to mean the Church of Rome – because he had come to be regarded as the principal apostle, the closest companion of Jesus, and the beneficiary of the famous 'Rock and Keys' text in the Gospel According to Saint Matthew. It was in about AD 250 that Roman churchmen began to draw attention to this passage, in order to demonstrate Rome's primacy (in the first instance with the specific purpose of reducing the voluble bishop of Carthage, St Cyprian, to size).

This raised the whole question of the conjunction of Peter and Paul. Their presumed association, at Rome, had become a central feature of the Christian faith; Ignatius bracketed them together, and by about 200, although they had differed to such a considerable extent during their lives, they were firmly linked with one another as residents and martyrs in Rome, by the approximately ten million Christians worldwide. As a result, their heads appeared conjointly on works of art.

But then there was a gradual change – involving the demotion of Paul. Its major cause was the 'heresy', in the second century, of

Marcion, who tried to elevate Paul to an immensely high position, declaring him to have been the only true apostle. This proved counterproductive because, by way of reaction against this extreme view, Paul, far from retaining that elevated position, lost any retrospective claim to have been the equal of Peter. So when the primacy of Rome came to be asserted, Peter, without Paul, was claimed to have been the founder of the Roman Church, and its first bishop, or Pope. The 'union' of the two men, however, was not altogether forgotten or dismissed, thus a mosaic in the Mausoleum of Constantia (S. Costanza) at Rome (c.345) depicts Jesus entrusting Peter and Paul with the scroll of the new Covenant, and in the same fourth century, also at Rome, there were great Basilicas not only of one of them, but of both. There is a fine fourth- or fifth-century relief with both their portraits, and the practice of conjoining them continued, since ten frescos of the later thirteenth century at St Peter's (destroyed by Pope Paul v, 1605–21) depicted both men.

Nevertheless the reputation and mystique of Peter, on his own, continued to persist and ultimately prevailed. In particular, the widely read writings of St Gregory I the Great, who occupied the Papacy between AD 585 and 604, induced belief in Peter's residence in Rome and in the miracles that he was supposed to have performed. Indeed, there was a popular, mystical conviction that Peter himself *was still bodily there*: that he had never ceased to dwell in the city.

Later, in the eighth century AD, this special connection of Peter with Rome was further stressed and exploited. His prestige increased, and so did the conviction that he was still among the people, as he had always been. This doctrine gained such emphasis and prominence in the eighth century because of political situations that had arisen, which meant that the relationship of Rome to the outside world needed to be defined in new ways and with a new intensity.

The most important of such situations arose when the Papacy's relations with the Byzantine empire deteriorated during the period after 726. One extraordinary development was the *Donation of Constantine*, which took the form of an alleged grant by the emperor Constantine the Great to Pope Sylvester I (314–35) – and, by deliberate implication, to all Popes after him – of spiritual supremacy over the other major patriarchates, and temporal dominion over the entire western world. But the Donation was a forgery, composed either at Rome or, more probably, in the Frankish empire during the second half of the eighth century. It was based on the conviction that Sylvester I, and all subsequent Popes, were direct successors of Peter as bishops of Rome. Indeed, its contents included a fictitious account of Constantine placing the document upon the body of Peter himself, as a gift to him.

Throughout all these centuries, and those that followed, the artistic depictions of Peter continued, although they remained entirely imaginary, since no one knew (or knows) what his physical characteristics were. Like Jesus, Peter was not reckoned important enough to be portrayed in his lifetime. 'The tradition whereby artists portray Peter as a stout, half-balding, elderly man clearly reflects the influence of his later Apostolic authority.'[2] Nevertheless, in spite of complete uncertainty about his appearance, representations abounded. Peter's miraculous catch of fish is a favourite theme in early art. 'Portraits' of Peter going back at least to the later second century have survived. The oldest certain representation was found in the catacomb under the Church of S. Agnese fuori le Mura at Rome. Fourth-century sarcophagi depict the lives of Christ and Peter in a single row of figures; and on some of these sarcophagi Peter is made to look like both Adam and Moses,[3] by no means owing to any supposed physical resemblance, but for typological reasons: like Adam he had Fallen, and like Moses he had led.

There is a thirteenth-century head in the crypt of Saint Peter's, and above ground, in the same church, can be seen the superb bronze seated statue of the Apostle, possibly a Constantinian or medieval adaptation (ascribed to Arnolfo di Cambio (c. 1248–1302), of a statue of a philosopher or senator, which is reproduced by a faithful copy in London's Brompton Oratory. Giotto (1266/7–1337) made a mosaic for Saint Peter's, the 'Navicella', of Peter walking on the Sea of Galilee.

Perhaps the finest conceptions of all are the frescos by Masaccio (c.1424) and Filippino Lippi, which are in the Church of S. Maria del Carmine at Florence, and have recently been cleaned. Peter also attracted the attention of Gentile da Fabbriano (c.1370–1427) (*Christ and Peter*), Conrad Witz (c.1400–45) ('*La pêche miraculeuse*') and Melozzo da Forlì (c.1480). Raphael's ten Vatican tapestries (1516–19), of which seven original cartoons were lent by the British Royal Collection to the Victoria and Albert Museum (where they are, for the present, not on show), display Jesus commanding Peter to 'feed my sheep' ('Christ's Charge to Peter'), Peter's Miraculous Draught of Fishes, his Healing of the Lame Man in the Temple, and his miraculous striking down of Ananias. Titian (c.1487/1490–1576) portrayed him in the church of the Frari (S. M. Gloriosa dei Frari), at Venice. El Greco (1541–1614) saw him as a poor simple man, and Guido Reni (1575–1642) made him look spiritual. Nicolas Poussin (1593/4–1665) depicted the *Sacrament of Ordination*.

Perhaps I may conclude with a personal view of how St Peter seems to me, after the examination of his career that I have attempted. It is curious that the Gospels have such a poor opinion of him, but this is due partly to conflicts on the subject within the Church, and partly also to the evangelists' desire to show up the disciples, of whom he was the leader, as fallible human beings in contrast to the divine driving force of Jesus to whom they owed everything.

It appears to be a historical fact that Jesus deliberately chose Peter as his principal apostle. Why did he do this? It would be too cynical to conclude that he did so primarily because Peter and his family had a convenient house in the Galilean region in which Jesus conducted his mission. There must have been more to it than that. True, there seems to be some substance in the traditional Gospel picture of Peter as impetuous, impulsive, hasty and not over-reflective. But he was utterly devoted to the personality and mission of Jesus. I think that it was because of Peter's wholehearted, unreserved devotion, dedication and faith – highlighted rather than diminished by incidents such as the Denials, if they are authentic – that Jesus selected him as his chief disciple, or as the representative of the rest.

If that is correct, then Peter was Jesus's principal follower, the second person in the story of Christianity, and thus a figure of enormous, overwhelming significance in the history of the world.

Next we come to that terrible, traumatic time after Jesus's death. I have said a good deal about the Resurrection of Jesus. And Peter, who was evidently an arch-visionary, figured prominently in what were claimed to be the Appearances of the risen Jesus, which played a large part in justifying the role which Peter proceeded to assume. That role was nothing less than the leadership of the little, scattered, sad and depressed band of those who still believed in Jesus and his mission. It was a remarkable achievement of Peter to sustain and encourage them, to hold them together and increase their numbers, and this success reveals a powerful additional facet of his character. Only a person of determination, authority and charisma could have seen his companions through this intensely difficult period, and now one begins to understand better why Jesus had felt such confidence in his qualities. They were shown to the full after Jesus was dead.

But then came the period when Peter was edged aside and lost his leadership of the group – under pressure from envoys of James. Paul declared that Peter had shown 'fear', but I have suggested in this book that what he rather displayed was diplomatic skill. For all his impetuosity, Peter was essentially the mediator, the man of compromise, the moderate figure who tried to bridge the gulf between extremists on either side. This is an unwelcome, unpopular part to play, but it is a valuable and essential role, and once again it throws some light on the reasons why Jesus had thought so highly of Peter. After a bit, however, some years after Jesus's death, Peter had to pay the inevitable penalty for this moderate, intermediary stance. For it cost him the leadership of the Jerusalem church.

As we have seen, what happened next is shrouded in some mystery, but it seems likely that Peter made his way to Rome and became one of the martyrs of Nero's persecution. What is beyond doubt is that his name and reputation thereafter became so elevated that he was seen as a mighty personage, and indeed, in the eyes of many Catholics, as the first Pope of their Church. Amid the fantastic

accumulation of legends about St Peter, there has been much concentration on this problem, so long and profoundly debated
between Catholics and Protestants, of whether St Peter is entitled
to a primacy from which the papal office and all true Christianity
since that time should be derived.

The present book has avoided these questions. It has endeavoured, instead, to find out who Peter really was, what he did and
what happened to him. Certainly, historians have to concern themselves with the vast proliferation of legendary material, in order to
see if any truth lies behind it – and in addition, because it has affected
the *history* of subsequent epochs. But these legends must be carefully
segregated and left aside when we set ourselves the task of trying to
reconstruct the life and person of Peter himself, which are quite
remarkable enough, indeed almost uniquely remarkable, even
without the gigantic superstructure of fabricated, controversial and
conflict-inspired accretions.

This superstructure has been erected because Peter has been
revered by innumerable people throughout the ages. 'No wonder
they like to petition Peter to intercede with the Almighty on their
behalf and that of their friends in the great community of the faithful.
They have done so since time immemorial.'[4]

There have been many books and articles about Peter – though far
fewer, owing to lack of material, than those relating to Paul. And
there have been many other writings which make incidental references to his life and career. The question may well be asked,
therefore, whether another book was needed, and whether it has
had anything to add.

I am inclined to answer this question by saying that, after all these
works have been read, Saint Peter still seems enigmatic. There is a
great deal in his career that appears evanescent and obscure, and it
was this that tempted me to the subject. I can only hope that I have
helped to clear some of the mysteries up, or at least to present them
in the terms that they deserve.

Part of the obscurity has been caused by prejudices. The writers
of the Gospels had strong prejudices of their own, and inherited

others from the communities to which they belonged. And the Christian churches which followed throughout the ensuing centuries added powerful biases of their own, which are, indeed, still with us, and are fully echoed and documented by the sources to which reference is made in this survey.

What I have tried to do is to approach the matter, and discuss its problems, without being influenced by any such prejudices. That is, of course, hard if not impossible, seeing that we are all brought up in an environment that cannot fail to affect us. Nevertheless, I have endeavoured to avoid such snares, while at the same time not ignoring the various points of view that others have expressed. I have also tried to see Peter, and the authors of the Gospels, in the light of what was being thought when they were alive: the discussion of miracles, visions and typology in Chapter 1 has something to say about this.

In any case it was, I am sure, a task that had to be attempted. As I pointed out at the start, Peter is one of the most significant people who has ever lived, and it must surely be worthwhile to bring together whatever facts can be known about him. Peter was significant for two reasons, both of which I have discussed in some detail, and both of which remain firmly fixed in the historical picture. In the first place Jesus chose him as his principal helper; the man who was assigned that remarkable honour and responsibility must have been very far from negligible. Second, after the appalling event of Jesus's Crucifixion, it was Peter who collected his disheartened followers together and formed them into a Christian community. This was a tremendously difficult task, and the person who was able to do it must have exercised an extraordinary influence. Moreover, unless Peter had done this, Jesus's endeavours would never have survived. Paul could not have achieved this without Peter's work immediately after the Crucifixion; and so, without Peter, there would have been no Christian Church either in the subsequent centuries or today.

Bibliographical note

On the Donation of Constantine, see W. Ullmann, *A History of Political Thought: The Middle Ages* (1965), pp. 81–5, 97f. For the Constantinian Basilica at Rome, see M. Grant, *The Emperor Constantine* (1993), pp. 204f.

The iconography of Peter is discussed by G. Duchet-Suchaux and M. Pastoureau, *Le Bible et les Saints: guide iconographique* (1990), pp. 263f. A. Grabar, *Christian Iconography: A Study of Its Origins* (1961). For Masaccio's Peter at S. Maria del Carmine at Florence, see M. Carniani, *S. Maria del Carmine and the Brancacci Chapel* (1992), pp. 55, 62–73.

REFERENCES

Chapter 1   *The Problems of Research*

1. R. E. Brown, K. P. Donfried and L. Reumann (eds), *Peter in the New Testament* (1973), p. 166.
2. O. Cullmann, *Peter: Disciple, Apostle, Martyr* (1962), pp. 69f.
3. *Acts* 2.22.
4. R. M. Grant, *A Historical Introduction to the New Testament* (1963), p. 315.
5. *John* 21.25.
6. *Exodus* 4.8, etc.
7. *Matt.* 17.27.
8. C. L. Mitton, *Jesus: The Fact Behind the Faith* (1973), p. 72; *cf.* E. P. Cox, *Saint Matthew* (1952), p. 117.
9. R. V. G. Tasker, *The Gospel According to Saint Matthew* (1961), pp. 145f.; *pace* C. P. Thiede, *Simon Peter: From Galilee to Rome* (1986), p. 217 n. 35.
10. *John* 11.4, 25.
11. *Matt.* 14.25; *John* 6.19; *cf. Job* 9.8 and *Psalms of Solomon* 39.8.
12. *Luke* 8.24.
13. E.g. *Apocalypse of Peter.*

14. *Mark* 9.2–8.
15. *Mark* 8.22–6.
16. *Acts* 5.15, 19.11.
17. R. Lane Fox, *The Unauthorised Version: Truth and Fiction in the Bible* (1991), pp. 10, 210.
18. M. Smith, *Jesus the Magician* (1978), p. 55.
19. J. Kahl, *The Misery of Christianity* (1971), pp. 121f.
20. *Cf.* G. Turner, *New Blackfriars*, LVI, 661, 1975, p. 273; C. W. Martini, *Theology Digest*, XXII, 2, 1974, p. 110.
21. Mitton, op. cit., pp. 53ff.
22. *Acts* 2.4.
23. *Acts* 2.11; *cf.* *1 Cor.* 14.4–6, 27.
24. *Acts* 2.13, 15.
25. A. W. F. Blunt, *The Clarendon Bible* p. 317.
26. H. Schonfield, *The Pentecost Revolution* (1985), pp. 110ff.
27. *Cf. Amos* 4.13; *Proverbs* 30.4.
28. W. D. Davies and D. C. Allison, *The Gospel According to St Matthew*, Vol. I (1988), pp. 491, 493.
29. *Testament of Zebulun* 6.6; *Luke* 5.1–11.
30. *John* 8.48f.
31. *Luke* 24.23.
32. *Acts* 7.55.
33. *Acts* 5.19, 12.7; Lane Fox, op. cit., p. 373.
34. *Acts* 10.17.
35. *2 Peter* 1.16.
36. *Acts* 9.3–9, 22.6–11.
37. *Pseudo-Clementine Homilies* 17.19.
38. *Exodus* 32.16.
39. *Numbers* 12.3.
40. *Matt.* 17.4, 10–12.
41. M. D. Goulder, *Theology*, LXXIX, 260, 1976, p. 211.
42. *Mark* 8.28.
43. *Luke* 4.17.
44. *Isaiah* 62.1–2.
45. *Psalms* 118.26; *Zechariah* 9.9.
46. *Luke* 22.64.
47. *Luke* 24.27.
48. *Mark* 14.49.

49. *Acts* 7.1–39.
50. *Acts* 3.25.
51. *Hebrews* 8.8–10, 12.24, 13.20.
52. *Acts* 26.22.
53. Justin Martyr, 1 *Apology*, 30.
54. Augustine, *City of God*, 22.30.
55. *Matt.* 5.17; *cf.* W. D. Davies and D. C. Allison, *The Gospel According to St Matthew*, Vol. I (1988), pp. 481–503, Vol. II (1991), p. 726.
56. J. Barr, *Holy Scripture: Canon, Authority, Criticism* (1983), p. 15; E. C. Hoskyns and N. Davey, *Crucifixion – Resurrection* (1981), p. 181.
57. B. Lindars, *New Testament Studies*, XXIII, 1976, p. 77.
58. *Matt.* 4.20; *Mark* 1.18; *Luke* 5.11; *cf. 1 Kings* 19.19–21.

Chapter 2   *The Sources*

1. On the *Gospel of Thomas*, and other non-canonical Gospels, see R. Cameron (ed)., *The Other Gospels* (1982).
2. E.g. *Luke* 1.1–4; *John* 20.30–1.
3. J. N. Wenham, *Redating Matthew, Mark and Luke* (1991); *cf.* J. A. T. Robinson, *The Priority of John* (1985).
4. E. C. Hoskyns and N. Davey, *Crucifixion – Resurrection* (1981), p. 297.
5. H. H. Hobbs, *The Gospel of Mark*, p. 111.
6. *Letter to Theodore*; M. Smith, *Clement of Alexandria and a Secret Gospel of Saint Mark* (1973), pp. 19–23; *cf.* C. P. Thiede, *Simon Peter: From Galilee to Rome* (1986), p. 248 n. 60, p. 234 n. 172.
7. *Mark* 13.14.
8. *Mark* 15.38.
9. *Cf.* J. A. Fitzmyer, *The Gospel According to Luke* (1981), p. 69; W. D. Davies and D. C. Allison, *The Gospel According to St Matthew*, Vol. I (1988), pp. 12, 327.
10. For modern writings on various aspects of Mark, see bibliographical note, p. 48
11. M. Goulder, *Theology*, LXXIX, 1976, p. 214 n. 1.
12. Eusebius, *Church History*, Vol. III, 39, 14f.
13. Ibid., 15.
14. B. P. Robinson, *Journal of Studies of the New Testament*, XXI, 1984, p. 101 n. 20.

15. On *Matt.*, see Fitzmyer, op. cit., pp. 35, 63f., 66, 89.
16. *Colossians* 4.14.
17. Fitzmyer, op. cit., pp. 42, 45f.
18. W. G. Kümmel, *Introduction to the New Testament* (1975), pp. 129f.
19. *Cf.* M. Grant, *Jesus* (1977), p. 121 and n. 46.
20. C. P. Thiede (ed,), *Das Petrusbild in der neueren Forschung* (1986), p. 225.
21. Fitzmyer, op. cit., p. 88.
22. R. Lane Fox, *The Unauthorised Version: Truth and Fiction in the Bible* (1991), pp. 124, 203ff.
23. R. E. Brown, K. P. Donfried and L. Reumann (eds), *Peter in the New Testament* (1973), pp. lxxxviiiff., xcii, xciv, 134 n. 285.
24. H. Schonfield, *Those Incredible Christians* (1985), p. 184; *cf.* pp. 180f.
25. *John* 21.24.
26. S. Brown, *The Origins of Christianity* (1984), p. 117 (*cf.* p. 144); F. J. Cwiekowski, *The Beginnings of the Church* (1988), pp. 168f.
27. *John* 19.5.
28. *John* 1.41.
29. A. H. Maynard, *New Testament Studies*, XXX, 1984; G. Snyder, *Biblical Research*, XVI, 1971, pp. 5–15.
30. *John* 20.1–9.
31. *John* 21.4, 8.
32. *John* 13.23f.
33. *John* 21.20–3.
34. *John* 20.2, 8.
35. R. E. Brown, *The Gospel According to John* (1966), p. 1007.
36. Ibid., pp. 1077–85.
37. W. C. van Unnik, *Studies in Luke-Acts: Essays presented in Honor of P. Schubert* (1966), p. 16.
38. Thiede, *Simon Peter*, op. cit., p. 234 n. 172.
39. *Acts* 16.10ff., 20.5ff.
40. *Acts* 1.1.
41. Fitzmyer, op. cit., p. 10; M. Grant, *Saint Paul* (1982), p. 178.
42. E.g. Thiede, op. cit., p. 251 n. 285; *cf.* pp. 175, 184.
43. *1 Peter* 1.1.
44. *1 Peter* 1.6.
45. *1 Peter* 5.13.
46. Ibid.

47. *1 Peter* 5.12; *cf. 2 Cor. 1.19; 1 Thessalonians* 1.1.
48. *Acts* 15.22, 17.4.
49. *1 Peter* 1.13.
50. *1 Peter* 5.1–3.
51. *1 Peter* 2.13–15.
52. *1 Peter* 1.19–21.
53. Thiede, op. cit., pp. 173, 181–3, 251 nn. 28ff., 252 nn. 306f.; doubted by J. L. McKenzie, *Dictionary of the Bible* p. 667.
54. *2 Peter* 1.16.
55. *2 Peter* 3.16.
56. *2 Peter* 2.9, 1.14.

Chapter 3   The Calling of Peter

1. *Mark* 1.16–18; *cf. Matt.* 4.18–20.
2. *Luke* 5.1–11.
3. *John* 1.35–42.
4. Herodotus III.42; R. Pesch, *Simon-Petrus* (1980), p. 35.
5. *1 Kings* 19.19–21.
6. E. C. Hoskyns and N. Davey, *Crucifixion – Resurrection* (1981), p. 212.
7. *Acts* 1.21f.
8. *Matt.* 8.14; *Mark* 1.29; *Luke* 4.38 (if chronology correct).
9. *John* 21.17.
10. *Isaiah* 9.1; *Matt.* 4.15.
11. *Matt.* 11.21; *Luke* 10.13.
12. D. Tiede, *Jesus and the Future* (1990), p. 36.
13. C. P. Thiede, *Simon Peter: From Galilee to Rome* (1986), p. 21.
14. *Mark* 9.49; *Luke* 14.34.
15. Strabo, *Geography*, XVI, 2, 45.
16. *Cf.* H. Mayr-Harting, *Times Literary Supplement*, 26 December 1986, p. 1447.
17. *Cf.* above, note 8.
18. *Matt.* 11.23; *Luke* 10.15.
19. S. and H. Shanks, in C. P. Thiede (ed.), *Das Petrusbild in der neueren Forschung* (1986), pp. 145ff.
20. *1 Cor.* 9.5.
21. Clement of Alexandria, *Stromateis*, VII, 63.3.

22. *Cf.* J. Lees-Milne, *Saint Peter's* (1967), pp. 14–17.

23. *Matt.* 16.18; *John* 1.42.

24. *Isaiah* 28.16; W. D. Davies and D. C. Allison, *The Gospel According to St Matthew*, Vol. II (1991), pp. 627f.

25. *Cf.* H. Maccoby, *Times Literary Supplement*, 31 January 1986, p. 114.

26. M. Wilcox, *New Testament Studies*, XXII, 1975/6, p. 85.

27. *Acts* 4.11; *cf. Shepherd of Hermas.*

28. *Isaiah* 8.14; R. E. Brown, K. P. Donfried and L. Reumann (eds), *Peter in the New Testament* (1974), pp. 94f. n. 218.

29. Clement of Alexandria (deprecating Peter), K. Lake, *Harvard Theological Review*, XIV, 1921, pp. 95ff.; Pesch, op. cit., p. 101 n. 26.

30. A. E. Harvey, *Companion to the Gospels* (1970), p. 68.

31. *Mark* 3.17.

32. Davies and Allison op. cit., p. 627; D. E. Nineham, *Saint Mark* (1963), p. 116; and D. Attwater, *Dictionary of Saints* (2nd ed., 1983), p. 185; R. Lane Fox, *The Unauthorised Version: Truth and Fiction in the Bible* (1991), p. 208.

33. *Genesis* 17.5.

34. *Matt.* 17.1; *Mark* 9.2; *Luke* 9.28.

35. *Mark* 5.37.

36. *Luke* 22.8.

37. *Matt.* 16.17.

38. *Mark* 9.34, 10.37ff.; *Luke* 22.24.

39. *John* 6.70.

40. Davies and Allison, op. cit., p. 152.

41. *Matt.* 19.28.

42. *Revelation* 21.12–14.

43. On these proselytes see M. Grant, *The Jews in the Roman World* (1973), p. 61.

44. *Matt.* 10.40; *Luke* 10.16.

45. *Luke* 9.2.

46. *Matt.* 6.24f.; *Luke* 12.22.

47. *Luke* 10.17.

48. *Matt.* 17.16.

49. *Job* 2.12.

50. *Letter of Barnabas* 5.

51. *Mark* 8.17f.; *cf.* 7.18.

52. *Mark* 14.50.

53. *Matt.* 8.26.

Chapter 4 Peter's Weaknesses and Strengths

1. *Matt.* 16.16 (*Luke* 9.20: 'the Christ of God').
2. *Enoch, Testament of Levi*; B. P. Robinson, *Journal of Studies of the New Testament*, XXI, 1984, p. 110 note.
3. *Mark* 8.29.
4. *Matt.* 16.20–3; C. P. Thiede, *Simon Peter: From Galilee to Rome* (1986), p. 33; R. E. Brown, K. P. Donfried and L. Reumann (eds), *Peter in the New Testament* (1973), pp. 67f. and n. 154, p. 160.
5. *Luke* 9.21.
6. M. Grant, *Saint Paul* (1982) p. 66 (references).
7. R. Harries, *Christ is Risen* (1988), p. 102; G. W. E. Nickelsburg, *Resurrection, Immortality and Eternal Life* (1972).
8. J. G. Davies, *The Early Christian Church* (1965), p. 27; M. Grant, *Jesus* (1972), p. 96.
9. *Mark* 8.33 (toned down by *Matt.* 16.17–19): O. Cullmann, *Peter: Disciple, Apostle, Martyr* (1962), p. 179; C. P. Thiede, *Simon Peter: From Galilee to Rome* (1986), pp. 34f.; J. C. Fenton, *Saint Matthew* (1963), p. 79.
10. *Matt.* 4.1–11; *Luke* 4.9–12, etc.
11. *Job* 1.6–12, 2.1–8.
12. *Gal.* 2.11–14.
13. *Mark* 9.5; *Matt.* 17.4; *Luke* 9.33.
14. *Mark* 9.6; *Luke*, loc. cit. (or 'did not know what to say').
15. *Mark* , loc. cit.
16. *Matt.* 15.16.
17. *Matt.* 14.31.
18. *Mark* 14.37.
19. *Luke* 22.51.
20. *Mark* 14.29–31.
21. *Mark* 14.66–72.
22. J. A. Fitzmyer, *The Gospel According to Luke* (1981), p. 1426; W. L. Craig, *New Testament Studies*, XXXI, 1985, p. 55.
23. *Matt.* 26.75; *Mark* 14.72; *Luke* 22.62.
24. *Matt.* 14.31.
25. *Acts* 4.13.

26. *Mark* 14.70.
27. *Luke* 5.8.
28. *John* 13.6–9.
29. A.-M. La Bonnardière, *Irénikon*, XXXIV, 1961, pp. 451–99; R. E. Brown *et al.*, op. cit., p. 95.
30. *Mark* 9.23; *cf.* 16.17, etc.
31. *Mark* 10.28.
32. *John* 6.67–9.

Chapter 5   Peter and Jesus

1. See the bibliographical note, p. 47.
2. *Matt.* 11.14.
3. *Micah* 5.2.
4. W. D. Davies and D. C. Allison, *The Gospel According to St Matthew*, Vol. II (1991), p. 469.
5. *Luke* 13.31.
6. *John* 1.7–8; *Matt.* 11.7–10.
7. *John* 1.8–9; *Matt.* 11.11.
8. *Mark* 10.14; *Luke* 18.15.
9. M. Grant, *Jesus* (1977), pp. 98ff.
10. *Matt.* 16.13–20.
11. *Matt.* 11.21, 23; *Luke* 10.13.
12. *Matt.* 16.21, 17.22–3, 20.18–19, etc.
13. *Matt.* 21.12; *Mark* 11.15; *Luke* 19.45; *John* 2.14.

Chapter 6   Peter and the Resurrection

1. M. Grant, *Saint Paul* (1982), p. 82.
2. *1 Cor.* 15.14.
3. J. S. Whale, *Christian Doctrine* (1957 ed. [1941]) p. 66.
4. *Rom.* 1.4.
5. *1 Peter* 1.3–4.
6. *1 Cor.* 15.55.
7. *2 Cor.* 5.17.
8. *Luke* 24.44–7.
9. *Mark* 13.24–7; *cf. Daniel* 9.27, 12.12.

10. *Testament of Benjamin*, 10.8; *2 Esdras* 7.35.
11. *Cf.* Tertullian, *De Carne Christi* 5.
12. *Acts* 17.18, 30–2.
13. *Mark* 6.14.
14. *Acts* 2.23.
15. *Gospel of Peter* 35–42.
16. *Mark* 9.9–10; *Luke* 9.22, 43–5.
17. J. Reuf, *Paul's First Letter to Corinth* (1971), p. 160; E. C. Hoskyns and N. Davey, *Crucifixion – Resurrection* (1981), p. 281 and n. 4, p. 288.
18. *Exodus* 3.4–6, 33.20–3; *Judges* 13.3–20.
19. J. A. Fitzmyer, *The Gospel According to Luke* (1981), p. 1557.
20. *1 Cor.* 15.3–8.
21. *Luke* 24.34; *Matt.* 28.1–10; *Mark* 16.1–10.
22. *1 Cor.* 1.23.
23. C. L. Mitton, *Jesus: The Fact Behind the Faith* (1973), p. 54.
24. *Acts* 10.41; *cf. 2.32, 5.32*.
25. *1 Cor.* 15.6.
26. *Luke* 24.11; *1 Cor.* 15.12; *cf.* Thomas, *John* 20.24–9.
27. *Luke* 24.12f.
28. Origen, *Against Celsus* 2.62/68.
29. *Luke* 24.33–51.
30. *1 Cor.* 15.5ff.
31. Ibid. 15.8.
32. S. Brown, *The Origins of Christianity* (1984), pp. 82ff.
33. R. Annand, *Scottish Journal of Theology*, XI, 1958, pp. 180–7; *pace* R. E. Brown, K. P. Donfried and L. Reumann (eds), *Peter in the New Testament* (1973), p. 125 n. 270.
34. F. Gils, *Ephemerides Theologicae Lovanienses*, XXXVIII, 1962, pp. 42f.
35. Fitzmyer, op. cit., p. 1569.
36. *Luke* 24.36f., 42f.
37. *Matt.* 22.30; *Mark* 12.25.
38. Augustine, *City of God*, XIII, 22.
39. *Acts* 1.3.
40. C. F. D. Monk, *New Testament Studies*, IV, 1957–8, pp. 58ff.; H. Hendrickx, *Resurrection Narratives* (1978), p. 15.
41. *Genesis* 29.3–10; *Joshua* 10.18.
42. Hendrickx, op. cit., p. 116; M. Brändle, *Theology Digest*, XVI, 1, 1968, pp. 18ff.

43. *Matt.* 28.13–15.
44. *John* 20.15; Tertullian, *De Spectaculis*, 30.
45. *Daniel* 7.9, etc.; *Matt.* 28.2ff.; *Mark* 16.5ff.; *Luke* 24.4 (two).
46. *Acts* 2.31 (Authorised Version).
47. *Mark* 16.19; *Luke* 24.50; *Acts* 1.9–11, 2.33, 3.21; *Philippians* 2.9. See also the bibliographical note, p. 102.
48. R. E. Brown, *The Gospel According to John* (1966), p. 1013.
49. *Acts* 3.20. See also the bibliographical note, p. 102.
50. R. E. Brown, op. cit., p. cxvii.
51. *Hosea* 6.2; *2 Kings* 20.5; *cf. Jonah* 1.17 and *Matt.* 12.40.
52. C. H. Dodd, in D. E. Nineham, *Studies in the Gospels: Essays in Honour of R. H. Lightfoot (1955)*.
53. *1 Cor.* 15.8; *Gal.* 1.16.
54. *1 Cor.* 15.42–9.
55. *John* 11.1–43 (39: 'there will be a stench').
56. Origen, *On the Resurrection*, 79.
57. *1 Cor.* 15.23 (36: 'what a stupid question!').
58. *Philippians* 3.10f.

Chapter 7   *The Leadership of Peter*

1. *John* 21.3.
2. *Matt.* 16.19.
3. *John* 1.42.
4. B. P. Robinson, *Journal for the Study of the New Testament*, XXI, 1984, p. 98; O. Cullmann, *Peter: Disciple, Apostle, Martyr* (1962), pp. 220ff.; R. E. Brown, *The Gospel According to John* (1966), p. 1088; R. Pesch, *Simon-Petrus* (1980), p. 96.
5. *Isaiah* 22.22.
6. *Cf. Revelation* 1.18; *2 Enoch* 40.9–11; *B. Sanhedrin*, 113a.
7. *Matt.* 23.13.
8. *Matt.* 18.18.
9. *Matt.* 16.18.
10. W. D. Davies and D. C. Allison, *The Gospel According to St Matthew*, Vol. II (1991), p. 613; *cf.* the Dead Sea Scrolls, ibid., pp. 611, 629; C. Rowland, *Christian Origins* (1985), p. 153.
11. *Luke* 22.32.
12. *John* 21.15–17.

13. H. Hendrickx, *Resurrection Narratives* (1978), pp. 63ff.
14. *Matt.* 16.18 (or 'the gates of death will never close on it').
15. *Mark* 16.7.
16. *Acts* 1.13.
17. *Gal.* 1.18.
18. *Acts* 4.3, 5.18, 12.3.
19. *Acts* 1.15, 2.5–6, 3.11, 6.1, 9.31.
20. *Acts* 1.26.
21. *Acts* 6.1–6.
22. H. Schonfield, *The Pentecost Revolution* (1985), pp. 102f., 146; *Those Incredible Christians* (1985), p. 180.
23. Pesch, op. cit., pp. 80, 102.
24. *Gal.* 2.9.
25. *Acts* 6.8, 7.1–53.
26. *Acts* 6.11, 14, 7.58–60.
27. *Acts* 8.1.

Chapter 8   The Speeches Attributed to Peter

1. *Acts* 1.15.
2. *Acts* 1.16, 20, quoting *Psalms* 41.9, 69.25, 109.8.
3. *Acts* 2.14, 22.
4. *Acts* 2.14–36, quoting *Joel* 2.28–32 and *Psalms* 16.8–11.
5. *Acts* 2.32–3.
6. *Acts* 2.46.
7. *Acts* 2.40.
8. *Acts* 3.12–26; *Deuteronomy* 18.15, 19; *1 Samuel* 3.20 and *Genesis* 22.18.
9. *Acts* 3.13–21.
10. *Acts* 4.8–12.
11. *Acts* 10.34–43.
12. C. L. Mitton, *Jesus: The Fact Behind the Faith* (1973), pp. 23f.

Chapter 9   Cornelius: Peter and the Gentiles

1. *Acts* 7.58–60.
2. *Acts* 11.19.
3. J. C. Fenton, *Saint Matthew* (1963), p. 370.

4. *Acts* 8.14.
5. *Matt.* 10.5; *John* 4.9, 8.48.
6. *Acts* 8.9–13.
7. *Acts* 8.14–17.
8. *Acts* 8.25.
9. *Acts* 9.32, 36, 10.5, 11.5.
10. *Acts* 11.18.
11. *Acts* 10.34.
12. *Matt.* 8.8–13; *Luke* 7.1–10.
13. J. A. Fitzmyer, *The Gospel According to Luke* (1981), p. 651.
14. G. Lüdemann, *Early Christianity According to the Traditions in Acts* (1989), pp. 125f.
15. M. Grant, *Jesus* (1977), p. 121 (references).
16. *Acts* 13.46–8, 18.6, quoting *Isaiah* 49.6.
17. X. Léon-Dufour, *The Gospels and the Jesus of History* (1967); *cf.* R. E. Brown, K. P. Donfried and L. Reumann (eds), *Peter in the New Testament* (1973), pp. 44f.; E. M. Blaiklock, *Acts* (1989), p. 97.
18. *Acts* 8.27.
19. *Acts* 10.45f., 11.18.
20. H. Hendrickx, *Resurrection Narratives* (1978), p. 13.

Chapter 10 The Clash with Paul

1. *Gal.* 1.18–20.
2. *Acts* 9.26–30.
3. *Acts* 15.25.
4. *Acts* 15.7.
5. *Acts* 12.17.
6. *Acts* 15.20.
7. *Acts* 10.13.
8. W. H. C. Frend, *The Early Church* (1991), p. 26.
9. *Mark* 7.6–8.
10. R. E. Brown, K. P. Donfried and L. Reumann (eds), *Peter in the New Testament* (1973), p. 49 n. 116.
11. *Acts* 15.2.
12. *Acts* 15.23.
13. *Cf.* Pesch, *Simon-Petrus* (1980), p. 84.
14. *Gal.* 2.1 (some omit 'again' in first sentence), 6–9.

15. *Acts* 16.3.
16. *Gal.* 2.9.
17. *Gal.* 2.10.
18. *Gal.* 2.12.
19. *Gal.* 6.7.
20. R. E. Brown *et al.*, op. cit., p. 54 n. 154.
21. *Acts* 11.26.
22. *Acts* 7.60.
23. *Gal.* 2.11ff.
24. O. Cullmann, *Peter: Disciple, Apostle, Martyr* (1962), p. 48.
25. By F. F. Bruce: C. P. Thiede, *Simon Peter: From Gailiee to Rome* (1986), p. 250 n. 276; R. E. Brown *et al.*, op. cit., pp. 30 n. 67, 162.
26. *Acts* 11.27f., 13.1.
27. Origen, *Homily on Luke*, VIIc.
28. Dionysius (*c.*AD 170) to the Romans: Eusebius, *History of the Church*, II 25.8.
29. *1 Cor.* 1.11ff.
30. *2 Cor.* 11.5; *Gal.* 2.4; Thiede, op. cit., p. 250 n. 281; C. K. Barrett, *New Testament Studies*, XI, 1964–5, pp. 138–53.
31. *2 Peter* 3.16.

Chapter 11 *Paul and James*

1. *Acts* 22.3.
2. *Gal.* 1.22.
3. *Acts* 7.58.
4. *Acts* 9.3, 22.6.
5. M. Braybrooke, *Christian–Jewish Relations: A New Look* (1992).
6. *Acts* 13.46–8, 18.6 (Antioch in Pisidia, Corinth).
7. *Acts* 18.12.
8. *Acts* 23.26.
9. *Acts* 25.11.
10. *1 Cor.* 9.16.
11. *2 Timothy* 4.2.
12. *Gal.* 1.19.
13. *Mark* 6.3; cf. 3.31ff. and *Matt.* 12.47ff.
14. Rejected by J. A. Fitzmyer, *The Gospel According to Luke* (1981), p. 724.

15. *Mark* 3.31ff.; *John* 7.5.
16. *1 Cor.* 15.7.
17. *Gal.* 1.19, 2.9.
18. *Acts* 15.19ff.
19. *Acts* 5.34–9.
20. Josephus, *Jewish Antiquities*, XX, 9, 1ff.; Eusebius, *Church History*, II, 23.
21. M. Baigent and R. Leigh, *The Dead Sea Scrolls Deception* (1991), pp. 186, 188.

Chapter 12 Peter in Rome

1. G. A. Wells, *The Jesus of the Early Christians* (1971), pp. 214–17.
2. *Gal.* 2.11ff.
3. *1 Clement* 5.
4. Ignatius, *Letters* 4.3.
5. Eusebius, *Church History*, III, 25.8.
6. Irenaeus, *Against Heresies*, III, 3.1.
7. *Rom.* 1.13.
8. *Cf.* O. Cullmann, *Peter: Disciple, Apostle, Martyr* (1962), pp. 213, 223f., 242.
9. *Rom.* 11.13.
10. *1 Peter* 5.1.
11. *Acts* 18.2, 26; *1 Cor.* 16.19; *Rom.* 16.3–5; C. P. Thiede, *Simon Peter: From Galilee to Rome* (1986), p. 251 n. 283.
12. Thiede, op. cit., pp. 107, 236 n. 177; *cf.* cautionary remarks of G. Masson, *Companion Guide to Rome* (1965), p. 325.
13. *Acts* 8.5–24. See also the bibliographical note, p. 151.

Chapter 13 The Death and Burial-Place of Peter

1. Tacitus, *Annals*, XV, 44.
2. *John* 13.36; *cf. Acts of Peter* 35 and *Martyrdom of Peter* 3.
3. *1 Clement* 5, 4.
4. *John* 21.18–19.
5. *John* 13.36. See also the bibliographical note, p. 157.
6. Eusebius, *Church History*, III, 31.4. On the sites see H. Chadwick, *The Early Church* (1967), pp. 162f.

7. *Acts of the Martyrs: Acta Petri cum Simone (Acts of Peter)* 40; *Acts of Peter and Paul* 84; *Martyrdom of Peter* 63; *Apocryphal Acts of the Apostles,* attributed to *Marcellus*; R. Pesch, *Simon-Petrus* (1980), p. 133; M. Guarducci, *Le reliquie di Pietro sotto la Confessione dela Basilica Vaticana* (1965), *La tomba di San Pietro* (1989), p. 14.
8. *Encyclopaedia Britannica* (1971), Vol. XVII, p. 735.

Epilogue

1. P. Johnson, *A History of Christianity* (1976), pp. 60f.
2. C. P. Thiede, *Simon Peter: From Galilee to Rome* (1986), p. 19.
3. G. M. A. Hanfmann, *Roman Art* (1975), p. 124 n. 142. On the iconography of Peter, see also the bibliographical note, p. 167.
4. J. Lees-Milne, *Saint Peter's* (1967), p. 327.

TABLE OF DATES

AD 14–37	**Tiberius**
30s AD	Calling of Peter
30/36	Crucifixion of Jesus
30/36–44	Leadership of Peter
37–41	**Gaius (Caligula)**
41–54	**Claudius**
43	Execution of James, the son of Zebedee
44	Third arrest and 'miraculous' escape of Peter
44	Death of King Agrippa I
40s	Peter one of three 'reputed pillars' of the Church
48/49	'Apostolic Council and Decree' (perhaps fictitious): James the brother of Jesus in charge
c.49	Peter's clash with Paul at Antioch
c.49–62	Paul's Letters to the churches (*1 Galatians* in 49 or 55/6: Paul visits Peter at Jerusalem; *1 Corinthians* in 54–6: party of Peter at Corinth)
54–68	**Nero**
Early 60s	Possible visit of Peter to Antioch
62	Execution of James the brother of Jesus

60s	Probable arrival of Peter in Rome
64/68	Probable execution of Peter in Rome
64/68	Supposed inauguration of Linus as Peter's successor in Roman bishopric
66–73	First Jewish Revolt (Roman War)
69–79	**Vespasian**
60s–*c.*120	The Four Gospels and the *Acts of the Apostles*
79–81	**Titus**
81–96	**Domitian**
*c.*96(?)	*1 Clement* refers to Peter
98–117	**Trajan**
*c.*107	Ignatius's Seven Letters
117–38	**Hadrian**
132–5	Second Jewish Revolt
138–61	**Antoninus Pius**
144	Marcion expelled from the Roman community
161–80	**Marcus Aurelius**
165	Execution of Justin Martyr at Rome
2nd century	Probable period of *Letters* (two), *Gospel, Acts* and *Apocalypse of Peter*
*c.*160/170	Tomb of Peter in Vatican
*c.*200	Gaius refers to monuments of Peter
235, 257–8, 303–11	Persecutions of the Christians (**Maximinus I, Valerian, Diocletian**)
258	Joint cult of Peter and Paul at Rome
*c.*258	Petrine supremacy invoked against Cyprian of Carthage
303(?)–24	Eusebius's *History of the Church* (died 339)
306–37	**Constantine the Great**
311	Galerius renounced persecution
313	'Edict of Milan' in favour of Christianity
324–49	Construction of Basilica of St Peter at Rome
fifth century	Petrine supremacy invoked by Popes Leo I the Great (440–61) and Gelasius II (492–6)
590–604	Papacy of Gregory I the Great, popularizer of Petrine presence and miracles

eighth century   Importance of Peter's connection with Rome fully understood and proclaimed. Forged 'Donations of Constantine'

BIBLIOGRAPHY

I   Ancient Writings

(1)   Greek

ACTS OF PETER. See PETER, ACTS OF.

ACTS OF THE APOSTLES. Book of the New Testament, traditionally attributed to Saint Luke, describing the history of the early Church and the leadership of Peter and career of Paul.

ACTS OF THE APOSTLES. Apocryphal, attributed to the senator Marcellus, but composed in the fourth century AD.

ACTS OF THE MARTYRS. Late and prolonged. For references to Peter (and individual works), see R. Pesch, *Simon-Petrus* (1980), pp. 8ff., 34ff., 84, 129, 133f.; O. Cullmann, *Peter: Disciple, Apostle, Martyr* (1962), p. 127.

APOCALYPSE OF PETER, see PETER, APOCALYPSE OF.

BARNABAS, LETTER OF. An allegorical treatise on the Old Testament, regarded as scriptural in Alexandria.

BENJAMIN, TESTAMENT OF. One of the Testaments of the Twelve Patriarchs (sons of Jacob), perhaps of the first or second century, AD: see also section 4.

CLEMENT OF ALEXANDRIA, *c.*AD 150–215. Head of the philosophical

Christian school of Alexandria. His numerous works included *Stromateis (Miscellanies)*.

CLEMENT OF ROME (SAINT). Bishop of Rome (Pope), *c.*AD 88/92–97/101. One of the Apostolic Fathers. Author of a Letter to the church at Corinth (*1 Clement*), much quoted with regard to the Apostolic Succession. See also next item.

CLEMENTINE HOMILIES. Part of the 'Clementine Literature' of the late fourth century AD, associated with the name of Clement of Rome (see above, Epilogue.

DIONYSIUS, *c.*AD 170. Bishop of Corinth, quoted by Eusebius (see below).

ENOCH. Three books preserved under the name of the patriarch Enoch (a fourth is no longer extant). *1 Enoch* (Ethiopic) is based on a Greek translation (*c.*AD 400) of the Hebrew original. *2 Enoch* (Slavonic) derives from a lost Greek original. *3 Enoch* is Hebrew.

EPISTLES (LETTERS). See BARNABAS, CLEMENT OF ROME, IGNATIUS, JAMES, PAUL, PETER, TIMOTHY.

EURIPIDES, *c.*485–*c.*406 BC. Athenian tragic poet.

EUSEBIUS, *c.*AD 260–340. Bishop of Caesarea Maritima in Syria Palaestina (Judaea). Writer of *Church History* and other works.

HEGESIPPUS, *c.*AD 160. A Christian writer, quoted by Eusebius (see above).

HERODOTUS of Halicarnassus in Caria, *c.*490/480–429/5 BC. Historian.

IGNATIUS (SAINT), executed as a martyr *c.*AD 110. Bishop of Antioch in Syria, and author of Letters to churches in the Roman province of Asia (western Asia Minor) and in Rome.

IRENAEUS (SAINT), *c.*AD 130/140–200. Bishop of Lugdunum in Gaul. Two of his numerous works survive (in Latin and Armenian translations, see sections 2 and 4).

JAMES, LETTER OF. New Testament Epistle, of which 'James' names himself author. It has often been attributed to James the Just, though a considerably later date (end of second century) has also been preferred from early times.

JOHN, GOSPEL OF. The fourth New Testament Gospel, often believed to be the latest. The writer's identity is uncertain.

JOSEPHUS, *c.*AD 37–after 94/95. Jewish historian in Greek, although (in some cases) the originals were Aramaic.

LETTERS (EPISTLES). See BARNABAS, CLEMENT OF ROME, IGNATIUS, JAMES, PAUL, PETER, TIMOTHY.

LEVI, TESTAMENT OF. See BENJAMIN.

LUKE, GOSPEL OF. The third New Testament Gospel. Traditionally the work of Luke the physician, an associate of Paul; but in fact later, and of uncertain authorship. The two Anchor Bible volumes on the Gospel are helpful about Peter.

MARCION, second century AD. The founder of a powerful Christian Church which regarded Paul as the only true apostle. None of his writings have survived.

MARK, GOSPEL OF. The second, and earliest, New Testament Gospel. Traditionally, but dubiously, the work of John Mark, 'interpreter' of Peter. See PAPIAS.

MATTHEW, GOSPEL OF. The first New Testament Gospel. Thus placed because its author was believed to be one of Jesus's apostles; but this is unlikely. There are volumes on Matthew's Gospel in the *International Critical Commentary* series.

ORIGEN, c.AD 185–254. The outstanding theologian of the Greek and Alexandrian Church, though frequently denounced for inserting pagan elements.

PAPIAS of Hierapolis, late first or early second century AD (?c.140). His various writings included an assertion that Mark's Gospel (see above) was based on information from Peter.

PAUL of Tarsus in Cilicia, deeply involved in the story of Peter recounted in this book. Author of New Testament Epistles (Letters) to Christian communities at Rome and Corinth (two), in Galatia, at Philippi and Thessalonica, and to Philemon. Letters to the Colossians and Ephesians attributed to him have been worked over subsequently. For Letters to Timothy, which bear his name but are of later authorship, see TIMOTHY.

PETER, ACTS OF, c.AD 312. They ascribe Peter's confrontations with Simon Magus to several locations, ending in Rome.

PETER, APOCALYPSE OF. One of the earliest and most important of the Apocalypses attributed to early Christian personages and classified as part of the New Testament Apocrypha (i.e. not finally admitted to the Bible). Perhaps written in c.AD 135. See also section 4.

PETER, GOSPEL OF, second century AD. A book of the New Testament Apocrypha; occasionally added to the Gospels as canonical, and claimed to be based on direct eyewitness, but attribution to Peter was already rejected before AD 200.

PETER, LETTERS OF. These two New Testament Letters, of which the first was addressed to Christian communities of Asia Minor, are of much disputed date and authorship.

PHILO (JUDAEUS) of Alexandria, *c.*30 BC–AD 40. The outstanding, Hellenizing philosopher of the Dispersion (Diaspora) and of the large Jewish community in Egypt.

PSALMS OF SOLOMON. See SOLOMON, PSALMS OF.

PSEUDO-CLEMENT. See CLEMENTINE HOMILIES.

Q (= German *Quelle*, source). The designation given to the special source or sources (unidentified) which *Matthew* and *Luke* have in common but do not share with *Mark*.

REVELATION, BOOK OF (*Revelation of St John the Divine*; *Apocalypse of St John the Apostle*). The last book of the New Testament, written much later than the time of John, the son of Zebedee, to whom it was attributed.

SHEPHERD OF HERMAS, *c.*AD 110–40. A work of the Apostolic Fathers which narrates allegories in the form of visions, and illustrates Christianity at Rome. According to tradition, Hermas was the brother of Pius I, bishop of Rome and Pope (*c.*AD 140–55). It is traditionally divided into *visions, mandates* and *similitudes*.

SOLOMON, PSALMS OF, first century BC. Eighteen poems by Pharisee authors, surviving in Greek and Syriac versions. The Hebrew original is not extant.

SOLOMON, WISDOM OF, first century BC or AD. Book of Old Testament Apocrypha, belonging to Wisdom Literature and influenced by Alexandrian Greek philosophy.

STRABO of Amasia (Amasra) in Pontus, 64/63 BC–at least AD 21. Writer of Greek history (lost) and geography (extant).

TESTAMENT OF BENJAMIN. See BENJAMIN, TESTAMENT OF.

TESTAMENTS OF THE TWELVE PATRIARCHS. Ibid.

THOMAS, GOSPEL OF. Ascribed to Jesus's disciple Thomas and containing 114 alleged sayings of Jesus, some unrecorded in the canonical Gospels, among which this book was not included. One of these sayings is quoted in Chapter 5, and another in the notes to that appendix, which indicates some studies of the work. The Gospel was found in 1945 near Nag Hammadi in Upper Egypt.

THUCYDIDES of Athens, *c.*460/455–?*c.*399/8 BC. Historian.

TIMOTHY, LETTERS TO. Two New Testament Letters forming, with the Letter to Titus, the Pastoral Letters or Epistles. They claim to have been written by Paul to his associate Timothy, but are of the early second century.

TWELVE PATRIARCHS, TESTAMENTS OF THE. See BENJAMIN, ZEBULUN.

WISDOM OF SOLOMON. See SOLOMON, WISDOM OF.

ZEBULUN, TESTAMENT OF. One of the Testaments of the Twelve Patriarchs (sons of Jacob, perhaps of the first or second century AD). See also section 4.

(2) Latin

AUGUSTINE (SAINT), AD 354–430. Born at Thagaste. Bishop of Hippo. Theologian; writer of *Confessions, The City of God,* etc.

CLEMENTINE RECOGNITIONS. Part of the 'Clementine Literature' of the late fourth century AD, associated with the name of Clement of Rome (section 1). The *Recognitions* have survived in Latin and Syriac translations.

CONSTANTINE, DONATION OF. Eighth-century forgery of supposed grant by Constantine the Great to Pope Sylvester I (AD 314–35) of spiritual supremacy.

CYPRIAN (SAINT), c.AD 200–58. Bishop of Carthage, who split with Pope Stephen I. Writer of pastoral addresses and letters applying juridical categories to the conception of the Church. Executed by the Romans.

ESDRAS, SECOND BOOK OF (The 'Ezra Apocalypse'), first century AD. It describes the return of Ezra to Palestine in the fifth or fourth century BC, and although originally in another language (see section 4), it has survived in a Latin version.

GAIUS, c.AD 200. Presbyter quoted by Eusebius (in Greek) as pointing out the tombs of the apostles at Rome, against the Montanist heresy (in Asia Minor).

IRENAEUS (SAINT), c.AD 130/140–200. See section 1. His work *Against Heresies* has only partly survived in the original Greek, but wholly in a Latin translation.

JEROME (SAINT), c.AD 348–420. Born at Stridon in Dalmatia. Founder of religious house at Bethlehem and theological and historical writer. Reviser and translator of the Latin Bible (Vulgate).

LIBER PONTIFICALIS. Begun in the sixth century AD. It purports to contain the official biographies of the Pope from earliest times (down to the Renaissance).

OVID, 43 BC–AD 17. Born at Sulmo (Sulmona), eventually exiled to Tomis. Elegiac and hexameter poet.

PHILOCALUS, fourth century AD. Writer of calendar in AD 354 for Pope Liberius.

TACITUS, c.AD 56–before or after 117. Probably of north Italian or Gallic origin. Historian (*Histories, Annals*) and writer of *Agricola, Germania* and *Dialogue on Orators*.

TERTULLIAN, c.AD 160–c.240. Born in or near Carthage. Theological writer and controversialist. The first Latin churchman.

VINCENT OF LÉRINS, died c.450. Perhaps born at Toul. Theological writer against heresies and (indirectly) Augustine.

(3) Hebrew

ABOTH (the Fathers) or PIRKE ABOTH (Sayings of the Fathers). A collection of ethical maxims from the Mishnah (see below).

AMOS, eighth century BC. Prophet of Israel, after whom the earliest prophetic book of the Old Testament is named.

BABA MEZIA (Middle Gate). A tractate of the Mishnah and Talmud (see below).

COMMUNITY RULE (or Manual of Discipline). Perhaps of later second century BC. One of the oldest Dead Sea Scrolls found at Qumran (see below).

DANIEL. The name of this Jew of the sixth century BC, in exile at the Babylonian court, was given to an Old Testament book written c.167–164 BC, in which the Messiah is forecast.

DEAD SEA SCROLLS. Manuscripts found in caves adjoining the Dead Sea, illustrating the religious views of the Jewish community at Qumran (see below). See also COMMUNITY RULE, HABAKKUK PESHER.

DEUTERONOMY. The fifth book of the Old Testament (and the Pentateuch). Its nucleus probably dates from the seventh century BC.

ENOCH. See section 1. *3 Enoch* is Hebrew.

EXODUS. The second book of the Old Testament. The name refers to the miraculous escape of the Israelites from their servitude in Egypt.

EZEKIEL. A Jewish priest and prophet who was taken into exile by the Babylonians on the downfall of Judah in the early sixth century. The Old Testament book bearing his name was perhaps completed in the following century.

GENESIS. The first book of the Old Testament, traditionally ascribed to Moses, but based on a number of sources.

HABAKKUK PESHER (Commentary). One of the writings of the sect at Qumran preserved on the Dead Sea Scrolls (see above).

HILLEL, late first century BC and early first century AD. Jewish sage and head of a school, remembered for many sayings and the 'Seven Rules'.

HOSEA, eighth century BC. Jewish prophet. The Old Testament book bearing his name includes additions and adjustments of a later epoch.

ISAIAH, eighth century BC. Jewish prophet. The Old Testament book named after him is the work of at least two principal authors. The second Isaiah, c.400 BC delineated the Suffering Servant, which was a partial prototype of the Messiahship of Jesus. See also section 4.

JEREMIAH, before and after c.600 BC. Jewish prophet. The Old Testament book bearing his name is based on a document dictated by himself but enlarged over a period of several centuries.

JOB. An Old Testament book describing the sufferings of the Edomite Job. It contains material of various dates from the sixth (or eighth?) century onwards.

JOEL. A Jewish prophet whose name was given to an Old Testament book. Peter was said in *Acts* to have quoted him twice as forecasting future salvation.

JONAH. Supposedly a Jewish prophet of the early eighth century BC. The subject of an Old Testament book, perhaps of the later fifth century. Jesus was said to have quoted him in relation to his three-day sojourn in the tomb, and as a warning.

JOSHUA. An Ephraimite who succeeded Moses as leader of the Israelite tribes. The sixth book of the Old Testament (sixth century?) bears his name and tells his story.

JUBILEES. An Apocryphal Jewish book of the first century BC, retelling *Genesis* and parts of *Exodus* in apocalyptic fashion. The Hebrew original is lost; but see section 4.

JUDGES. The seventh book of the Old Testament, describing Israelite history in continuation of Joshua (see above).

KINGS. Two Old Testament books recounting the history of Solomon and of the two Hebrew kingdoms, Israel and Judah. Originally a single book, perhaps completed c.600 BC and re-edited c.550 BC.

MIDRASH (from *darash*, to search or investigate). A term applied to Jewish writings employing certain methods of biblical exposition. The earliest extant collections date from the second century AD.

MISHNAH ('repetition' in Hebrew). Jewish sacred book. A collection of traditional precepts in Mishnaic Hebrew, completed early in the third century AD and forming one of the two main parts of the Talmud (section 4). See also ABOTH, BABA MEZIA.

PENTATEUCH. See DEUTERONOMY, EXODUS, GENESIS. For the Hebrew Bible (the *Torah*), see M. Grant, *History of Ancient Israel* (1984), p. 253.

PSALMS, BOOK OF (or Psalter). Old Testament collection of 'songs of praise' long ascribed to King David (tenth century BC) but reflecting all periods of Judaism from the thirteenth to the sixth or fifth centuries BC.

PSALMS OF SOLOMON. See section 1 (SOLOMON). The Hebrew original is not extant.

QUMRAN community (Khirbet Qumran near the Dead Sea). Residence of a Jewish sect dating from *c.*140/130 BC until the First Jewish Revolt (AD 66–73). Many of its Dead Sea Scrolls (see above) have been found in adjoining caves: see COMMUNITY RULE, HABAKKUK PESHER. Recent discussions: R. Lane Fox, *The Unauthorised Version: Truth and Fiction in the Bible* (1991), pp. 100–5; G. Vermes, *The Times*, 27 December 1991, p. 12; J. Muddiman in J. L. Houlden (ed.), *Judaism and Christianity* (1988), p. 31.

SAMUEL, 1, the first of two historical books (originally one) named after the national and religious leader who brought monarchy to Israel in the eleventh century BC. Its nucleus goes back to the time of David or, more probably, Solomon (*c.*965–927 BC).

(4) Other Languages

ASCENSION OF ISAIAH. See ISAIAH, ASCENSION OF.

BENJAMIN, TESTAMENT OF. One of the Testaments of the Twelve Patriarchs which have survived not only in Greek (section 1), but also in Armenian and Slavonic.

CLEMENTINE RECOGNITIONS. Part of the 'Clementine Literature' of the late fourth century AD, associated with the name of Clement of Rome (section 1). The *Recognitions* have survived in a Syriac as well as a Latin translation.

ENOCH. See section 1. *1 Enoch*, as it has come down to us, is Ethiopic, and *2 Enoch* is Slavonic.

ESDRAS, SECOND BOOK OF (the 'Ezra Apocalypse'). The book has survived in Latin (section 2), but its original version was probably in Aramaic.

HEBREWS, GOSPEL ACCORDING TO THE (*or* OF THE NAZARENES). Second century AD, probably written in Aramaic, in Egypt. Known chiefly from quotations by Clement of Alexandria and Jerome (sections 1, 2).

IRENAEUS. See sections 1, 2. His *Demonstration of Apostolic Preaching* exists in an Armenian translation.

ISAIAH, ASCENSION OF. A composite Jewish–Christian work dating in its extant form from about the third century AD. The work survives as a whole in Ethiopic (though there are Greek, Latin and Slavonic fragments).

JOSEPHUS. See section 1. Some (at least) of his works were translated from Aramaic into Greek.

JUBILEES. See section 3. The only complete known version is an Ethiopic translation from the original Hebrew.

NAZARENES, GOSPEL OF. See HEBREWS.

PETER, APOCALYPSE OF. See section 1. There is also an Ethiopic version.

PSEUDO-CLEMENT. See CLEMENTINE RECOGNITIONS.

SOLOMON, ODES OF. A collection of forty-two hymns reflecting eastern Christianity of the second century AD. The only complete version is Syriac, which is probably the original language.

SOLOMON, PSALMS OF. See section 1. A Syriac as well as a Greek version is extant, but not the Hebrew original.

TALMUD. Jewish sacred book, comprising the Mishnah (section 3) and Gemara ('completion'). The Gemara, an interpretative commentary on the Mishnah for which the designation 'Talmud' is generally reserved, comprises the Palestinian (Jerusalem) and Babylonian Talmuds, of the fourth (and earlier) and fifth centuries AD, in Western and Eastern Aramaic respectively.

THOMAS, GOSPEL OF. A Coptic document found in 1945 near Nag Hammadi in Upper Egypt. It contains 114 sayings described as 'secret sayings' of Jesus, which 'Didymus Judas Thomas wrote'. The question arises whether any of these sayings are derived from a tradition separate from, and perhaps prior to, the Gospels. See also bibliographical note, p. 47.

TWELVE PATRIARCHS, TESTAMENTS OF THE. See BENJAMIN, LEVI and ZEBULIN (section 1). These Testaments have survived not only in Greek but in Armenian and Slavonic versions.

II   Modern Books

(1)   On Peter*

F. D. ARCAIS, P. BREZZI and J. RUYSSCHAERT (eds), *Pietro a Roma* (1967).

T. W. ALLIES, *St Peter: His Name and his Office* (1923).

E. BAMMEL, *Jesu Nachfolger: Überlieferungen in der Zeit des frühen Christentums* (1988).

A. BEA (etc.), *San Pietro* (1967).

J. BLANK, *The Person and Office of Peter in the New Testament* (1973).

R. E. BROWN, K. P. DONFRIED and L. REUMANN (eds), *Peter in the New Testament: A Collaborative Assessment by Protestant and Roman Catholic Scholars, 1973* (1974).

F. F. BRUCE, *Peter, Stephen, James and John* (US edn of *Men and Movements in the Primitive Church* (1979).

C. C. CARAGOUNIS, *Peter and the Rock* (1990).

O. CULLMANN, *Peter: Disciple, Apostle, Martyr* (1962).

W. DIETRICH, *Das Petrusbild der Lukanischen Schriften* (1972).

J. D. G. DUNN, *Jesus' Call to Discipleship* (1992).

G. E. ELTON, *Simon Peter: A Study of Discipleship* (2nd edn, 1967).

W. R. FARMER, *Peter and Paul in the Church of Rome* (1990).

U. M. FASOLA, *Petrus und Paulus in Rom* (1980).

F. J. FOAKES-JACKSON, *Peter: Prince of the Apostles* (1927).

C. FOUARD, *Saint Peter and the First Years of Christianity* (1892).

P. GAECHTER, *Petrus und seine Zeit: Neutestamentliche Studien* (1958).

S. GAROFALO and M. MACCARONE (etc.), *Studi Petriani* (1968).

D. GEWALT, *Petrus: Studien zur Geschichte und Tradition des frühen Christentums* (1966).

K. G. GOETZ, *Petrus als Gründer und Oberhaupt der Kirche und Schauer von Gesichten nach den altchristlichen Berichten und Legenden* (1927).

U. HOLZMEISTER, *Vita Sancti Petri* (1937).

J. M. HULL, *Touching the Rock* (1990).

C. JOURNET, *The Primacy of Peter from the Protestant and Catholic Point of View* (1954).

O. KARKER, *Peter and the Church: An Examination of Cullmann's Thesis* (1963).

---

* There is a further bibliography of Peter in R. E. Brown, K. P. Donfried and L. Reumann (eds), *Peter in the New Testament* (1973), pp. 169ff.

E. KIRSCHBAUM, *The Tombs of St Peter and St Paul* (3rd German edn, 1974).

J. LEES-MILNE, *Saint Peter's* (1967).

J. LOWE, *Saint Peter* (1956).

M. MACCARONE, *La concezione di Roma, città di S. Pietro e di Paolo* (1985).

H. MARTIN, *Simon Peter* (1869; new edn, 1984).

A. MÉHAT, *Simon dit Képhas: la vie clandestine de l'Apôtre Pierre* (1989).

F. MUSSNER, *Petrus und Paulus: Pole der Einheit* (1976).

D. W. O'CONNOR, *Peter in Rome*, 2 vols. (1969, 1975).

A. PENNA, *Saint Pierre* (1958).

R. PESCH, *Simon-Petrus* (1980).

K. B. QUAST, *Peter and the Beloved Disciple* (1990).

H. N. RIDDERBOS, *The Speeches of Peter in the Acts of the Apostles* (1962).

A. RIMOLDI, *L'apostolo San Pietro* (1958).

J. DE SATGÉ, *Peter and the Single Church* (1981).

R. SCHNEIDER, *Petrus* (1955).

T. V. SMITH, *Petrine Controversies in Early Christianity* (1985).

C. P. THIEDE, *Simon Peter: From Galilee to Rome* (1986).

C. P. THIEDE (ed.), Das Petrusbild in der neueren Forschung (1987).

J. M. C. TOYNBEE and J. WARD-PERKINS, *The Shrine of St Peter and the Vatican Excavations* (1956).

J. J. WALSH, *The Bones of St Peter* (1983).

M. M. WINTER, *Saint Peter and the Popes* (1960).

(2)   The Resurrection*

D. C. ALLISON *The End of the Ages has Come* (1985).

J. E. ALLSOP, *The Post-Resurrection Appearance Stories* (1975).

P. BADHAM, *Christian Beliefs about Life After Death* (1976).

K. BARTH, *The Resurrection of the Dead* (1933).

E. L. BODE, *The First Easter Morning* (1970).

R. E. BROWN, *The Virginal Conception and Bodily Resurrection of Jesus* (1973).

P. CARNLEY, *The Structure of Resurrection Belief* (1987).

* For lists of additional writers, see J. D. G. Dunn, *Christology in the Making* (1989), p. 270 n. 16; J. A. Fitzmyer, *The Gospel According to Luke* (1981), pp. 1549–53; and for Appearances, ibid., p. 1570.

N. CLARK, *Interpreting the Resurrection* (1967).

C. B. COUSAR, *A Theology of the Cross* (1990).

J. D. CROSSAN, *The Cross That Spoke* (1988).

J. D. M. DERRETT, *The Anastasis: The Resurrection of Jesus as an Historical Event* (1987).

E. DHANIS (ed.), *Resurrexit: Actes du Symposium International sur la Résurrection de Jésus, 1970* (1974).

C. S. DUTHIE, *Resurrection and Immortality* (1979).

C. F. EVANS, *Resurrection and the New Testament* (1970).

R. T. FRANCE and D. WENHAM (eds), *Gospel Perspective*, Vol. I, 1980/1.

R. H. FULLER, *The Formation of the Resurrection Narratives* (1972).

M. GOGUEL, *La foi à la résurrection de Jesus dans le christianisme primitif* (1933).

N. R. GOLDBERG, *Resurrecting the Body* (1993).

K. GRAYSTON, *Dying We Live* (1990).

R. HARRIES, *Christ is Risen* (1988).

J. P. HEIL, *The Death and Resurrection of Jesus* (1991).

H. HENDRICKX, *Resurrection Narratives: Studies in the Synoptic Gospels* (1978).

E. C. HOSKYNS and N. DAVEY, *Crucifixion – Resurrection* (1981).

J. L. HOULDEN, *Backward into Light* (1987).

A. KEE, *Fram Bad Faith to Good News* (1991).

G. KEGEL, *Auferstehung Jesu: Auferstehung der Toten* (1970).

G. KOCH, *Die Auferstehung Jesu Christi* (1959).

W. KÜNNETH, *The Theology of the Resurrection* (1966).

G. E. LADD, *I Believe in the Resurrection of Jesus* (1979).

G. W. H. LAMPE and D. M. MACKINNON, *The Resurrection* (1966).

P. LAPIDE, *The Resurrection of Jesus: A Jewish Perspective* (1984).

X. LÉON-DUFOUR, *The Resurrection and the Message of Easter* (1974).

W. J. LUNNY, *The Sociology of the Resurrection* (1989).

W. MARXSEN, *The Resurrection of Jesus of Nazareth* (1970).

J. I. H. MCDONALD, *The Resurrection: Narrative and Belief* (1989).

V. MESSORI, *Pati sotto Ponzio Pilato?* (1992).

C. F. D. MOULE (ed.), *The Significance of the Message of the Resurrection for Faith in Jesus Christ* (1968).

G. W. E. NICKELSBURG, *Resurrection, Immortality and Eternal Life in Intertestamental Judaism* (1972).

R. NIEBUHR, *Resurrection and Historical Reason* (1957).

D. E. NINEHAM (ed.), *Studies in the Gospels: Essays in Memory of R. H. Lightfoot* (1968).

G. O'COLLINS, *Jesus Risen* (1987).

W. PANNENBERG, *Jesus God and Man* (1964).

P. PERKINS, *Resurrection* (1984).

J. PERRET, *Ressuscité? Approche historique* (1984).

N. PERRIN, *The Resurrection According to Matthew, Mark and Luke* (1977).

M. PERRY, *The Resurrection of Man* (1975).

A. M. RAMSEY, *The Resurrection of Christ* (1961).

A. M. RAMSEY, 'What was the Ascension?', in *History and Chronology in the New Testament* (1965).

K. H. RENGSTORF, *Die Auferstehung Jesu* (1967).

G. ROCHAIS, *Les récits de résurrection des morts dans le Nouveau Testament* (1981).

L. SCHENKE, *Auferstehungsverkündigung und Leeres Grab* (1968).

J. SCHMITT, *Jésus ressuscité* (1949).

P. SELBY, *Look for the Living: The Corporate Nature of Resurrection Faith* (1976).

K. STENDAHL (ed.), *Immortality and Resurrection* (1965).

P. DE SURGY, *La résurrection du Christ et l'exégèse moderne* (1969).

B. G. THOROGOOD, *Risen Today* (1987).

D. H. VAN DAALEN, *The Real Resurrection* (1972).

H. WANSBRUGH, *Risen from the Dead* (1978).

U. WILCKENS, *Resurrection: Biblical Testimony: An Historical Examination and Explanation* (1977).

H. A. WILLIAMS, *Jesus and the Resurrection* (1961).

H. A. WILLIAMS, *The Resurrection* (1972).

H. M. WINDEN, *Wie kam es zum Osterglauben? Darstellung und Beurteilung durch R. Pesch ausgelösten Diskussion* (1979).

(3)   Other Books*

R. H. BAINTON, *Early Christianity* (1960).

E. BAMMEL (ed.), *Jesu Nachfolger* (1988).

---

* Commentaries and bibliographies on individual New Testament books are not included here, although they have been recorded in the references and bibliographical notes; see also W. G. Kümmel, *Introduction to the New Testament* (1975), pp. 555–61. But at the risk of being invidious, I should like to mention three, owing to the fullness of the information they

W. BARCLAY, *Jesus as They Saw Him* (1991).

J. BARR, *Holy Scripture: Canon, Authority, Criticism* (1983).

S. C. BARTON, *The Spirituality of the Gospels* (1992).

H. W. BARTSCH (ed.), *Kerygma and Myth: A Theological Debate* (1961).

O. BETZ, *What Do We Know About Jesus?* (1968).

H. BOERS, *Who Was Jesus?* (1990).

G. BORNKAMM, *Early Christian Experience* (1969).

G. BORNKAMM, *Jesus of Nazareth* (1973).

J. BOWDEN, *Jesus: The Unanswered Questions* (1988).

P. BRADSHAW, *The Search for the Origins of Christian Worship* (1992).

S. BROWN, *The Origins of Christianity* (1984).

F. F. BRUCE, *The New Testament Documents* (1960).

R. BULTMANN, *New Testament and Mythology: the Other Basic Writings* (1985).

R. A. BURRIDGE, *What Are the Gospels? A Comparison with Graeco-Roman Biography* (1992).

D. A. CARSON (ed.), *Biblical Interpretation and the Church* (1984).

H. CHADWICK, *The Early Church* (1967, 1993).

J. CLARKE, *Encyclopaedia of the Early Church* (1991).

D. COHN-SHERBOK, *The Crucified Jews: Twenty Centuries of Christian Anti-Semitism* (1992).

D. COHN SHERBOK, *The Jewish Faith* (1993).

R. F. COLLINS, *Introduction to the New Testament* (revised edn, 1987).

H. CONZELMANN, *History of Primitive Christianity* (1973).

J. D. CROSSAN, *The Historical Jesus: The Life of a Mediterranean Jewish Peasant* (1991).

H. CUNLIFFE-JONES and B. DREWERY (eds), *A History of Christian Doctrine* (1978, 1993).

F. J. CWIEKOWSKI, *The Beginnings of the Church* (1988).

E. DABROWSKI, *La Transfiguration de Jésus* (1939).

J. G. DAVIES, *The Early Christian Church* (1965).

A. DI BERARDINO, *Encyclopaedia of the Early Church* (1991).

provide. They are R. E. Brown, J. A. Fitzmyer and R. E. Murphy (eds), *The New Jerome Biblical Commentary* (1968, 1990), R. E. Brown, *The Gospel According to John* (1966), J. A. Fitzmyer, *The Gospel According to Luke* (1981), and W. D. Davies and Dale C. Allison, *The Gospel According to Saint Matthew*, 3 vols (1988, 1991 and in press). For some of the most recent books on Jesus, see note on Chapter 15.

C. H. DODD, *History and the Gospel* (1964).

J. DRANE, *The Bible: Fact or Fantasy?* (1989).

J. D. G. DUNN, *The Evidence for Jesus* (1985).

J. D. G. DUNN, *Christology in the Making* (1989).

J. D. G. DUNN, *Unity and Diversity in the New Testament* (1990).

D. L. EDWARDS, *The Real Jesus: How Much Can We Believe?* (1991).

J. K. ELLIOTT, *Questioning Christian Origins* (1982).

C. F. EVANS, *The Beginning of the Gospel* (1968).

J. FOSTER, *Church History I: The First Advance (AD 29–500)* (1972).

W. H. C. FREND, *The Early Church: From the Beginnings to 461* (1991).

W. H. C. FREND, *The Rise of Christianity* (1993).

R. W. FUNK, *The Poetics of Biblical Narration* (1991).

G. J. E. GOEHRING etc. (eds), *Gospel Origins and Christian Beginnings* (1990).

L. GOPPELT, *Apostolic and Post-Apostolic Times* (1970).

M. GRANT, *Jesus* (1977).

M. GRANT, *Saint Paul* (1982).

P. GRANT, *Reading the New Testament* (1989).

R. M. GRANT, *A Historical Introduction to the New Testament* (1963).

R. M. GRANT, *Jesus and the Gospels* (1990).

D. GUTHRIE, *New Testament Introduction* (1990).

E. HAENCHEN, *Die Apostelgeschichte* (1957).

R. P. C. and A. T. HANSON, *The Bible Without Illusions* (1989).

A. E. HARVEY, *Companion to the Gospels* (1970).

A. E. HARVEY, *Jesus and the Constraints of History* (1982).

V. A. HARVEY, *The Historian and the Believer* (1967).

I. HAZLETT (ed.), *Early Christianity: Origins and Evolution to AD 600* (1991).

M. HENGEL, *The Son of God* (1976).

M. HENGEL, *Between Jesus and Paul* (1983).

M. HENGEL, *Earliest Christianity* (1986).

M. HENGEL, *The Cross of the Son of God* (1986).

M. HENGEL, *The Hellenization of Judaea in the First Century after Christ* (1990).

J. L. HOULDEN, *Backward into Light* (1987).

J. L. HOULDEN, *Jesus: A Question of Identity* (1992).

J. L. HOULDEN (ed.), *Judaism and Christianity* (1988).

A. M. HUNTER, *Introducing the New Testament* (1972).

J. ISAAC, *Gesù e Israele* (1976).

P. JOHNSON, *A History of Christianity* (1976).

W. KASPER, *Jesus the Christ* (1976).

H. C. KEE, *What Can We Know About Jesus?* (1991).

W. G. KÜMMEL, *Introduction to the New Testament* (1975).

K. J. KUSCHEL, *Born Before All Time? The Dispute Over Christ's Origin* (1992).

R. LANE FOX, *Pagans and Christians* (1986).

R. LANE FOX, *The Unauthorised Version: Truth and Fiction in the Bible* (1991).

H. LIETZMANN, *History of the Early Church*, Vol. I (1993 ed.).

G. LÜDEMANN, *Early Christianity According to the Traditions in Acts* (1989).

D. LÜHRMANN, *An Itinerary for New Testament Study* (1991).

A. E. MCGRATH, *Christian Theology: An Introduction* (1993).

A. E. MCGRATH (ed.), *The Blackwell Encyclopedia of Modern Christian Thought* (1993).

J. P. MACKEY, *Jesus: The Man and the Myth: A Contemporary Christology* (1979).

J. MACQUARRIE, *Jesus Christ in Modern Thought* (1990).

L. H. MARSHALL, *The Origins of New Testament Christology* (1976).

W. MARXSEN, *The Beginning of Christology* (1969).

W. MARXSEN, *Jesus and the Church* (1993).

F. J. MATERA, *Passion Narratives and Gospel Theologies* (1986).

W. H. MEEKS, *The First Urban Christians* (1983).

J. P. MEIER, *A Marginal Jew: Rethinking the Historical Jesus* (1992).

B. F. MEYER, *The Aims of Jesus* (1979).

V. MESSORI, *Ipotesi su Jesu* (1966).

B. M. METZGER, *The Early Versions of the New Testament* (1977).

B. F. MEYER, *The Aims of Jesus* (1979).

C. L. MITTON, *Jesus: The Fact Behind the Faith* (1973).

A. MODA, *Il Cristianesimo nel primo secolo* (1986).

J. MOLTMANN, *The Way of Jesus Christ* (1990).

S. D. MOORE, *Literary Criticism and the Gospels* (1989).

C. F. D. MOULE, *The Origin of Christology* (1977).

C. F. D. MOULE, *The Birth of the New Testament* (1981).

J. NEUSNER, *Judaism in the Beginning of Christianity* (1984).

J. NEUSNER, *A Midrash Reader* (1990).

J. NEUSNER, *Jews and Christians* (1991).

A. NOLAN, *Jesus Before Christianity* (1992).

P. PERKINS, *Jesus as Teacher* (1991).

B. REICKE, *The New Testament Era* (1969).

H. J. RICHARDS, *The Miracles of Jesus: What Really Happened?* (1983).

J. RICHES, *The World of Jesus: First-Century Judaism in Crisis* (1991).

J. M. RIST, *On the Independence of Matthew and Mark* (1991).

A. ROBERTSON, *Jesus: Myth or History* (1949).

J. A. T. ROBINSON, *Relating the New Testament* (1976).

C. ROWLAND, *Christian Origins* (1985).

E. P. SANDERS, *Jesus and Judaism* (1985).

E. P. SANDERS, *Judaism: Practice and Belief 63* BCE–*66* CE (1992).

E. P. SANDERS, *The Historical Figure of Jesus* (1993).

S. SANDMEL, *We Jews and Jesus* (1973).

E. SCHILLEBEECKX, *Christ* (1991).

H. SCHONFIELD, *The Pentecost Revolution* (1985).

H. SCHONFIELD, *Those Incredible Christians* (1985).

E. SCHWEITZER, *Theological Introduction to the New Testament* (1992).

L. SEBASTIANI, *Transfigurazione* (1992).

F. F. SEGOVIA, *Discipleship in the New Testament* (1985).

M. SMITH, *Jesus the Magician* (1978).

G. STANTON, *The Gospels and Jesus* (1989).

B. H. STREETER, *The Primitive Church* (1929).

G. THEISSEN, *Social Reality and the Early Christians* (1993).

G. THEISSEN, *The First Followers of Jesus* (1978).

G. THEISSEN, *The Miracle Stories of the Early Christian Tradition* (1983).

G. THEISSEN, *The Shadow of the Galilean* (1987).

C. P. THIEDE, *Jesus: Life or Legend?* (1990).

C. P. THIEDE, *The Heritage of the First Christians* (1992).

B. THIERING, *Jesus the Man: A New Interpretation from the Dead Sea Scrolls* (1992).

W. M. THOMPSON, *The Jesus Debate* (1985).

D. TIEDE, *Jesus and the Future* (1990).

G. VERMES, *Jesus and the World of Judaism* (1983).

G. VIDAL, *Live from Golgotha* (1992).

A. W. WAINWRIGHT, *A Guide to the New Testament* (1965).

J. WEISS, *Earliest Christianity* (1959).

G. A. WELLS, *The Jesus of the Early Christians* (1971).

BIBLIOGRAPHY

A. WESSELS, *Images of Jesus* (1990).

M. WILES, *The Making of Christian Doctrine* (1967).

R. L. WILKEN, *The Myth of Christian Beginnings* (1979).

T. C. WILLIAMS, *The Idea of the Miraculous* (1990).

A. N. WILSON, *Jesus* (1992).

I. WILSON, *Jesus: The Evidence* (1984).

N. T. WRIGHT, *Who Was Jesus?* (1992).

Index

Abilene 22
Aboth 191
Abraham (Abram) 21, 24, 58, 90, 112
Achaea, see Greece
Acts of Peter (*Acta Petri*) 101, 151ff., 181f., 184, 188
Acts of the Apostles 22, 31, 43–6, 50, 59, 64, 69, 71, 102, 106–9, 111–27, 132, 134, 137, 143, 147, 149, 151, 153f., 192
Acts of the Apostles (apocryphal) 182, 186
Acts of the Martyrs 186
Adam 136, 162
Aenon 85
agrammatos, see education
agriculture 55
Agrippa I 123, 140
Agrippa II 22
Alexandria 30, 35, 39, 188f.; see also Clement
allegory 8, 189
Alphaeus, see James 'the Less'
Amasia (Amasra) 130, 189
Amos 17, 191
Ananias 25, 163
Ananus 141
Andrew, St 40, 53f., 57, 64
angels, 60, 107, 109; see also miracles
Announcement, see *kerygma*
Antioch in Pisidia (Yalvaç) 36
Antioch in Syria (Antakya) 13, 30, 32, 35f., 39, 116, 119, 123f., 126ff., 130, 134f., 138f., 147, 151, 153, 187
Antoninus Pius 184
Apocalypse of Peter 184, 188, 194
Apocalypse of St John, see *Revelation*
Apocrypha (Old Testament) 100, 192
Apollos 130

Apostles, Twelve 59ff., 70, 93, 108 n.1
'Apostolic Council' 44, 122–7, 137, 141
'Apostolic Decree' 44, 124f., 127
Apostolic Succession, see Primacy of Peter
Appearances of Jesus 69, 92–100, 103, 107, 115, 140, 164
Appian Way, see Via Appia
Aquila 150
Aquinas, St Thomas, see Thomas
Arabia (Nabataea) 135f.
Aramaic 27, 30ff., 48, 58, 65, 71, 106, 111, 113, 187, 194
Arcene 22
Aretas IV 135
Arimathea (N. of Jerusalem) 155
Aristophanes 55
Arnolfo di Cambio 162
arrest, see prison
'*asar*, see Binding-Loosing
Ascension of Isaiah 157, 194
Ascension of Jesus 98, 102, 114
Asia (province) 46
Asia Minor 137; see also Cappadocia, Cilicia, Galatia, Pontus
Assumption, see Mary (Virgin)
Assyria 75
Athens, Athenians 91
Augustine, St 23, 70, 191
Augustus 55
Aurelius, Marcus see Aurelius

Baba Mezia 191
baptism 76, 85, 119, 150
'Babylon' 46
Babylonia 75, 191, 194
Barnabas, Letter of, see *Letter of Barnabas*
Barnabas, St 123f., 126, 128, 137, 147; see also *Letter of Barnabas*

Basilicas of St Paul, St Peter, see Saint
   Paul, Saint Peter
Beatitudes 47
belief, see faith
Beloved Disciple 39–43, 49, 59, 108
Benjamin 132; see also Testament of
   Benjamin
Bethany 85
Bethlehem 76
Bethsaida 12, 55
Binding-Loosing 104, 109
bishops of Rome, see Popes
Bithynia 46
bn 58
Boanerges 58
Boeotia 36
bones of St Peter 156ff.
Byzantine empire 161
Byzantium (Constantinople) 16

Caesarea Maritima (Sdot Yam) 13,
   117f.
Caesarea Philippi (Banyas) 36, 65,
   103f.
Calendar of Philocalus, see Philocalus
Caligula, see Gaius
Capernaum (Tell Hum) 56, 118f.
Cappadocia 46
Cappella Paolina (Vatican) 157
Carthage 160, 190f.
Catholics, Catholicism (Roman), see
   Primacy of Peter
centurion 118f.
Cephas, see Rock
children 37, 79
Chloe 130
Church (ekklesia) 94, 105f., 108ff.,
   114, 143, 149, 160, 163; see also
   Primacy of Peter
churches, see their names
Cilicia 124, 132, 135f.
cilicium 133
circumcision 124ff., 131, 137, 141, 153
Claudius 183
Clement of Alexandria 28, 48, 140,
   173 n.29, 186f., 194
Clement of Rome 142, 148, 152, 187,
   193; see also Letters of Clement
'Clementine' Homilies 142, 187
'Clementine' Recognitions 142, 190,
   193
coins, coinage, see money
Colossae (near Honaz) 188

Commissioning of Peter 33, 104, 106f.
Community Rule (Manual of
   Discipline) (Qumran) 191
compassion 37, 79
Confession of Peter 4, 33, 71
Constantia (S. Costanza) 161
Constantine I the Great 154, 156, 161,
   167, 184; see also Donations of
   Constantine
Coptic 194
Corinth, Corinthians 91f., 102, 119,
   130f., 138f., 148, 187; see also Paul
Cornelius 45, 118–21
corner-stone, see Rock
Council, Apostolic, see 'Apostolic
   Council'
Covenant 17, 21f., 112, 161
Crucifixion of Jesus 83f., 92f., 95ff.,
   102f., 107, 112, 120, 122, 129, 131,
   134, 139f., 166
cures, see healing
curses 68f.
Cyprian, St 160, 190
Cyprus 116, 137
Cyrene 36

Damasus 99, 126, 135f.
Damasus I, Pope 155
Daniel 90f., 37f., 191
David 21, 74, 77, 80, 111f., 193; see
   also Psalms of David
Dead Sea Scrolls, see Qumran
Decree, Apostolic, see 'Apostolic
   Decree'
demons, see devils
Denials of Peter 68f., 71f., 106, 163
desposynoi 142
Deutero-Isaiah, see Isaiah
Deuteronomy 191
devils, demons 61; see also Satan
diaspora, see Dispersion of Jews
Didymus Judas Thomas, see Thomas,
   Gospel of
diet, see food
Diocletian 184
Dionysius of Corinth 148, 187; see
   also Letter of Dionysius
Dispersion (diaspora) of Jews 132,
   137, 189
Docetism 40, 49f., 96, 101
Domitian 184
Donation of Constantine 161f., 167,
   190

doublets 119
drunkenness 15

Easter, see Resurrection
ecstasy 14
'Edict of Milan' 184
Edom 192
education 56, 69f., 72
Egypt 16, 19, 48, 191, 194
ekklesia, see Church
El Greco 163
Elijah 12, 17, 21, 24f., 54, 67, 75, 90
Elisha 16f., 19, 21, 24, 54
Emmaus (S.W. of Jerusalem) 94
Empty Tomb, see Tomb of Jesus
End of the World (Last Days) 47, 102,
   157
England 151
Enoch, *I*, *II*, *III Enoch* 90, 187, 191
Ephesus (Selçuk) 39, 138, 188
Ephraim 192
episcopacy, see bishops
Epistles, see *Letters*
escape from prison, see prison
II Esdras (Ezra) 91, 190
Essenes 4
Ethiopia, Ethiopic 120, 193f.
Eucharist 15, 101
Eudoxia, Aelia 16
Eudoxia, Licinia 16
eunuchs 120
Eusebius
evangelists, see *John, Luke, Mark,
   Matthew* (Gospels)
Exodus 191f.
exorcisms 4
Ezekiel 17, 191
Ezekiel Apocryphan 100
Ezra, see *II Esdras*

faith, belief 13, 68, 90, 96, 106, 110,
   114, 156
'fear' of Peter 129, 164
Feast of the Tabernacles, see
   Tabernacles
Felix, Marcus Antonius 138
Festivals 101, see also Jerusalem,
   Romulus, Tabernacles
Festus, Publius Porcius 138
Fire of Rome, Great 139
First Jewish Revolt, see Jewish
   Revolt, First

fishermen, fishing 3, 9, 11, 15, 41, 53–
   6, 103, 162f.
Five Thousand 15, 61
food, diet 15, 61, 123f., 126f., 129
forgiveness 78f., 105, 137; see also
   repentance
Foundation Stone, see Rock
Four Regulations 123, 125
Four Thousand, see Five Thousand
Franks 162
Frari, Church of, see Santa Maria
   Gloriosa dei Frari (Venice)

Gaius (Caligula) 183
Gaius (presbyter of Rome) 154f., 184,
   190
Galatia, Galatians 46, 107, 122, 125–8,
   131, 139f., 147; see also Paul
Galerius 184
Galilee, Galileans 10, 30, 49, 55f., 63,
   68f., 75ff., 81f., 95, 97, 103, 163
Galilee, Sea of (Lake Gennesaret) 41,
   53, 55f., 69, 162
Gallio Novatus, Lucius Annaeus 138,
   143
Gallio, Lucius Junius 143
Gamaliel 132, 141
Gelasius II, Pope 184
Germara 194
Genesis 192
Gennesaret, Lake of, see Galilee, Sea
   of
Gentile Christians, conversions 35–7,
   39, 62, 116–21, 123–9, 131, 136, 141
Gentile da Fabbriano 163
Giotto (di Bardone) 162
glossolalia, see Pentecost
Gnostics 49, 151
goat's hair, see *cilicium*
God-Fearers (*sebomenoi*) 150
Gospel According to the Hebrews (or
   of the Nazarenes) 47f., 194
Gospel of Peter 92, 97, 101
Gospel of Thomas 26, 73, 79, 143, 189,
   194
Gospels, canonical, see *John, Luke,
   Mark, Matthew*
Greece, Greeks (Achaea, Hellenism,
   Hellenistic world, Seleucids) 39,
   68, 75, 91, 101, 109, 126, 129, 133f.,
   136, 138
Greek language 32, 36f., 55, 109, 114,
   133, 186–90, 194

Gregory I the Great, St, Pope, 161, 184

Habakkuk Pesher 192
Hades, see Hell
Hadrian 184
Hanina 25
harmony, one-mindedness (among disciples: *homothumadon*) 122, 124f., 147
harmony (with Rome) 44
Hasmonaeans, see Maccabees
healing, cures 4, 25, 61, 78, 112, 163
Hebrew language 27, 54, 58, 106, 114, 191–4
Hebrews, see Jews
Hebrews, Letter to the, see *Letter to the Hebrews*
Hebrews (Nazarenes), Gospel According to the, see *Gospel According to the Hebrews*
Hegesippus 141, 187
Hell (Sheol) 98, 109
Hellenism, Hellenistic world, see Greece, Greek language
Hermas, Shepherd of, see *Shepherd of Hermas*
Herod Agrippa I, see Agrippa
Herod Antipas 75, 77, 81f., 119
Herod the Great 55, 65, 75
Hierapolis (Pamukkale) 49, 188
High-Priest (chief priest) 66, 75; see also Malchus
Hillel 116, 192
Hispania, see Spain
Holy Apostles, Church of (Constantinople) 16
homothumadon, see harmony (among disciples)
Honi 25
Hosea 17, 192

iconography of Peter 162, 167
Ignatius, St 148f., 151, 160, 187
Irenaeus, St 148, 187, 194
Isaac 21, 90, 112
Isaiah (and *Deutero-, Second Isaiah*) 17, 19f., 58, 66, 104f., 192; see also *Ascension of Isaiah*
Israel (kingdom, with Judah) 74, 192
Israel, Israelites (Hebrews), see Jews
Italian cohort 118, 121
Ituraea 22

Jacob 21, 90, 112, 186
James, Letter of, see *Letter of James*
James 'the Great', St (son of Zebedee) 11, 38, 54, 56, 58, 108, 140
James 'the Just', St (brother of Jesus) 122–30, 137–44, 164
James 'the Less', St (son of Alphaeus) 140, 143
jealousy (*zelos*) 152f.
Jeremiah 17, 19, 192
Jerome, St 48, 129, 140, 194
Jerusalem (Zion) 13, 20, 23, 28, 45, 56ff., 66, 77, 82, 94f., 97, 112, 116, 118, 122, 124–7, 130, 132, 134, 136ff., 140, 142, 149, 155, 164
Jewish Christians (Judaeo-Christians) 29, 35, 42, 61, 67, 69, 120, 123, 138, 150
Jewish Revolt, First (First Roman War) 28f., 35, 39, 61, 142, 193
Jews (Hebrews) 5, 14, 17, 21, 29f., 35, 37, 39f., 55, 59ff., 66, 74, 77–85, 90f., 97, 100f., 106, 109, 112, 116–21, 123, 128, 132–8, 141; see also Covenant, Dispersion, Essenes, Israel, Jewish Christians, Jewish Revolt, Judah, Midrash, Mishnah, Pharisees, rabbis, scribes, synagogues, Talmud, Torah (Pentateuch), Tribes
Joan of Arc 16
Job 11, 61, 66, 192
Joel 102, 112, 192
John, Book of Revelation of, see *Revelation*
John Chrysostom, St 35, 129
John, Gospel According to St 10, 25, 37–43, 49, 54, 57, 59, 70f., 73, 85, 101, 103f., 107f., 118f., 151ff.
John Mark, see Mark, St
John, St (son of Zebedee) 11, 27, 31, 38, 42, 54, 56, 58, 73, 108f., 112, 117, 121, 125f.
John the Baptist 21, 55f., 75–8, 80, 82, 85, 92
John the Elder 31, 38, 42
John the Priest 108
Jonah 21, 55, 192
Jonah (Johannes), father of Peter 55
Joppa (Jaffa) 117, 121
Jordan, River 76f.
Joseph (husband of Mary) 77, 140
Joseph of Arimathea 155

Josephus 141f., 187
Joshua, Book of 192
Jubilees, Book of 91, 192
Judaea (Palestine) 28, 31, 55f., 74f., 83,
  102, 126, 129f., 132, 136, 138, 194
Judaeo-Christians, see Jewish
  Christians
Judah 74, 191f.
Judaism, see Jews
Judas Iscariot 82f., 85, 108, 111
Judges, Book of 192
Julia (daughter of Augustio) 55
Julias, see Bethsaida
Justin Martyr 22f., 148f.

Kefa, see Rock
kerygma (Announcement) 114
Keys 104f., 109, 160
Khirbet Qumran, see Qumran
Kingdom (Kingship) of God, Heaven
  11, 20, 23, 27, 29, 33, 37, 60, 75,
  77ff., 82, 104f.
Kings, Books of 192

Lamb of God 54
Last Days, see End of World
Last Supper, see Eucharist, Passover,
  Supper
Latin language 190f., 193f.
Law, Jewish, see Torah
Lazarus 10, 99
Leo I the Great, St, Pope 184
Letter of Barnabas 61, 186
Letter of Dionysius 148
Letter of James 50, 142f., 187
Letter of Jude 50
Letter to the Hebrews 22
Letter to Titus, see Letters of Paul
Letters of Clement 148, 187
Letters of Paul, see Ephesus, Galatia,
  Paul, Rome, Thessalonica,
  Timothy, Titus
Letters of Peter (I, II) 37, 45ff., 50, 90,
  131, 150
Letters to Timothy 139, 189
Liber Pontificalis 190
Liberius 155, 191
Linus 184
Lippi, Filippino 162f.
Livy 29
Lord's Supper, see Supper
Lucania 36
Lugdunum (Cyan) 187

Luke, Gospel According to St 5f., 35–
  8, 44, 47ff., 54, 61, 71, 73, 79, 118f.
Luke, St 27, 32, 36, 43, 66f., 73
Luke – Acts, see Acts of Apostles
Lydda (Lod) 117, 121

M material 34
Maccabees (Hasmenaeans) 75
Macedonia 138
Magdala (Majdal), see Mary
  Magdalene, Taricheae
magic 12; see also miracles
Malchus 68, 85
Manual of Discipline, see Community
  Rule
Marcan Secret, see Secret
Marcellus 155, 186
Marcion 160f., 188
Marcus Aurelius 184
Mark, Gospel According to St 5, 11f.,
  19, 21, 25, 28–33, 35f., 38, 46, 48, 53,
  61ff., 65ff., 72f., 91, 95, 97, 113; see
  also Secret (Messianic, Marceen)
Mark (John Mark), St 27f., 31f., 44,
  46, 73
Martyrdom of Peter 181f.
Mary Magdalene 40, 101
Mary the Virgin (mother of Jesus) 77,
  102, 140
Marys 19
Masaccio 162f., 167
Matthew, Gospel According to St 5f.,
  12, 21, 33ff., 38, 47, 58, 61, 63ff., 73,
  97, 102, 104f., 107, 118f., 121, 151,
  160
Matthew, St 27, 32–6, 57, 63
Matthias 108, 111
Maximinus I Thrax 184
mediation, see moderation
Mediolanum (Milan), see 'Edict of
  Milan'
Melozzo da Forli 163
Messianic Secret, see Secret
Micah 76 n.3, 175
Michelangelo 157
Midrash 8, 192
miracles 4–16, 19, 25, 44f., 54, 78, 93,
  99, 103, 107ff., 118, 152, 161f., 166,
  184
Mishnah 191, 193f.
missionary activity 3, 44f., 77, 81, 112,
  116, 118, 123f., 127ff., 136, 138f.,
  150, 153; see also Gentile Christians

moderation, mediation 129, 164
money (coins, coinage) 11, 133; see
    also finance
Montanists 14, 190
Moses 12, 16f., 19, 21f., 25, 35, 67, 90f.,
    112, 162, 192
myths 15; see also miracles

Nabataeans, see Arabia
Nag Hammadi 189, 194
Nazareth, Nazarenes 5, 19f., 48, 68,
    76, 101, 194
Nero 46, 139, 152, 164, 183
Newman, Cardinal J. H. 3
Nietzsche, Friedrich 18

oaths, see curses
Odes of Solomon 194
Old Testament, see typology
ophthe, see Appearances
oral traditions 32
Origen 70, 94, 99, 140
oth, see Sign
Ovid 191

Palestine, see Judaea
papacy, see Popes
Papias 31f., 49, 188
parables 8, 55, 78
parousia, see Second Coming
Passover 122; see also Supper
pathemata 46
Patriarchs, Twelve 186, 190
Paul, St 4, 13, 20, 22, 24, 28f., 33, 44f.,
    47, 50, 67, 89, 92f., 95, 99, 102, 106f.,
    118f., 122–39, 142f., 147–50, 154f.,
    159ff., 164f.
penitence, see repentance
Pentateuch, see Torah
Pentecost 14f., 101, 112, 121
Pentecostalists 14
Peraea 75, 81
persecutions, see Diocletian,
    Maximus I, Nero, Valerian
Persia, Persians 75
Peter, Letters of, see Letters of Peter
Peterborough Abbey Church 151
petra, petros, see Rock
Petronilla 57
Pharisees 4, 81f., 91, 105, 124, 132,
    134, 141f.
Philip (apostle) 117
Philip ('evangelist', one of the Seven)
    117, 120, 151

Philip (tetrarch) 55, 65, 75
Philippi 188
Philo Judaeus 39, 189
Philocalus 154, 191
Phoenicia 116
Piero della Francesca 92
Pilate, Pontius 40, 83
'Pillars', the Three 108, 126
Pirke Aboth, see Aboth
Pisa 151
Pisidia 36
Pius I, Pope 189
Pontius Pilatus, see Pilate
Pontus 46, 130, 150
poor, the 37, 55f., 79, 127
Popes, papacy (bishops of Rome) 155,
    158, 161, 190
Porcius Festus, Publius, see Festus
Poussin, Nicolas 163
Praxedis (Prassede), St 150
Primacy of Peter (Apostolic
    Succession) 34, 143, 149, 155, 161f.,
    164f.
Prisca, Priscilla, St 150
prison (arrest, escape) 5, 13, 108,
    139
procurators 141; see also Felix, Festus,
    Pilate
Pronouncement Story, see
    Commissioning of Peter
prophets, prophecy, predictions 18f.,
    22f., 25, 33, 58, 76, 80, 92, 101f.,
    111f., 114, 191f.; see also Amos,
    Ezekiel, Hosea, Isaiah, Jeremiah
proselytes, Jewish 60
Psalms of David 18, 111f., 157, 193;
    see also David
Psalms of Solomon 11, 189, 193f.; see
    also Solomon
Pseudo-Clement, see Clementine
    Homilies, Recognitions
pseudonymous literature,
    pseudepigrapha 48, 151
Pudens 150
Pudentiana 150; see also Santa
    Pudenziana (Church of)

Q material 32ff., 36, 48f., 189
Quadratus 13
Quo Vadis? 152
Qumran (Dead Sea Scrolls) 29, 39, 43,
    48, 58, 100, 108, 141, 144, 191ff.;
    see also Community Rule

rabbi 6, 8, 12, 54, 69, 72
Raphael 163
Regulations, Four, see Four
  Regulations
Reni, Guido 163
repentance (penitence) of sinners 37,
  76, 78, 112, 137
Restorer, see *taleb*
Resurrection 21f., 32, 64, 71, 83f., 89–
  104, 107, 110, 114f., 164
Revelation of John, Book of 60, 157,
  189
Revolt, First Jewish, see Jewish
  Revolt
Rock (Cephas, Kefa), foundation-
  stone, corner-stone 37f., 60, 63f.,
  71, 104f., 112f., 160
Rome, Romans 131, 138f., 147–58; see
  also Paul
Romulus 154, 158
ruach, see wind

Sadducees 82f., 142
Saint Paul Outside the Walls, Basilica
  of (Rome) 154f.
Saint Peter, Basilica of (Rome) 156–9,
  162, 167
Salim 85
salt 56
Samaria, Samaritans 109, 116f., 121,
  151
Samuel, *I Samuel*, 112, 193
San Paolo Fuori le Mura, see Saint
  Paul Outside the Walls
San Piero a Grado, Church of (near
  Pisa) 151
San Pietro in Montorio, Church of
  (Rome) 157
San Pietro in Vincoli, Church of
  (Rome) 16
San Sebastiano, Church and
  Catacomb of (Rome), see Via Appia
Sanhedrin 75, 112, 134
Sant'Agnese fuori le Mura, Church of
  (Rome) 162
Santa Costanza, Church of (Rome)
  161
Santa Maria del Carmine, Church of
  (Florence) 162f., 167
Santa Maria Gloriosa dei Frari
  (Church of Frari, Venice) 163
Santa Prisca, Church of (Rome)
  150

Santa Pudenziana, Church of (Rome)
  150
Santa Trinità dei Monti, Church of
  (Rome) 156
Sapphira 25
sarcophagi 162
Satan 11, 66f., 71, 106
Saul, see Paul
scribes 66, 69
Sea of Galilee, see Galilee
sebomenoi, see God-fearers
Second Coming (*parousia*) 98, 102
Second Isaiah, see Isaiah
Secret, Messianic, Marcah 29f., 48, 65f.
Seneca, Luceus Annaeus 143
Serà, see Binding-Loosing
Seven, The 108f., 117
Shammai 116
shelters, see tabernacles
Sheol, see Hell
Shepherd of Hermas 63, 189
sign (*oth*) 11, 109; see also miracles
Silas 46
Silvanus 46
Silvester (Sylvester) I 161f., 190
Simon Magus 117, 148, 150f., 188
Sinai 17
Sinope (Sinop) 130
sins, see repentance
sirocco, see wind
Sixtus IV, Pope 157
slaves, servants 112, 118; see also
  Malchus, Suffering Servant
Slavonic 193f.
Solomon 21; see also *Odes, Psalms of
  Solomon*
Son of Man 80f.
Soter, Pope
Spain 138f.
speaking with tongues, see Pentecost
speeches attributed to Peter 111–15
Stephen, St 109, 116f., 134
Stephen I, St, Pope 190
Strabo 189
Suffering Servant 66, 192
Sulmo (Sulmona) 191
Supper, Last, Lord's Supper 41f., 59,
  72, 123
Sylvester, see Silvester
symbolism 6, 93, 101; see also signs
synagogues 56, 59, 80, 118, 137
Synoptic Gospels, see *Luke, Mark,
  Matthew*

Syria 124, 136f.; see also Antioch
Syria–Cilicia 135
Syriac 142, 193f.

Tabernacles (*skenai*, shelters, tents)
    67, 71
Tabernacles, Feast of 71
Tacitus 29
taleb (Restorer) 116
Talmud 8, 191, 193f.
Taricheae (Magdala, Majdal) 56
Tarsus 132, 134f.
Tasseli, Domenico 156
taxation 9, 55
Teacher of Righteousness 141
Temple, the (Jerusalem) 9, 22, 28, 35,
    57, 82, 112, 141, 163
tent-makers 150
Tertullian 140, 191
Testament of Benjamin 193
Testament of Zebulun 190
Testaments of the Twelve Patriarchs
    186, 193
Theophilus 36, 44
Thessalonica (Salonica) 102; see also
    Paul
Third Day, see Resurrection
Thomas, Gospel of, see *Gospel of
    Thomas*
Thomas, St 47; see also *Gospel of
    Thomas*
Thomas Aquinas, St 101
Three, The 58f., 108, 131
Tiberius 183
Timothy 126, 139; see also *Letters to
    Timothy*
Titian 163
Titus (companion of Paul) 125
Titus (emperor) 184
Tomb of Jesus (Empty Tomb) 38,
    40ff., 94, 97f., 101f., 192
Tomb of Peter 155–9

Torah, Jewish Law (Pentateuch) 17ff.,
    23, 25, 35, 60, 105, 116, 118, 129,
    138, 141, 191, 193
Trajan 184
Transfiguration 11f., 19, 25, 59, 67
Tribes, Jewish 59
tropaia 155
Twelve, see Apostles, Tribes (Jewish)
typology 17–24, 82, 90, 92, 97f., 111f.,
    114, 166

unanimity, see harmony (among
    disciples)

Valerian 155, 184
Vatican Hill 154, 156ff., 163
Vespasian 184
Via Appia (Appian Way; San
    Sebastiano) 154f., 158
Via Maris 55
Via Ostiensis 154
Vicus Patricius (Via Urbana) 150
Vincent of Lérins, St 13, 191
visions (hallucinations) 16, 93, 99, 135,
    164, 166

widows, see women
wind (*ruach*) 15
Wisdom Literature 38
Wisdom of Solomon 91, 189
Witz, Conrad 163
women 79f., 101, 107f.

ybny 58

Zaddik, see James the Just
Zebedee 56, 58; see also James and
    John (his sons)
zelos, see jealousy
Zebulun, Testament of, see *Testament
    of Zebulun*
Zion, see Jerusalem